Men in White

To Our darling Deepu,
With lots of love
from,
Chittappans, Chithas,
Vijü, Vidya
+ Vinu
8/8/07

Men in White

A Book of Cricket

MUKUL KESAVAN

PENGUIN
VIKING

VIKING
Published by the Penguin Group
Penguin Books India Pvt. Ltd, 11 Community Centre, Panchsheel Park, New
Delhi 110 017, India
Penguin Group (USA) Inc., 375 Hudson Street, New York, New York 10014,
USA
Penguin Group (Canada), 90 Eglinton Avenue East, Suite 700, Toronto,
Ontario, M4P 2Y3, Canada (a division of Pearson Penguin Canada Inc.)
Penguin Books Ltd, 80 Strand, London WC2R 0RL, England
Penguin Ireland, 25 St Stephen's Green, Dublin 2, Ireland (a division of Penguin
Books Ltd)
Penguin Group (Australia), 250 Camberwell Road, Camberwell, Victoria
3124, Australia (a division of Pearson Australia Group Pty Ltd)
Penguin Group (NZ), 67 Apollo Drive, Rosedale, North Shore 0632, New
Zealand (a division of Pearson New Zealand Ltd)
Penguin Group (South Africa) (Pty) Ltd, 24 Sturdee Avenue, Rosebank,
Johannesburg 2196, South Africa

Penguin Books Ltd, Registered Offices: 80 Strand, London WC2R 0RL,
England

First published in Viking by Penguin Books India 2007

Copyright © Mukul Kesavan 2007
Photographs copyright © Pradeep Mandhani 2007

10 9 8 7 6 5 4 3 2 1

ISBN-13: 978-0-67099-953-8   ISBN-10: 0-67099-953-9

Typeset in Sabon by Mantra Virtual Services, New Delhi
Printed in India by Gopsons Papers Ltd, Noida

For Sudhakar Kesavan (aka Babboo)
for Pandara Park cricket,
Feroz Shah Kotla mornings,
Test Match Special on an old Philips radio,
and more.

Contents

Introduction

I've never connected the excitement of Test matches with a result. This isn't on account of any special insight into the game or superior spectatorial virtue; it has to do, I think, with my initiation into the complicated business of following Test cricket. The first Test series I remember was a five-Test marathon played against M.J.K. Smith's MCC side in 1964, where every match ended in a draw. I was seven. Despite being a second-rate series against a third-rate team, this was a first-rate introduction to the slow burning excitement kindled by a long Test tour. My winter was warmed by twenty-five days of Test cricket that were meant to achieve a cumulative result (winning or losing the series) but which, despite five successive draws, were absorbing in themselves.

It was my blooding as a spectator that dated back to the MCC tour; as a player I had made my debut three years earlier. I first played cricket in the gully or lane that ran along my maternal grandmother's house in Kashmere Gate. This was a neighbourhood in old Delhi, just within the city walls that had been a genteel shopping district in the days of the Raj but had declined rapidly after Independence.

I played with my brother and four older boys: Anand, Pooran, Heera and Kamal, who lived in tenements down the lane from Nani's rented middle class home. I knew they were poor because they played barefoot. This was the first time I had played with children who were obviously poorer than I was. It was also the only time. From Kashmere Gate we moved to a neighbourhood of civil servants in New Delhi where class distinctions were rigidly enforced. The poor in Kashmere Gate were tenants in their own right; in Pandara Park, the poor were tenants-at-will. Anand, Pooran, Heera and their parents were unequal neighbours; their counterparts in Pandara Park were proximate menials. I didn't know it then, but I can see now that Kashmere Gate was a real neighbourhood while Pandara Park was correctly described as a government *colony*.

Cricket was one of the games I played in that rutted lane in Kashmere Gate. I also learnt to play pitthu, marbles and football. Cricket was just one of four games to me; nothing marked it out as special. We had heard of the one-eyed nawab who had just become our captain but that wasn't enough to make cricket our main game.

Cricket took over my life around the same time English did. I might have had some passive knowledge of English when I was darting down the gully with Anand and Pooran but the one language I could speak till I was nearly six was Hindi. Then I was sent to a school run by Jesuits and in short order, by the time I was in Class II, I had lost all but functional literacy in my mother tongue. (It was, more accurately, my mother's tongue. My mother was a Hindi-speaking north Indian. My father was a Kannadiga who spoke so many south Indian languages that his confused children never learnt any.)

It wasn't a coincidence that the first Test series that I followed was played the same year that I became fluent in English. I can date this accurately to 1964 because I finished reading my first full-length novel, Enid Blyton's *The Rubadub Mystery* while sitting by the side of the road, waiting for Nehru's funeral cortege to trundle down Rajpath. It was also the year that I acquired enough English to follow All India Radio's Test commentary. English consolidated the place of cricket in my life; it invested it with public significance—there was no All India Radio (AIR) commentary on marbles or pitthu, nor, so far as I knew, on football—and it gave me the words to enter the adult world of newspapers and magazines like *Sport & Pastime*. Cricket helped me practise reading English and reading English helped me fall deeper into love with cricket. For me, as for many Indian boys of my class, English was an inseparable part of the romance of cricket.

Reading and the radio made cricket and English one thing, not two. Enid Blyton and Richmal Crompton, being females, never had cricket in their stories, but a year or two into reading English, I found in Anthony Buckeridge's Jennings books and Frank Richards' Billy Bunter series, books that sometimes worked cricket in. The boarding school Frank Richards invented, Greyfriars, was carefully furnished with beaks, fags, tuckshops, studies . . . and cricket. With the exception of Bunter, who was too fat and too lazy, his form, the Remove, played cricket. One of his classmates was an Indian, Hurree Jamset Ram Singh, aka Inky, who, naturally, was a fine spin bowler. Young though I was, I was old enough to know that Hurree Jamset Ram Singh was an absurd name. Jamset, I suspect, was Frank Richards' way of investing the Nabob of Bhanipur with the Jam Saheb's aura, but with the severity of a ten-year-old critic, I objected to the tin-eared name because its implausibility spoilt my enjoyment of Bunter's difficulties at Greyfriars.

No, I didn't want to read about unlikely Indian nabobs playing cricket in England; like any English medium type, I wanted to read about *English* boys playing cricket in England. This happened when I was thirteen and I discovered *Mike at*

Wrykyn and *Mike and Psmith*, the two best cricket novels ever written. These are proper cricket novels in that everything that happens in the books happens on account of cricket. Mike's need to play cricket and to play it well is the engine that drives the action of these books in which P.G. Wodehouse takes the boarding school story and makes it plausible. It's hard to think of Wodehouse introducing *realism* into a genre but in his early cricket stories he did, and by doing this, he made the boarding school a believable setting for heroic cricket. And because this was Wodehouse, these novels told great cricket stories with a virtuoso delight in the telling that spoke directly to the Indian schoolboy's growing interest in being clever with English. English, like carpentry or Kathak, was an acquired art, and children enjoy showing off their skills.

The written word's twinning of cricket and English was reinforced by the more direct influence of the spoken word. My brother, who was two years older, was a radio buff. So year after year we listened to live commentary on the Wimbledon finals (I can remember stroke by stroke accounts of Newcombe's triumph and Stan Smith's and Arthur Ashe's deconstruction of Jimmy Connors' game), Tony Blackburn's *Top Twenty, Just a Minute* and, crucially, *Test Match Special*.

In the sixties, the BBC World Service's newsreaders and cricket commentators spoke in what I can only describe as the old Empire style. Indians understood this speaking manner to be the Real Thing and All India Radio's broadcasters tended to aspire to it. Surajit Sen, Latika Ratnam and Pamela Singh read the news beautifully but it was always a performance: they were skilled high wire artists, intently going through their routines. But for Brian Johnston, Christopher Martin-Jenkins and Trevor Bailey, English was level ground and I listened, entranced by the marbled perfection of their accents.

I disapproved for years of John Arlott, a veteran member

of the *Test Match Special* commentary team, because I couldn't completely understand his Hampshire burr, but also because it sounded provincial and defective and I believed that remote cricket, that is, any cricket that had to be read about or listened in to, had to be written and spoken in Standard Received English. Trevor Bailey's pursed vowels and cut glass consonants were nearly too much of a good thing, but Billy Bunter, the BBC, and the anxieties of a recently post-colonial middle class had persuaded me that those accents were cricket's natural medium, the ether in which the game lived and breathed.

It was only in high school that I learnt that Brian Johnston, despite his jolly patter about cakes and his air of bluff good humour, was an unreconstructed supporter of cricket relations with racist South Africa. It was John Arlott of the defective accent who had taken the lead in getting Basil D'Oliveira to England from South Africa in 1960 where he couldn't play first-class cricket because he was classed as coloured. And it was Arlott who supported the cricket boycott of South Africa when his clubby *Test Match Special* colleagues spent their time finding excuses for the apartheid state. But though I came to my politically correct senses in the seventies and spent many happy hours subsequently listening to Arlott illumine the game, I can't deny that my cricketing childhood was spent in slavish worship of posh speech. This reverence was closely related to my belief that *My Fair Lady* was the best film ever made, but that's too large a digression for this introduction ... though, if you stop to think about it, Rex Harrison as Higgins would have been a natural for *Test Match Special*.

I read recently that Rupert Murdoch's Sky network had trumped the BBC for the rights to telecast and broadcast Test cricket in England. Just when broadband connections had made listening to *Test Match Special* online a real prospect, without twiddling knobs in anguished search of elusive shortwave frequencies, the BBC had gone and lost its right to turn Test cricket into the spoken word. Dismay doesn't cover it; I felt an epoch-ending gloom—the sort of desolation mercantilists must have felt when the pound abandoned the gold standard.

If my enthusiasm for cricket was distorted by this fetish about diction, it was redeemed by the absence of television coverage. The only way I could watch Test cricket was by buying a cheap seat in Feroz Shah Kotla whenever a match came round. Kids still watch cricket at the stadium but something fundamental has changed. Since the advent of the sponsored cricket telecast, stadium audiences in the eyes of Indian cricket administrators have become an irrelevant variable in the staging of a Test match. The local cricket board in Delhi or Cuttack or Jaipur makes so much money through its share of the television revenues that it isn't interested in the gate money. Selling tickets is too much trouble; it's easier to let them in for nothing.

The result is that the stadium spectator in India is no longer central to the economy of cricket; he lives off the fat of its television earnings. He is, in the strict sense of that word, a parasite. And when a game, any game, loses the paying fan, it loses a vital part of its being.

Stephen Jay Gould, neo-Darwinian, palaeontologist and baseball fan, spent his life rooting for the New York Yankees. Every time he went to a baseball match, even after he became a very grand professor, he bought a ticket, packed a pencil and a scorecard and took the subway to the stadium because the trains were full of baseball nuts like him and he wanted to feel the adrenalin rush that only communal fandom can bring.

That scorecard is important. Gould was going to the stadium to watch the ball game. Watching meant immersion:

keeping score was a way of sustaining that trance of absolute attention. He forced Alan Dershowitz, the celebrated lawyer, to switch off his cellphone when he tried to take a call while an inning was in progress. A ball game was sacred; would you take a call in the middle of a service in a synagogue?

But to the non-paying desi spectator, the stadium is a Roman circus. In place of a scorecard he carries a large placard with a large 4 or 6 printed on it. Instead of using the scorecard as a way of attending to the game, he waves that boundary placard to draw attention to himself. When you can watch the same game on television in the comfort of your home, the only reason to travel to the stadium is to be seen on camera.

It wasn't always like this. The Feroz Shah Kotla in Delhi is and has forever been a dreadful cricket stadium with miserable facilities. But forty years ago (I was nine), you had to queue from early in the morning to have a chance of buying the five-rupee daily tickets before they ran out. Even in the early seventies, the ticket buying spectator was enthusiastic enough for there to be lots of policemen to keep the queues in order. I was once a law-abiding part of a very long queue when some lumpen muscled in. In the angry confusion that followed, the constables of the Delhi police restored order in the way they knew best, by swinging metal-tipped lathis. One such swing had its arc interrupted by my bottom. 'Speechless with pain', I learnt that day, was not a metaphor, it was a realistic description.

The point of the story is not police brutality but the fact that after being brutalized (you should have seen the weal), I queued up again and bought my ticket. I wasn't (yet) your free-loading desi fan; I was a paying customer and I paid my dues. This meant getting to the cricket ground at five in the morning, hours before the match began, to get the good seats next to the sight screen. Early winter morning starts, blankets, packed tiffin, cold concrete terraces to sit on and transistor radios murmuring in my ear, that was my version of Gould's rituals of spectatorship. I swear I'd do it all over again . . . but they don't sell tickets any more.

To return to the modern Indian spectator we have to leave the stadium because he generally watches cricket on television. It's important to remember that not only is he non-paying, he's also non-playing in the sense that very few Indian men play cricket or anything else. Indians leave sport behind on the road to grown-up-ness. The first of the Men Commandments is: Thou Shall Not Play. As a result their devotion to cricket is a form of vicariousness. This is true to some degree of all kinds of spectatorship, but in countries where sport is participatory, this vicariousness is moderated by a practical understanding of the game and its challenges, by the empathy created by experience even if that experience was gained at a much lower level of skill. The Indian spectator is purely a fan. This has consequences for the way in which he watches cricket, the expectations he brings to the television set.

Not having played in years (or ever) he has no understanding of the contingencies that can turn a match, no first-hand experience of defeat. Cricket on television isn't, for him, that different from a movie or a cartoon: it unfolds on the same slick surface. He has a happy ending in mind and when that end doesn't come to pass, it has to be on account of cheating opponents, conspiring umpires, malevolent match referees or slack, spoilt, dishonest, traitorous players unworthy of India. Seduced by the tidy perfection of televised cricket, failure, in his book, is inexcusable.

This bulletproof sense of entitlement is nursed and fed and watered by television reruns which either show matches that India won, or excerpt great Indian innings from matches that India unaccountably lost. The big difference between this generation of spectators and mine is that when I was young, India lost at cricket all the time. Now, apart from contemporary defeats watched live (and it's to the credit of the Indian team that these are fewer than before), nearly every match shown on television is won by India. There's a cricket programme called *India Glorious* on television that specializes in reruns. No prizes for guessing how often India loses on that show.

The most satisfactory cricket match ever played from the point of view of the contemporary fan is not listed by *Wisden* because it was played in a country that the ICC doesn't recognize: the colonial India confected by Aamir Khan in *Lagaan*.

But that's a cheap shot. Rereading the pieces that make up *Men in White*, I realize that I can't, in good conscience, sneer at the modern couch potato from the vantage point of the virtuously enthusiastic child that I once was. After forty years and more of rooting for India, I may not contain multitudes but I know that I have to make room for at least two people: that middle aged, free-loading, non-playing slob on the sofa *and* the child on the concrete terraces for whom the sight of Farokh Engineer swaggering down the steps of Willingdon Pavilion to open the Indian innings was a doorway to heaven. Separately and sometimes together, both of them wrote this book.

The Long Game

Not Watching but Drowning

Newspapers in England sometimes carry reports on their sports pages about a game called Real Tennis. Someone explained to me that this was an archaic version of the modern game with bizarre features like sloping side walls, asymmetric courts and fiendishly complex rules. Bizarre, I thought, thinking of the lucidity and elegance of the modern game. But when the Board of Control for Cricket in India (BCCI) recently said yes to Twenty20 cricket, for a nightmarish instant I pictured my children's children reading a boxed report on Test cricket, thinking to themselves, how weird is this. Then I thought of all the reasons this couldn't, wouldn't happen, and wrote them down as reassurance.

Remember the rest day? As if five days weren't long enough.

Test cricket has intervals that correspond with mealtimes: lunch, drinks, tea. Night falls on it; you dream about the game's possibilities, you wake to it in the morning. You can't drink six packs and crunch chips to it. NRIs who try, make the mistake of confusing American ball games with cricket. They aren't the same thing; not even baseball comes close. A few hours of action and a result: cricket isn't like that.

Cricket is to other games what Vyas is to V.S. Pritchett, what the Mahabharata is to a short story. A short story demands a resolution; every element within that story works towards that resolution, is subordinate to it. Test cricket is different. It has self-contained sub-plots that may or may not contribute to the end. It has epic losers. Winning is important but individual digressions give pleasure in themselves. That's why cricket audiences celebrate great losing innings. It's like watching Karna fight in vain: tragedy heightens the heroism of the performance.

Despite Marqusee's fine book, *Anyone But England*, it's hard to explain or understand cricket in wholly materialist terms. I can't think of any other game, bourgeois or plebeian, pre- or post-industrial, that lasts the best part of a week and has an audience willing to go along. Complete immersion over five days: there is no parallel in sport.

That's why watching or listening to matches in different time zones is so unsettling. Cricket is meant to follow the day. When it follows someone else's day, you're dislocated, left dangling. Up at 5 a.m. to tune in to Tests in Oz, to catch Alan McGilvray's odd flat voice over the static, then asleep in the school bus going home—I knew jet lag before I'd ever been on a plane. Following cricket in Australia was exciting because it was hard to do and shortwave radio made me feel travelled in a second-hand way, but those Tests were over by noon and I had an empty day to live through. On school days, the day's play Down Under was done before I got home from school. Cricket fans my age discovered time-zone trauma decades before young men and women in call centres did.

To people who don't know it, Test cricket is the playground equivalent of dhrupad: tedious, repetitive and impossibly long. Everything about the game is inhumanly drawn out, indifferent to mortal attention spans or even comfort. The nature of Test match supervision has two men stand near motionless for thirty hours, semaphoring their judgements through terrible heat or bitter cold. This requires not merely fitness but stoicism and a capacity for suffering. And though we know better, we aren't immune to the world's bafflement. The most passionate fan frets about Test cricket's future, wonders if it's too queer for the contemporary world. We shouldn't worry.

Test match spectators are the modern world's last audience for epic narrative. Peter Brook's *Mahabharata* was made for us; we're its perfect audience, only we never went to watch because there was a Test on the telly. Aamir Khan, in his movie, *Lagaan*, got people to sit through a four-hour film by the simple device of building a cricket match into the movie. Knowing his audience, he shrank the contest between imperialism and nationalism into a cricket match and tapped into the vast reservoir of patience and passion learnt from watching cricket. Once he had persuaded the paying public that nationalism was best understood as a fuzzier form of Test cricket, he had it hooked.

Test cricket is best understood in terms of epic theatre. Think of the Ram Lila: it used to be and still is, a performance played out over days, like a Test match. Every year, as a child, I sat through a long sequence of daily performances that led to Ravana burning. The Ram Lila is not for everybody; it is badly acted and boring and Sita's often a hairy man, but there's nothing quite like it, that accumulation of action by night and day, that intense, gradually developed sense of an ending. But, as with Test matches, there's a popular, abbreviated version. There is the one-day or single-evening Ram Lila, pioneered in Delhi by the Bharatiya Kala Kendra. The production uses the idiom of classical dance and drama eclectically to create a condensed, boutique narrative that goes down well with Delhi's middle classes. It's the limited-overs version of the Ram Lila, but the real thing still exists and people watch it.

Like the Ram Lila, Test cricket needs a special kind of watching. Long hours spent sleeping on chairs and cement steps, or slumped on a slope of grass, dozing. Test cricket takes you over, creates terrible mood swings, even suicidal depressions because so much of your life is invested in it. You watch, drifting, surrounded by the thing. It's like living underwater.

But unlike the Ram Lila, cricket isn't a dwindling tradition in need of private or public subsidy because in television, Test cricket has found its natural medium. All sport has been remade by television and the commercial possibilities it created, but none more so than cricket. CNN discovered that there was money to be made in telecasting breaking news round-the-clock, that people would watch endless shots of night skies lit up by missile trails and anti-aircraft flashes so long as they thought there was a contest on and particularly if they felt that they had a dog in the fight. There was a market for the action and there was a market for the talking heads who glossed the action: retired generals, retired politicians and embedded correspondents.

Like war, Test cricket allows you to fill days and weeks of television programming with reliable action that pulls in reassuring viewership numbers. For the game's followers, every Test match is breaking news, and every tour is a new campaign. The American public's support for that country's wars is more easily understood if you think of the American people as a television audience and their armies as their touring sides.

The nature of Test cricket allows television spots at the end of every over and the longer intervals in play that occur every two hours can be filled with cricket talk, so the punditry and the commercials never stop. And as if a seven-hour day wasn't enough, the sports channels have an hour of talk before the day begins and an hour of talk after. The point is this: far from cricket having to mutate into increasingly compact forms—limited-overs cricket and now the absurd twenty-over format—in order to survive in the modern world, the modern world, i.e., televison, wants Test cricket to be ever more itself. If anything, television does its best to prolong Test matches. Doordarshan has recently taken to replaying the whole day's play, unedited, so something like fifteen hours of the day are filled with men in white.

Test cricket has designs on both our attention and our lives. Television and Test cricket offer not just diversion and entertainment, they hold out the insidious pleasure of an alternative, voyeuristic existence. Cricket is meant to be spun out and elaborated: television does just that. The pitch reports, the coin toss, the on-field interviews, the scrutiny of technique, the constant reruns of matches we've won, create on television a continuous, enveloping world. It is cricket as wallpaper.

We were depressed, rightly, by empty stadiums when India played a Test series in Pakistan. Great contests deserve packed houses. But when empty stands are theorized into symptoms of an anachronistic game's inevitable decline, polite scepticism is in order. Test cricket needs people at the ground to make the contests passionate and real, but for two decades now the spectators who sustain the game have been watching it on television.

Ironically, technology has come to the rescue of this intractably old-world game. NRIs in America record inconveniently timed Test matches on DVD recorders to watch after work. Living in Brooklyn, I watched the 2003 World Cup final on my computer via broadband webcast. The marvels of computer-aided telecasts have helped millions of viewers tell the difference between a top-spinner and a flipper thanks to SpinVision; to understand the complexities of the leg before wicket (lbw) law thanks to Hawk-Eye, and most of all, to understand bowling and batting techniques in an unprecedented way. Television hasn't just consolidated an audience for the game; it has created more literate and informed spectators than any the game has had before. The sophistication and knowingness with which young children mimic Warne and Tendulkar is a tribute to the teaching skills of television.

It doesn't always seem that way when you watch crowds in Kolkata riot during a World Cup match, but if you must watch one-day cricket, what can you expect? And the reason the rest day was done away with was not because the rhythms of Test matches didn't suit the modern world, it was because the modern world wanted more Test matches. To paraphrase some poet or the other, we couldn't bear the eyelessness of a day without Test cricket. Now, thanks to television, that need never happen.

Cricket in My Neighbourhood

Tennis, however amateurishly played, is recognizably the same game at every level. So is football. The game you play in the park is the same as the ones you watch in the Premiership. Not so cricket. Childhood cricket, in its lack of basic kit, in its home-made rules, in its duration, was planets apart from the game Pataudi played. Test cricket and the five- or six-a-side matches we played in our neighbourhoods sometimes had only the bat and ball in common. But they were enough; Pataudi and us, we played different versions of the real thing.

I speak for no one but the boys I played with forty years ago. The cricket we played each afternoon in Pandara Park wasn't the authorized version but nor was it authentically local. It wasn't representative of neighbourhood cricket in India or even Delhi. It was the kind of cricket boys played in government colonies: localities where civil servants and their children lived. These neighbourhoods were concentrated in the city the British built to serve as colonial India's capital, so I suppose our version of the game could reasonably be called the Lutyens Variant.

This wasn't cricket as it was played on the maidans of Bombay or Calcutta. New Delhi wasn't a high density metropolis where a public maidan like Shivaji Park was shared out in a hundred games. New Delhi was a capital town and Pandara Park was an expansively built colony, laid out at a time when space was no consideration. When we moved into the double-storeyed house that my father had been assigned ('allotted' was the official term), my brother and I had a choice of parks to play in. Pandara Park's hundred or so semi-detached houses were built around two reasonably level hedged-in greens that were made for cricket. Some perversely placed trees, mainly neem, kept them from being perfect playing fields and ugly flowerbeds crammed with red cannas were natural ball traps, but we were privileged children: we had the park to ourselves.

Every day in the mid-sixties, at four in the afternoon (four-thirty in summer), a dozen children converged on the triangular park (because it was larger than the round one at its wide end) carrying between them four stumps, a bat, a ball and sometimes, gloves and pads. The gloves and pads depended on the fat boy who lived in C-1/ . . . Since the basic action of the game could occur without protective gear—boy with ball bowls to boy with bat—our salaried parents weren't keen to spring for extras. Even stumps. It was technically possible to play without stumps: you marked a wicket on a tree and bowled to it from twenty-two paces, but the tree's emerging root structure meant you had to stand yards in front of it to get predictable bounce. But between a dozen sets of parents, we could generally raise four stumps. Nobody had six—that would have been showing off, because we needed just one to mark the bowler's end and if the batsman was short of the bowler's crease, breaking the wicket at the other end counted as a run out. All the stumps we ever used then had their business ends shod in wicked pointy metal, the better to drive them into the ground with. I never saw a set that ended in blunt wooden points.

The boy in C-1/ . . . had political parents, so he owned a proper kit: pads, gloves, six stumps, keeper's gloves, even four separate bails! He couldn't play at all, but he was biddable and content to stand by the hedge at the edges of the action in return for the use of his property. He didn't come out to play every day, though, which was inconvenient and strange. Sometimes servants would be sent to call him in before the evening was done and that was really annoying because we had to take off his gear, gather his stuff, and give it to him in the middle of play.

But things got better and by the time we entered our teens (otherwise a foreign time of life which made no difference to our standing at home or school), we had pads and gloves of our own. But no one wore two pads even when two were available. Their straps cut into the skin of those who wore shorts (as most of us did) and they were so wide across the knee that they rubbed together and twisted round and made us waddle between wickets like we had a dhobi itch. The general practice was to wear one on the front leg. This allowed us to rehearse the rudiments of technique like getting in line or playing forward.

Without pads on pitches with uncertain bounce, the first order of business as a batsman was to keep both shins outside the line of the ball. Nobody took guard in colony cricket but I used to station my feet a few inches outside leg stump and my instinct, when we played without protective gear, was to slide my left foot towards midwicket, so that when the ball arrived I could take a swing at it without risking injury. Injury and pain had taught us a simple cricketing truth: you couldn't bat-and-pad without pad.

Our wickets were often longer than the official twenty-two yards. We would walk twenty-two paces as an approximate measure and because we were children, we over-compensated by taking big steps. The depth of the crease was, conversely, less than what it should have been. It was measured by laying the bat perpendicular to the line of the stumps and then adding the length of the bat handle to the length of the bat. Since our bats were less than full size, our creases tended to be shallow. Small boys bowling on outsize pitches meant that apart from one or two exceptional players, most of us bowled long-hops that bounced mid-pitch and sat up to be hit, or bounced again before getting to the batsman. The only way we knew of getting the ball to pitch on a goodish length was to bowl an over-arm lob that steepled upwards and fell to earth somewhere near the batsman. These lob balls, more launched than bowled, were called 'donkey drops'.

Bats tended to be small because they were the most expensive part of cricket's kit and had to be kept going a long time. The small bat and the absence of protection together produced the Mohalla Stance. This was an open, two-eyed stance, the left shoulder pointing towards midwicket, the bat grounded *between* the batsman's feet as he stood crouched in a near squat to fit himself around his tiny instrument. Not everyone stood in this way, but the low stance was a useful height from which to jam down on the surra, or shooter which, given the surfaces we played on, arrived every over. When the ball bounced, the open stance was a good preliminary position from which to play the cross-batted swipe or lappa.

The etymology of lappa is uncertain. I've always thought (and still do) that it's taken from colloquial Hindustani and is related to words like lappar (a slap) or lappeybaaz (a person, like Shahid Afridi, given to lappas). But I was recently confounded by the entry for 'lap' in Michael Rundell's *Dictionary of Cricket*:

lap n 1 a cross-batted stroke—somewhat like a pull—
played especially to a ball pitching on or outside off-
stump and sending it into the area between midwicket
and square leg.

I couldn't have come up with a better definition in English
of a lappa if I had tried, so I came to the conclusion that this
English use of lap was a colonial derivation from the
Hindustani lappa. Notice that this definition of 'lap' in a
book published twenty years ago, is different from the current
use of 'lap' which generally refers to the paddle sweep favoured
by batsmen like Dravid and Tendulkar, as in, '. . . he lapped
it very fine between keeper and leg slip'.

As an adult, I think of the ball as the most beautiful object
in cricket—the polished red leather, the seam, the way it can
be worked and twirled, the perfect size of it—but for us as
children, the fetish object was unquestionably the bat. There
was a ritual attached to it. New, it had to be seasoned with
linseed oil for two, three weeks before it could be used. We
had no idea what the oil did, except turn the unmarked off-
white of the bat face piss-yellow. I oiled reverently; what I
hated doing was the other part of breaking the bat in,
pounding it with a ball, because the process disfigured the
brand new bat face with red blotches. My understanding was
that the pounding got the new bat used to the rigours of
impact. I think we saw bats as inert but living creatures that
had to be treated gently and not rushed into experience. I
say this because there was another kind of bat which we
treated like a dead thing, like an instrument, merely: the
parchment bat. This was a ready to use bat that didn't have
to be seasoned: it came with its blade wrapped at intervals in
three-inch wide bands of thread and sheathed in a thick
membrane. The only reasons to buy it—besides the labour

saved on seasoning it—were that it was cheaper than a willow bat and also more durable because the membrane (probably some kind of intestinal skin) and the bands of thread kept its blade from chipping. But no one bought parchment bats if they could help it, because they were hideous to look at and, more importantly, had no 'stroke'.

A bat's 'stroke' was a compound quality made up equally of the feel of its sweet spot and the way the ball travelled on impact. Bad bats—and parchment bats were the worst—had no 'stroke' at all: all the batsman felt when ball struck bat was a jarring shock that travelled up the arm, and the ball just didn't 'go'. The good bat produced a low, cushiony thhunk when the ball was middled and the ball flew.

Most bats were used well after they began to go at the splice: it was common to see a batsman, in between deliveries, holding the bat in front of him, face down, and shaking it hard to test the extent of give. Quikfix was always used to join a dislocated splice. It never worked, but we tried. There was, generally, just one good bat in the neighbourhood; the non-doing bat carried by the non-striker was there to be grounded in the event of a sharp single and, more generally, to avoid the unbalanced awkwardness of running between wickets empty-handed. Every time a single was taken, the batsmen met mid-pitch to exchange bats. This was preceded by the ritual of gently slapping bat faces in solidarity, a sort of pre-modern high five. All batting occurred at one end of the pitch, the one with three stumps, and if a batsman ran a single off the last ball, he walked back to the batting end to take strike.

The scariest kind of bowling to face on those 'pitches' was fast left-arm spin of the sort Derek Underwood once bowled for England. Saten was the local left-arm bowler. He bowled over the wicket, pitched it a foot outside leg, from where it turned square across the stumps. Around the time it pitched, the batsman lost sight of it and was likely to be hit, depending on the bounce, anywhere between his shins and his solar plexus. When the surface was particularly uneven or the batsman specially inept, it was customary to tell the demon bowler: 'No fast bowling, oye.'

Six balls made up an over, the end of which was signalled by someone shouting, 'Over up!' No Pandara Park umpire ever said 'over' because for us, 'over' was a noun, a name given to a set of six deliveries, not a verb meaning 'done'.

The order of play was settled in two ways, depending on turnout. If there were upwards of, say eight players present, we played teams. The two best players would be nominated captains and they would select players alternately from the talent available. It was embarrassing being left till the last, but the consolation was that selection was guaranteed. When the turnout was too small to make up teams, say a small uneven number like seven, the batting order was settled by 'numbering': one boy stood behind another and mimed numbers from one to seven by holding up his fingers; the boy in front assigned each mimed number without knowing what it was, to the assembled batsmen (batting was all we were interested in, no one ever fought for a turn to bowl).

The turnout also determined the rules for run making. There were never enough players, especially in the two-team version, to field behind the wicket, so batsmen were seldom allowed to run for shots placed backward of square on either side. No one wasted any time practising the cut or the glance. For years I imagined that the cut was an involuntary or voluntary edge that slid through slips; only much later did I learn that it was a stroke played with the face of the bat. (I also thought, for purely phonetic reasons, that lbw was lpw and sightscreen was sidescreen. Like an illiterate, I knew what the sound signified without knowing how it was written.) When the attendance at the ground was especially poor, onside runs were banned as well. Hedges and ball obscuring flower-beds were dead zones: if the ball got lost in them, batsmen stopped running. There were two other rules not found in the laws of cricket. (1) Double touch was out: if your bat touched the ball twice, either unwittingly or to keep it from trickling on to the stumps, you were out; and (2) the idiot law which laid down that when one of a team's last pair of batsmen was out, the innings was over, had no traction in neighbourhood cricket. Last Man Batting was an iron law. The last wicket in Pandara Park really was the last wicket, not a weaselling description of the second-last wicket.

The interesting thing about the Lutyens Variant or Pandara Park cricket was that it existed in itself. Nothing depended on it and it led to nothing: it was as purely recreational as a game could get. It wasn't part of a league, for example. Bangalore had a many-tiered league as did Bombay. Delhi had some club cricket but its government colony babalog lived and played within the bounds of the neighbourhood. Very occasionally there'd be a Sunday match against some similar sarkari locality nearby, but whole seasons could pass without such a contest. The ambitious, talented ones developed their skills through other institutions: either school cricket or by joining the coaching class at the nearby National Stadium.

Neighbourhood cricket depended on our enthusiasm for the game and our membership, courtesy our parents, of Pandara Park. There was an innocence about that immersion in cricket, that unconditional pleasure in each other's company and the game itself. Time and distance and nostalgia make it shimmer like some amateur Eden. But it wasn't that. Tangavelu, who was my age and lived in Pandara Park and loved cricket, didn't play with us in the triangular park because he lived in our servants' quarters. There were two servants' quarters to every house, so there was no shortage of the servant young. They didn't play cricket in the park, not even at inconvenient hours when the bona fide children of the neighbourhood weren't using it. Like all amateur idylls, Pandara Park cricket was based on a rule of exclusion. Still, it's hard not to love it looking back because it was ours and there was joy in those afternoons and we took the world as we were given it, in New Delhi in the sixties. These would be better memories, though, if I had asked Tangavelu to play.

Why Not Hockey?

In Regal Cinema in Connaught Circus, some time in the sixties, they screened a half-hour documentary on India's legendary hockey goalkeeper, Shankar Laxman, before the main feature. Hockey was huge: what Bradman was to the Aussies, the great Dhyan Chand was to us. We watched his son, Ashok Kumar, with desperate hope, willing him to dribble us back to his father's glory days. When India lost to Pakistan—and by the sixties we lost more often than we won—we bled inside. My children don't know that India has a hockey team. What happened?

Let's eliminate the bad arguments for cricket's popularity. Cricket takes precedence over every other game in the minds and hearts of Indians because of the following reasons intrinsic to its nature:

1. _____
2. _____
3. _____

You can fill in the blanks with the reasons you like—the longeurs of Test match cricket suit the Indian conception of time; the physical demands of the game are minimal which makes it the one sport unfit Indians can play; cricket's intricate laws, its worship of orthodoxy, its capacity to generate statistical trivia, appeal to the pedantry of the upper-caste mind; its stop-start rhythm makes it the perfect vehicle for television commercials—and they will all sound plausible and they will all be wrong.

Stephen Jay Gould, great neo-Darwinian and lifelong baseball fan, drew upon his understanding of evolution to criticize theories that tried to explain baseball's popularity amongst American intellectuals in terms of baseball's intrinsic nature. He wrote in *Triumph and Tragedy in Mudville: A Lifelong Passion for Baseball*, (W.W. Norton, New York, 2003):

'We live in a basically unpredictable world, featuring histories dominated by contingency—that is, actual patterns that make good sense and become subject to interesting and sensible explanation once they unfold as they did, but that could have proceeded along innumerable alternative routes that would have yielded just as sensible a history, but that did not gain the good fortune of actual occurrence.

Thus, if it be true that intellectually inclined American sports fans tend to enjoy and follow baseball at a higher frequency than other popular national sports, I don't for a moment attribute such favouritism to any inherent property of the game itself.'

Gould's caution could serve as a corrective to the Indian need to connect the nature of cricket to the nature of desis. Matching Essences is a diverting parlour game, but if we are looking for non-mystical explanations for cricket's popularity, we should try, instead, to dig up and record those accidents that nudged cricket centrestage in India and then embark upon the interesting and plausible explanations that make sense of its subsequent development. We need empirical histories of cricket to answer the question, not generalities about Cricket Eternal and the Indian Mind. Put another way, Ramachandra Guha's *A Corner of a Foreign Field* is a more reliable guide to the game in India than Ashis Nandy's *The Tao of Cricket*.

Though Guha's book doesn't set out to answer our question, it does so en passant. Introducing the book, Guha makes a large claim. He says that it isn't so much a history of Indian cricket as a history of India through cricket. It isn't unusual for academics to make inflated claims for their work (thus a book with a title like *Empire, Hierarchy & Being* could be the memoir of a colonial clerk with a tenure-seeking introduction as long as the memoir), but Guha's history of Indian cricket lives up to that ambitious description. Through the book, Guha shows us how cricket becomes an arena where arguments and quarrels about defining issues like race, class, caste, religious community and nation are played out. In Guha's narrative, the early dispute between Parsees in Bombay and the white official class about the right of colonial subjects to play cricket on public turf also claimed by polo-playing Englishmen, pushes cricket on to the highway of Indian history, where it takes on more and more passengers, some muttering about race, others about caste or community or nation, all of them united by a shared passion for an unlikely game.

Returning to Gould's emphasis on the role of contingency, this dispute could just as well have been about football, another English team sport that Indian subjects learnt from their colonial masters. Maybe it was cricket because the Parsees, being middle class natives, wanted to play a game favoured by upper-class Englishmen. Or perhaps it was, as Gould suggests in another context, pure happenstance. I don't know enough to say for sure, but reading Guha's book, it seems reasonable to conclude that the polo–cricket dispute gave cricket in India a political headstart over other team games and that subsequently cricket became the vehicle of choice for several sorts of Indian striving.

Still, the world changes and once dominant games cede ground to others. England, the home of cricket, has seen the game marginalized by the massive passion for soccer. In Gould's own country, baseball, the national game, is now a distant third in the popularity stakes, behind American football and basketball. So the reasons adduced for cricket's hold on the consciousness of urban, middle class Indians during the Raj can't by themselves explain the continuing grip of the game over its contemporary public.

Why, for example, did hockey not sustain its challenge to cricket's pre-eminence in India? In the last years of colonialism and the early years of the Republic, it was hockey that symbolized the ability of Indians to compete and excel on the global stage. Our hockey teams won gold medal after gold medal at the Olympics and the standing of a legend like Dhyan Chand in the sixties when I was a boy, rivalled, indeed surpassed the standing of most cricket greats. Compared to Dhyan Chand's wizardry in the Olympics, the deeds of a Nayudu in the Pentangular seemed provincial.

So why didn't hockey become the standard bearer of Indian aspiration? In the absence of any serious work on the subject, we can speculate. In the early years of independence, hockey in India wasn't given the attention that it deserved since, compared to cricket, it was the less posh sport. Middle class children played hockey, but cricket was more desirable because it was the saheb's game. This preference might have changed had India's hockey team sustained its global dominance, but it didn't. Two things happened. The European teams that controlled international hockey changed the rules in ways that discounted the virtuosity that characterized Indian hockey. So Indian hockey lost its grip on the world game and with it, that gold-plated glint of success so necessary to wean Indians from cricket. Worse, Pakistan, the arch-enemy, began to beat us regularly, taking top international honours like the World Cup or Olympic gold despite the rule changes that handicapped the subcontinental style. Being bested by Pakistan snuffed out hockey's hopes of rivalling cricket in our affections.

Our love for cricket was born of a sense of self-preservation. Post-colonial elites find cunning ways of nurturing their obsessive need for international recognition. India, under the stewardship of the anti-imperialist Nehru, stayed within a Commonwealth headed by the English monarch because as Britain's largest former colony, India counted for more within the Commonwealth than it did in larger assemblies of nations. Cricket was a sporting version of the Commonwealth: a game played by a small group of colonial and ex-colonial countries. It was a small club and India was very much a junior member, patronized by the MCC and willing to defer to it, because it was better to count for something in a little pond than to count for nothing in the wide open spaces of world sport. In that world, all we had to cherish were a couple of semi-final appearances by Ramanathan Krishnan, two fourth-place finishes by Milkha Singh and P.T. Usha and Vijay Amritraj's fleeting membership of the ABC (Amritraj, Borg, Connors) of tennis.

In team games like football, our rank in the world read like our position on the UN's human development report. In hockey, our team strove mightily, but between Dhyan Chand and Dhanraj Pillay, there had occurred a fall from grace too steep to be easily reversed. And Pakistan beat us still. So cricket remained, by default, the team sport of choice, and when cable television and its commercial opportunities came calling, cricket was the chief beneficiary. For those of us who have followed cricket from the time before television, it is hard to appreciate how massively television expanded the audience for the game. But had there been a contender, had Indian hockey hung in there and retained its niche in the affections of the nation's sporting public till the arrival of cable television, cricket's Indian imperium might not have been the foregone conclusion that it seems today.

You could object that too much weight has been given in this account to the middle class and its anxieties and not enough to the actual practice of sport in India. After all, in Kerala, West Bengal, the North East and many other parts of India, hockey and football are the team sports most played by the general public. This is a reasonable point, but it's worth remembering that games can be widely played and yet remain peripheral to the public life of a nation. Take soccer in the US: soccer is the sport most played by American schoolchildren, both boys and girls. But in the US media market, in American writing, in cinema, in the American imagination, soccer counts for nothing. In computerspeak, football in America has no mindshare.

Cricket's near-monopoly in India doesn't mean that it shall be forever thus. In a world globalized by cable television, cricket is at a disadvantage: it is plainly not a global sport. Given the length of a Test match, the world of cricket will never be much larger than it is today; the year isn't long enough to accommodate more than ten or so Test-playing nations. In a world where Indians skim through global league tables looking for Indian contenders, a globally played game like soccer has enormous potential. The sports channels have made Manchester United, Arsenal, Real Madrid, Juventus and their stars household names in urban India. If, by some miracle, a soccer league of semi-decent standard were to emerge in India, or if a couple of home-grown footballers were to make a mark in the European leagues, football could cause an enormous stir. The reception given to Sania Mirza's relatively minor triumphs in an individual sport like tennis is a preview of what could happen with soccer.

This doesn't mean that cricket will be dethroned any time soon. Its installed base is so large that it'll take some shifting. But if the game is mismanaged, as it frequently is by the ICC and its affiliated boards, if it is devalued by no-contests featuring teams like Bangladesh and Zimbabwe and consequently begins to feel like a tawdry, uncompetitive, provincial game, India's vain middle class may well decide that it is too small and tarnished a mirror to properly reflect its self-esteem. Were that to happen, some future historian might explain the decline of cricket in terms of the remarkable fit between the essence of soccer and the Indian mind.

Change, for Better and Worse

God's Eye View: Cricket and the Camera

I followed the great 1971 tour of the West Indies in the sports pages of the Times of India. *Cricket in the Caribbean was frustrating for the desi fan; there was no ball-by-ball commentary, no counterpart to* Test Match Special. *Tony Cozier came afterwards. So Gavaskar's monster debut happened in radio silence as did Sardesai's great double century. Then, after the tour, Doordarshan announced that it was going to show twenty-six minutes of footage of the entire tour. And here's the thing: my friends and I (we were fourteen or thereabouts) didn't think this was paltry. We thought it was a gift.*

The contemporary spectator's relationship with cricket is so wholly shaped by the television camera that it takes an effort of will to recognize that cameras were once peripheral to the game. Cricket's relationship with the camera has passed through three distinct stages. In the beginning the camera existed to record cricket for posterity. Don Bradman is sometimes available on television in black and white, demonstrating his trademark shots in some long-dead nets. I remember watching, in my final year in school, the film of the tied Test between Australia and the West Indies in the school's auditorium. Some years ago, there was a documentary film shown on a sports channel about Graeme Pollock and I watched, mesmerized, because it was the first time I had seen footage of the great man at the crease. Movie cameras in those early years produced a scrappy and incomplete visual record of cricket gone by.

With the coming of television, the camera took on another function; it now existed to relay cricket to contemporary audiences. To start with, that was all it did; it was radio commentary with moving pictures. The commentators talked just as much as they had on radio till they learnt that their descriptive function had become largely irrelevant. We didn't need to be told that Sobers was running in to bowl because we could see that for ourselves. Nor was the commercial potential of camera-relayed cricket exploited. Cricket associations made no money from the telecast of their product because it was seen as an elaboration of radio commentary and therefore a form of public service broadcasting. Also, their commercial horizons were limited to gate money and the paying public, so in many countries matches weren't telecast in the city they were being played in to make sure that local fans didn't stay home and watch for free.

Slowly, people got used to the medium and began to understand and exploit it better. Commentators stopped narrating the game and began to explain it instead, in brief asides. The audiences that television made possible began to attract commercial sponsors and money came into the game on a scale that was unimaginable before television. Today, cricket's economy is largely based on television revenues.

Cricket is made for television in a way that no other team game is (with the possible exception of American football). There are many reasons for this, but the most basic one is that thanks to the zoom lens and the close-up, you can see the game better on television than you can in the stadium. You could argue that this is true for all sports but you'd be wrong. Take football. In football the action happens more or less continuously over the whole pitch; in cricket it is largely confined to a single set-piece repeated over and over again on a twenty-two-yard strip in the middle of the ground: it's a bit like watching a tennis match from a distance of seventy metres. While the stadium spectator in football gets a view of the action that is broadly comparable to camera coverage because the ball is large and the action spread over the field, the cricket camera delivers pictures that are incomparably better than anything you could see from a stadium seat.

You can see the ball turn, you can see it swing and reverse swing, you can watch the seam hit the ground upright or wobbly, you can watch McGrath's mouth make obscenities and if the stump microphones have been left on 'accidentally', you can hear him. And then, you can watch it again . . . on the slow motion replay. What you miss most in the stadium is the luxury of seeing things again and savvy stadium administrators have plugged that hole by erecting giant replay screens. Now spectators and players test what they have seen with their own eyes against the omniscience of the television camera.

Spin Vision, the Snickometer, the virtual strip used to assess lbw decisions are elaborations of the close-up and the slow motion replay: they make an arcane game with complex laws graphic and explicit. But doesn't this happen with every game? No, it doesn't, not to the same extent. Partly because in no other game is stadium spectatorship so difficult and limiting. But the main difference between cricket and football is that the continuous nature of football makes the replay much rarer. In football there is no equivalent for the dead time between one ball and another, so a replay happens only after a goal or whenever the ball goes out of play for a reasonable length of time. The slow motion replay as a way of clarifying real time action dominates cricket like it does no other sport.

The nature of cricket has helped make the television camera authoritative. Thanks to Kerry Packer and Channel 9, the camera's record has become the authorized version. This brings us to the latest role that the camera has begun to play in cricket: that of regulation. The camera not only records and relays cricket, now it also regulates it. Since the South Africans pioneered the third umpire for adjudicating run outs via slow motion replays, we have seen more and more decisions referred to the third umpire: dubious catches, marginal stumpings and close boundary calls have all begun to fall within the jurisdiction of the camera and its slow motion replay. In an astonishingly short time, cricket's audiences have begun to take the camera's jurisdiction for granted. The umpire sketching a rectangle in the air, so bizarre when it first happened, now seems normal, so normal that we forget that cricket is singular and exceptional in its routine use of the replay. In football the referee makes all his decisions without reference to video footage. To some extent this difference is explained by the tempo of football: it isn't possible to hold the game up while an off-field referee decides if the offside call was good. But surely marginal decisions about goals (did the ball cross the line before it was intercepted, was it Maradona's hand that knocked it in or his head?) could be referred to the camera without disrupting the game, since a goal creates an interval in play.

So why doesn't football use the camera's testimony in the way that cricket has enthusiastically begun to do? Why doesn't tennis? Why isn't the dodgy ace or the baseline clipping ground shot quickly reviewed by the camera angles that are available to the viewer? It can't be the hold-up in play because play is routinely held up by players disputing line calls. On clay in the French Open, it isn't unusual for the umpire to climb down from her perch to inspect the mark left by the ball on the surface to confirm or overrule a call. So why do these games not use the available technology in the way that cricket does?

I think the answer to this is that in cricket the camera's view of the game is (a) so patently superior to anything the human eye can see, and (b) so frequently aired via slow motion replays that cricket watchers, administrators and players have become conditioned over time to accept the camera's testimony as conclusive. In no other game do these two conditions apply to the same extent. Neither is the difference between the naked eye and the camera so great nor is the camera given so many opportunities to rehearse its omniscience. In these games, therefore, the camera's view has not had the opportunity to become hegemonic.

Alone amongst major sports (again with the exception of American football), cricket has chosen to submit its decisions to the judgement of the camera. Most other games choose to live with a margin of human error, but cricket in recent years has been seduced by the prospect of perfection. There's nothing necessarily wrong with this, so long as cricket's administrators are consistent in their use of technology. During the Pakistan tour of Australia in 1999, we heard Australian cricketers past and present criticize the minute examination by camera of the bowling actions of Brett Lee and Shoaib Akhtar. Chappell said that many fast bowlers in the past whose actions were accepted as legitimate had kinks in their action similar to those of Lee and Akhtar; only now these kinks were being blown out of proportion because superior cameras made them apparent. Rackemann suggested that the question of chucking be left to the unaided judgement of the umpires in the middle. Justin Langer opposed any action against them because they were great entertainers who helped bring crowds back to cricket.

These three opinions add up to a permissive position on chucking which is plainly wrong. Chappell's argument is inconsistent. When the camera captures a batsman a hair's breadth short of the crease or on the line, nobody complains that it is being pedantic or too literal in its interpretation of cricket's laws. Similarly, if the camera spots a kink, however small, that falls within the definition of chucking; its evidence needs to be used. The idea of an allowable 'kink' is hugely unfair to bowlers like Donald, Akram, Ambrose, Srinath and Walsh, who suffered terrible physical stress trying to bowl fast within the definition of a legal delivery.

To argue, as Langer does, that Lee and Akhtar ought to be exempt from a rigorous enforcement of the law because they are entertainers who bring colour to the game and crowds is appalling because it reduces cricket to the level of WWE wrestling matches. Cricket is entertainment because it is a credible contest. It is credible because it is defined by strict laws. Bend or break those rules in the name of entertainment and you convert cricket into a dishonest spectacle where players become performers instead of contestants, ingratiating themselves with an audience rather than battling each other. To the extent that the 15 degree 'flexion' allowed by the ICC legitimizes dodgy fast bowlers, it damages cricket. Having brought the camera into cricket, cricket's authorities can't use its testimony selectively. The camera is a stern god: it demands complete submission.

When Hearing Was Believing: Cricket on the Radio

We had a giant Philips radio at home with an aerial wire that was tied to a stick on the roof. It had six piano keys, SW1, SW2, SW3, SW4, MW and Phono. Nothing happened if you pressed Phono; the rest brought us, variously, Vividh Bharati, Radio Ceylon, Test Match Special at 3.30 p.m. on the BBC, crack-of-dawn commentary on Radio Australia and the signature tune that led into AIR's Test match broadcast: teeeen, diddy di deeen, diddy di deeen . . .

Till Doordarshan began telecasting matches in the seventies, cricket's audience listened to the game more than watched it. Cricket, like revealed religion, depended on the Word and its interpreters. Radio commentary was religion because it transported you to unseen, unknown realms. 'This is All India Radio. We now take you over to the Eden Gardens for a running commentary on the fifth day of the fourth cricket Test between England and India. Our commentators are . . .' When I started listening in the mid-sixties, these commentators were Chakrapani, Pearson Surita, and the unspeakable Maharajkumar of Vijianagram aka Vizzy. Fortunately, A.F.S. Talyarkhan had stopped broadcasting by then; if his columns in *Blitz* were anything to go by, he must have been a dreadful windbag. Vijay Merchant used to do the expert commentary. Devraj Puri and Anant Setalvad came later. So did Suresh Saraiya, but once he got into the box he never stopped talking: it was commentary as a continuous loop of speech with no beginning or end, where to pause was to admit defeat, where radio silence was dead time.

Hindi commentary used to be broadcast on a separate frequency till AIR thriftily merged English and Hindi commentary on a single frequency, so that every twenty minutes the listener travelled from a game in which the ball was bowled to one in which the ball was thrown because Hindi didn't have a word for bowled and was too proud to borrow an English one. The definitive Hindi commentator was Jasdev Singh. He knew nothing about the game but his voice was calm, and he conveyed the events on the field to you with a kind of prissy accuracy which was a welcome departure from the chronic agitation of other Hindi commentators who tried to make up for their lack of cricketing lore and insight with bursts of hysterical excitement: 'aur veh OUT!!'

Anyway, the mid-sixties was also the time when portable transistor radios became affordable and the respectable urban poor, wobbling on cycles, could be seen carrying largish sets, with their antennae extended, and their speakers crackling with Vividh Bharati, Radio Ceylon or cricket commentary. Cricket, though enjoyed for its own sake, was also tied in complex ways to an aspiration to be respectable and middle class. While the rich and the poor form part of cricket's audience in India, it mainly appeals to the people in between. This conveniently elastic category isn't really the middle class: it is, rather, that class of urban Indian that has some English, from just howzatt at one end of the spectrum to Hazlitt at the other. The reason cricket's spectators were generally peaceful was that they wanted to belong, unlike English football crowds for whom football stadiums were arenas where they could act out their alienation from a bourgeois world.

Sociology and psychology, disciplines anxious to generalize, have given football fans the academic treatment for years: anomie, plebeian male bonding, inner city tribalism, the decline of community, the rise of working class racism, every ready-to-wear idea has been tried on football hooligans to kit them out as subjects fit for scholarly attention. Nobody has done the same for cricket fans. This is in part because cricket's followers tend not to be alienated and violent; at least they don't routinely go berserk (though spectators at Eden Gardens have been known to turn matches on and off at will).

The relative tameness of cricket's audiences has also something to do with cricket's fans being raised, till recently, on radio commentary. Listening to a complex game being described needed concentration, attention span, an engagement with the game's traditions, and some use of the imagination to fill in the bits the commentators left out. Radio socialized thousands of Indians into cricket, but it also taught them deference: it gave them a set of second-hand opinions on everything and left them dependent on authoritative commentary.

Till the eighties, it was commonplace to see spectators at the ground watching the action in the middle with a transistor radio pressed to their ears. They were in the stadium watching, but to understand what was happening they needed those familiar voices naming the fielders, describing the shots played, measuring out praise and blame. Most of all they needed those familiar phrases ('runs in to bowl', 'played back along the pitch', 'walks back to the top of his bowling mark') to set out the leisurely rhythms of the game. Test cricket is to sport what shastriya sangeet is to music: both set great store by tradition, arcana and connoisseurship. Radio commentary in the terms of this analogy is the reassuring tanpura drone that anchors the performance.

We should acknowledge that cricket crowds aren't always peaceful. I can remember the time Brabourne Stadium erupted when umpire Shambu Pan gave Venkatraghavan out in the 1969–70 series against Bill Lawry's Australians. The crowd disagreed and decided to burn and otherwise damage the stadium. Significantly, this vandalism had been provoked by the observations of a radio commentator, Devraj Puri. Puri declared that Venkatraghavan had been wrongly given out by the umpire. For the thousands of fans inside Brabourne Stadium who depended on the wise men inside their radios to understand what was going on, for whom Akashvani supplied the first and last word on the game, it was as if a higher authority had struck down the verdict of a fallible earthbound umpire. Even in their violence they were deferential.

With the ascendancy of one-day cricket and the related capture of the game by television, cricket's following in India changed. The game became more accessible. Watching was more literal than listening: you didn't need a commentator to bring you the game entire, you needed him for a gloss on the visible action. The game became a spectacle for the simple reason that you could see it. The limited-overs game dramatized the spectacle by simplifying the game and thus making it even more accessible to those who had neither the time nor the inclination to learn to like the five-day version.

Untutored in the deference taught by radio, these television-raised generations of spectators go to the stadium not to watch the game (that can be better done at home via slow motion replay) but on the off chance that the cameras might be watching them. Where an earlier generation had been taught to revere cricket by a broadcasting monopoly, this one grew up watching the game as one entertainment among many supplied by cable television, all meant to sell colas and tyres. Television money revived the game, but it also trivialized it because entertainment isn't as serious a matter as religion. So where once angry cricketing crowds at Brabourne Stadium burnt the stadium down, the last time Indian crowds stopped a match at Eden Gardens, the 1996 World Cup semi-final between India and Sri Lanka, they did it by throwing plastic cola bottles on the pitch. In the age of ESPN cricket, even the violence feels sponsored.

On Walking

*Team stereotypes are fixed in childhood. So the
Australians, for my brother and me, were hard-nosed
men. Feroz Shah Kotla, winter, the 1969–70 tour, the
ball slipped out of the hand of an Indian bowler and
dribbled to a stop halfway down the pitch. Doug
Walters (or was it Ian Redpath?) walked up to the
stationary ball and teed off for four runs. I didn't
grudge him that boundary, nor did I particularly resent
the sledging and effing that the Aussies pioneered in
the years afterwards, but it did make it harder for me
to take contemporary Australian cricketers seriously
when they spasmodically committed themselves to
chivalry, fair play and the spirit of the game.*

'Walking' broke out like dengue during the Chennai Test,
the second of the Australian tour of 2004. Adam
Gilchrist walked, then Jason Gillespie, then Michael
Kasprowicz. Yuvraj Singh and Parthiv Patel reciprocated
reluctantly, coerced by Gilchrist's example. Dean Jones, in
the commentary box, confessed he'd never walked through
his career but, carried along by the rising tide of Australian
virtue, declared walking was good for the game.

It made me queasy, all this goodness. It was a bit like being
carsick in childhood: the kind of sickness that didn't set in
immediately, but took you by surprise after a few sharp turns.

When Gilchrist walked, I felt okay. He's always been a walker; walking fits the way he plays. He lays about himself with honest good cheer, mashing up bowling attacks without malice: it's hard to think of Gilchrist nicking one and dissembling. Gilchrist was walking before Yuvraj, who had taken a falling catch, had hit the ground. Gillespie, who followed suit, hesitated a fraction before acknowledging that he had gloved the ball by walking away. It was, for Gillespie, a political act, not a spontaneous one. Kasprowicz's self-incrimination was when I felt my gorge rise. Kasprowicz hung around long enough for David Shepherd to give him not out—before succumbing to Gilchrist's example and tearing himself away from the crease, frowning with embarrassment and exasperation at being forced into this brazen show of goodness.

The pragmatic argument against walking was concisely stated by former Australian opening batsman Michael Slater. If you walk every time you're out and are also given out a few times when you aren't (as all batsmen are in the course of their careers), things don't even out. So, in a competitive team game, walking is, at the very least, irrational behaviour. Secondarily, there is a strong likelihood that your opponents won't walk, so every time you do, you put yourself or your team at risk.

This isn't, of course, a moral argument; it is a cynical, prudential argument based on experience. The moral argument against this prudential case is simple. The rules of cricket define dismissals and if you know you're out within that definition, you are morally obliged to aid the umpire and walk. The assumption that you're entitled not to walk because others don't, is self-serving: by that logic, everything from tapping the water mains (because your neighbours do it) to cooking the books (because all shopkeepers do it) is justified. Also, the moralists argue that an innings prolonged by dishonesty is a devalued innings and for cricket lovers this is, or should be, a reasonable argument. The affection that Viswanath, Gilchrist and Lara inspire has something to do with the fact that they are walkers who have made their runs strictly within the rules of the game.

If there are good arguments for walking, why is standing your ground an acceptable position, acceptable not just to professional cricketers but even cricket's public? Matthew Hayden declared in a newspaper article that he wouldn't walk and even Gilchrist made it clear that walking was an individual decision, not team policy. Why isn't this tantamount to publicly declaring that the decision to not cheat isn't team policy but a matter of individual preference?

The usual defence invokes the umpire. This is how Allan Border put the non-walker's case: 'I believe, as do many others, that umpiring decisions tend to even themselves out over the years. I am of the opinion that just as the batsmen and bowlers have a job, the umpires have a specific job of making decisions, and it is best to leave it to them.'

For most people, this shifts responsibility from the individual competitor to the neutral official. The reason this rhetorical move is so successful is that cricket is deeply embedded in the procedures and metaphors of law.

A batsman is given out only when the fielding side appeals to the umpire; without an appeal the umpire is under no obligation to make a decision. You don't appeal for a goal in soccer, but you must appeal for a dismissal in cricket.

Not all forms of deception are seen as equally culpable by umpires or the cricketing public and this hierarchy of guilt is closely related to procedural distinctions made in law. For example, when a fielder claims a catch that he hasn't taken cleanly, his appeal is seen as sharp practice, liable to punishment. But the batsman who doesn't walk, knowing he has edged the ball, is deemed to be simply exercising the accused person's time honoured right to not be forced to incriminate himself.

But the right to remain silent is based on the presumption of innocence and that presumption is hard to sustain in the presence of cameras. Every time you nick the ball and don't walk, the camera is likely to show you taking advantage of human fallibility. The procedures of law are created in large part to enshrine the benefit of doubt because judges and lawyers know that in a court of law you can't have God as a witness. But today, on a cricket pitch, you can and you do.

The television camera's omniscience is beginning to create a crisis for the hard men who refuse to walk and Gilchrist, Australia's acting captain for the tour of 2004 was prescient enough to see the rocks ahead. Australia, despite Gilchrist and because of Steve Waugh, is widely seen as the most hard-nosed of teams, committed to never giving a sucker an even break. It is an image that has begun to damage Australian cricket's standing at home and abroad.

Behaviour once seen as merely tough or hard-bitten such as not walking or sledging becomes harder to gloss over when the camera picks up the nick and the stump microphone captures the obscenities. It's revealing that when Virender Sehwag was given out lbw to McGrath in Bangalore and the camera clearly showed a huge inner edge, McGrath didn't attempt the umpire-knows-best defence. Instead, he went to great lengths to emphasize that he appealed because he believed that at the time that Sehwag was out. The leeway traditionally granted to certain kinds of cricketing deception is threatened by the television camera's unblinking gaze.

The remedy Gilchrist proposes, walking as a matter of individual conscience, is more a gesture than a solution. It's a form of gallantry that should have become redundant or obsolete in this age of televised cricket. When batsmen of an earlier age, like Viswanath, walked, their gesture served a purpose: it disclosed information that no one else could be privy to. When Gilchrist (or Kasprowicz or Yuvraj or Lara) walk today, they merely corroborate what the camera is about to show or has already revealed. This is evidence that should be made available to the judges, the umpires, in every case. That it isn't, is a testament to a perverse amateur ethic that sentimentalizes human error—I once heard Ian Chappell declare that dealing stoically with bad decisions was one of cricket's tests of character! When livelihoods and careers turn on umpiring decisions, we should make sure that umpires have all the help they need to make the right ones. Once that happens, this unnecessary, reinvented distinction between gents (who walk) and pros (who don't) will disappear: everyone will walk because there won't be any bad decisions to be evened out.

Men in White

Sports channels replay lots of archival footage of long-ago matches these days. The one-day matches always seem curiously dated because the design of the coloured uniforms changes with every tournament. In contrast, a vintage Test match, like India's win at the Oval in 1971, can be watched as if it were a contemporary contest (if you can ignore the haircuts revealed by the missing helmets).

Appearances matter in cricket. My father, who was born nearly a hundred years ago, spent a summer in England following Bradman's Australians as they toured. One image from that summer stuck in his mind and whenever he talked cricket, he'd pull it out of storage and relive for us the memory of Duleepsinhji walking out to the middle to bat for England, his cream silk shirt *billowing* out behind him. I must have heard him tell the story dozens of times and it changed in the telling, but the shirt remained silk and it consistently billowed.

In my father's mind, the silk shirt both defined Duleep's delicate genius and marked him out as oriental, therefore ours, despite the fact that he played for England. That a more or less white shirt was freighted with such meaning in my father's mind has something to do with Test cricket's austere dress code: precisely because both teams are confined to white, small differences in texture and manner and style leave an impression and are invested with significance.

For Indians who began following cricket in the early sixties, the white neck-kerchief separated cricket's cavaliers from its dour roundheads. Chief amongst the kerchief dandies was that great Hyderabadi stylist and opening batsman, M.L. Jaisimha and his friend, teammate and honorary Hyderabadi, M.A.K. Pataudi, who captained Jaisimha for India and was captained by him in return, when the Nawab turned out for Hyderabad. The kerchief is a Hyderabadi tradition that has endured: the antique cricketing cool associated with this uniform accessory can still sometimes be glimpsed on a hot day when V.V.S. Laxman walks out to bat with his collar raised, his kerchief casually knotted round his neck.

If style was conveyed by the kerchief, attitude was signalled by the collar and its elevation. All the great Hyderabadis favoured the raised collar, but alone amongst them, Azharuddin built his on-field persona around it. An amulet on a string replaced the kerchief-cravat, his neck telescoped into the raised collar and he moved with that odd lopsided lope that looked like a limp but wasn't: it was Azhar's variation on cool cricketing swagger. So powerful was the raised collar as a sign of on-field machismo in the Nizam's domain that even Venkatapathy Raju who resembled Mr Bean more than he did the Terminator, affected one.

Given the uniformity of whites, spectators attended closely to the way they were worn. Gavaskar was perfectly turned out, his trouser cuffs neatly rolled and tucked under the lower straps of his pads. Mohinder Amarnath was amongst the world's worst dressed cricketers, his trouser bottoms sticking out behind him like tail wings, and he often wore coloured socks instead of white ones. The seventies were a terrible time for cricketing fashions: this was the era of the snug, short-sleeved T-shirt which replaced the loose, long-sleeved shirts that Pataudi's men had worn. Gavaskar and Kapil Dev both patronized this body-hugging style for a while before Kapil pioneered three-quarters length sleeves without cuffs to bowl in. Cricket has successfully resisted the abbreviated clothes that modern sportsmen favour. There are periods where utilitarian considerations prevail and T-shirts rule, but eventually, orthodoxy prevails. The reason for this has to be purely aesthetic: to preserve the look and feel of cricket. Anyone with sense can tell that cricket would be unwatchable if it were played in shorts. The quickest way to test this is to watch international players in the nets in shorts, their thigh protectors on view: they look like imposters.

I've seen the extinction of one uniform accessory: the floppy hat. Till the late seventies, the floppy hat had, as advertised by its name, a soft, floppy brim. Pataudi used to sometimes wear it and I remember one flying off his head as he chased down a ball in a Test against New Zealand. Then Majid Khan killed them off. He began wearing a white hat with a stiff brim that looked vaguely like a cut down Stetson with a less ambitious crown. Gavaskar, who used to favour the floppy to bat in, switched to the Majid-style hat and now the floppy is gone.

Going the way of the floppy hat is the cricket cap, at least with subcontinental teams. While the Australians wear their baggy green in the traditional style with pride, Indians and Pakistanis have embraced the baseball cap as their own. Everything about the new-style cap is wrong: its crown is too high, its peak too large, and the little strap at the back makes Test cricketers look like petrol pump attendants. The cap is the emblem of the national cricket team; to be capped for India is a great and resonant metaphor, and it doesn't work with a baseball cap. Someone should scrap them.

English whites used to be made of flannel. When Indian

cricket writers and commentators spoke of Indian players in 'flannels' I assumed that this was a traditionalist deference to the vocabulary of cricket. But talking to the great Madras leg spinner V.V. Kumar, about the old days, I discovered that in his time, they actually wore flannels. They wore them in the wet heat of Madras and Kumar remembered the time when he took five wickets against Hyderabad on first-class debut and was gifted a set of flannel shirts and trousers by Balu Alaganan in recognition of his achievement. Flannel next to the skin! The untold story of Indian cricket must be the nappy-rash epidemic that never made the sports pages.

By the sixties, mercifully, flannel had given way to cotton. Madan Lal, one of a string of medium-pace utility players that India fielded in the sixties and seventies, used to wear whites that were so cream they were nearly yellow. As a metaphor for the way he played fast bowling, the colour was appropriate. This was the time before helmets and my most vivid mental picture of Madan Lal is a radio memory: I was listening to Radio Australia's commentary on a Test match in Australia where Madan Lal was playing Jeff Thomson in a style that helmets made obsolete even for tail-end rabbits. The way the commentators described it, he backed away from the leg stump and swung and managed to hit Thomson for some boundaries before he fell. There was no shame in doing what Madan Lal did: Tendulkar, Azharuddin, Ganguly and Laxman amongst others have been pinged on the head by bowlers considerably less ferocious than Thomson. Without helmets, some of these players, Ganguly for example, might have considered the Madan Lal gambit.

Talking about helmets, protective gear is the one area where cricket has visibly changed. Gavaskar pioneered the elbow guard, and the world followed. Mohinder Amarnath tried reintroducing the sola topi, but that didn't take because the world embraced the helmet instead. It didn't help that the one time he wore it, he fell in a heap on his stumps trying to get out of the way of the ball. I don't recall cut-off or specially small pads for wicketkeepers till Kirmani started wearing them in the late seventies. Engineer wore the big ones and I remember a picture of Don Tallon, crouched in his keeper's stance, peering over enormous pad flaps.

The concealed padding grew bigger. Ganguly and Dravid pioneered extra large thigh pads and in the nineties, more and more players began to affect the semi-pregnant look against fast bowling as the chest protector crept downwards like a shortstop's armour.

For the layperson, the most puzzling change in concealed protective gear is the strapless box or guard. I distinctly remember that the box used to be tied on with straps, but now there are none. So what changed? Unless modern batsmen come with attachments that earlier models didn't have, it can't be evolution. It must be technology, then. My bet is suction cups, but I'm open to correction.

The least nice thing about the modern cricketer's rig is the jewellery. Admittedly, Gavaskar used to wear a rudraksha bead on a string round his neck and an elephant-hair bracelet, but at least those had the saving grace of idiosyncrasy. Now it's all gold in a grotesque jumble round the neck. Ganguly wears so much, he looks like a shady trinket vendor without a licence, but even the wonderfully cultivated Dravid and Kumble do gold under the collar. Eeeew! If they must wear jewellery, why not a nice earring? And why gold? Why not elephant hair?

The coolest thing in the contemporary cricketer's kit is his shades. I like the shape and colour of them and I'm sorry that their use seems limited to fielders. I think Indian batsmen should wear them against Australia to thwart McGrath: even a glowerer like him might find it hard to eyeball tinted plastic.

First Do No Harm

The growth of limited-overs cricket has had one unintended but disastrous consequence: the growth of a cricketing bureaucracy in the shape of the International Cricket Conference (ICC). From being a skeletal talking shop, it has become a centralizing corporation that threatens the bilateral nature of Test cricket.

I didn't know it as a cricket-mad kid in the sixties, but an era in the game's history was coming to an end. As I tracked my heroes on the radio, in the sports pages of newspapers, in *Sport & Pastime* and the colour pages of the *Illustrated Weekly of India*, I was bearing witness to the last decade of cricket's life as an unstandardized, bilateral, amateur sport.

Cricket at the highest level, even at the Test match level, wasn't played by a set of standard rules. In England, where it drizzles all the time, pitches were routinely left uncovered overnight; everywhere else they were protected from the weather. In its early years as a Test-playing nation, Pakistan played most home Tests on matting wickets. In Australia, umpires called over after eight balls: everywhere else this was done after six. Throughout the sixties and early seventies, Test matches in India were two and a half hours shorter than they were anywhere else because the post-tea session was an hour and a half long instead of the customary two hours, divided into two forty-five minute periods by the drinks break.

This tolerance of difference was connected to Test cricket's peculiarly bilateral nature. While Test cricket was an international sport, it was only played by seven countries and unlike any other sport, there was no contest in which more than two countries could participate. Team sports like hockey and football could integrate an encounter between two teams into a larger championship like the Olympics or the World Cup or the European Cup. Till the invention of one-day cricket, there were no cricketing tournaments: international cricket always meant one country's team touring another country to play a Test series. The outcome of the series or rubber clarified one country's standing vis-à-vis the other. It made no difference to the international cricket rank of either country because there was no formal way of reckoning rank: no point system, no league, no international calendar of matches. The West Indies were acknowledged as the best team in the world for decades till Australia took over in the nineties, simply because they hadn't lost to anyone for as long as people could remember.

International cricket meant series that went on for months, with the touring team playing several first-class matches against regional sides in between the main course of three or five Test matches. In the absence of a world championship (the length of a Test match made such a thing impractical), 'world champion' was an informal title earned by the side that had beaten enough countries at home and away to be consensually recognized as Test cricket's alpha male.

Test rubbers were agreed upon and scheduled by the cricket boards of two Test-playing nations. No considerations of fairness or equality encroached upon their discretion. The idea that cricket's calendar ought to be organized to let every Test-playing country play every other country never occurred to anyone. After Bill Lawry's Australians toured India in

1969–70, no Australian team visited India for a decade.

In this context, where playing conditions had to be agreed to by the two concerned countries, accommodating local differences wasn't difficult. The reason cricket came late to neutral, or third-country, umpires was because international cricket was so wholly bilateral in its structure and thinking that it just couldn't imagine how the supervision of a Test match could be anyone else's business.

The countries that made up the cricket-playing world were not a community of equals. England and Australia acted as the veto-wielding permanent members, while the rest were content to be junior or associate members. The custodian of the game was a private cricket club, the MCC. Seven countries played international cricket, of which India only ever played against four. We didn't play Pakistan because of Kashmir and only white, racist cricket boards like those of England, Australia and New Zealand played apartheid's all-white Springboks till they too were shamed into a boycott of South African cricket.

With the exception of county cricket, there was no professional first-class league anywhere in the cricketing world. Everywhere else, cricket was played as an amateur or shamateur sport, subsidized by the private sector and the government's goodwill. Cricket was dependent on gate receipts for its revenues. Television and radio coverage was provided by public sector broadcasting organizations as a public service. All India Radio and the BBC paid nothing for the rights to radio and television.

The slow transformation of cricket into a modern sport (a process not yet complete, nor wholly successful) had to wait upon the invention of one-day cricket. The act of framing rules for a new version of the game made it easier for administrators to rethink aspects of the longer game.

For example, the idea that the Test match day was to be measured not in minutes or hours but in overs, is a consequence of one-day cricket. Slowing the over rate to thwart a run chase, once an acceptable form of gamesmanship, became outlawed because one-day cricket taught us that the opportunity to score runs was better measured in terms of overs played than time spent at the crease. The current rule that makes the bowling of ninety overs in a day mandatory flows directly from that lesson.

One-day cricket came of age at a time when Test cricket had slowed down. It was plagued by draws, slow over rates, declining attendance in countries like England, and a gathering sense that Tests went on too long for cricket to survive in the modern world. With hindsight, it's clear that the shorter version of the game changed Test cricket. Along with television, One-day Internationals widened the appeal of the game, transformed the organizational structure of international cricket and raised the tempo of Test matches.

The ways in which television remade the economics of cricket are well known. Kerry Packer was the first to recognize cricket's commercial potential and World Series Cricket played a large role in refining the one-day game and making it marketable. Here it is enough to say that the revenues made possible by television provided the incentive to 'modernize' the game.

To play Test cricket, all you really needed was the MCC rule book and consultation between two national boards. To organize a World Cup every four years, on the other hand, cricket-playing nations needed a permanent international organization to work out schedules, agree on playing conditions and share revenues.

The significance of the World Cup didn't sink in immediately. You can see the influence and weight of tradition in the location and organization of the first three World Cups. England, historically the home and hub of the game, claimed the World Cup as its birthright and the other countries acquiesced in this monopoly, till the financial implications of the tournament became apparent to them. And when they did, the ICC mushroomed.

The growth of the ICC from being an insignificant adjunct of the MCC to its present position as the governing body of the sport is a classic instance of bureaucratic modernization. From being an unequal confederation of national associations, international cricket now has a federal centre located in that great nursery of cricket: tax-free Dubai! The move to Dubai is symbolically significant: not only does it indicate that the ICC has formally severed its last link with the MCC by choosing a location outside the major cricketing nations, it also signals its independence of all of them.

This new federal government has all the accoutrements of a modern organization: a chairman, a chief executive, a public relations department, standing committees, and a law enforcement machinery represented by federal agents called match referees. The Feds are ostensibly there to help the local policemen, in this case the umpires, but their authority and jurisdiction are wider and grander than those of an umpire whose authority is limited to a single match. Match referees can suspend a player, fine him, even suspend a delinquent captain for slow over rates.

All the controversies in the last few years—the Mike Dennesss affair, the controversy about playing Zimbabwe, Denis Lindsay's extraordinary punishment of Ridley Jacobs, the endless furore about chucking—stem from the attempt by a central organization to assert its authority and its collision with constituent members unused to federal jurisdiction and unwilling to lose their prerogatives. Like any central authority, the ICC constantly seeks to enlarge its sphere of authority and diminish the freedom of manoeuvre of the national boards. It does this, for example, by creating an annual schedule of fixtures that makes room for all cricket-playing nations. The ICC has ruled that Test series should be no longer than four Test matches to allow minor countries an opportunity to play Test cricket. There are exceptions made for series haloed by tradition like the Ashes, but it's clear that the ICC expects the scheduling of Test matches to be done in consultation with it.

Similarly, the creation of official ICC rankings for individual cricketers as well as national teams, complete with end of year ICC awards, are all part of a single enterprise: the creation of an 'authorized' framework for international cricket.

The centralization of international cricket is by itself neither good nor bad. Most games have undergone a similar process, but models derived from other games aren't always an appropriate guide to action for Test cricket, because of the singular nature of the beast. The duration of a Test match rules out the main justification for a central overseeing body like the FIFA or the IOC or the IHF, that is the organization of international tournaments. The second justification for a central sports organization is to spread the game globally. The ICC has done its share of proselytization with mixed results. Bangladesh and Zimbabwe have proved (in the case of the latter, for reasons beyond cricket) to be premature inductees into Test cricket. But this in itself is not a serious problem. The bigger issue raised by the induction of Zimbabwe and Bangladesh is whether Test cricket can fit more than ten countries into an already crowded calendar. It probably can't, so the role of cricket's evangelist isn't one that can justify the ICC's existence.

Not content with a minimalist, coordinating function, the ICC began to invent responsibilities for itself. This ambition has begun to threaten the game the ICC was set up to nurture. Two examples of unnecessary intervention by the ICC have been a) the invention of the position of the match referee and b) the ICC's decision in recent years to stage matches between its champion side and a Rest of the World team.

The position of the match referee undermines the umpires, institutes a kangaroo court that conducts post-match court martials which generate endless bad feeling, and invents a class of arbitrarily appointed officials with no specialist credentials. It exists to give the ICC a sphere of patronage of its own.

Similarly, the invention of the new class of ICC-owned matches between World Champions and the Rest of the World, is intended to establish a new sort of contest that can only be organized by the ICC. The ICC is not satisfied with servicing and facilitating Test cricket because Test matches are owned by national boards. Super Series matches, on the other hand, can only be put together by a supranational organization like the ICC. The ICC wants to play impresario: it wants to produce and direct.

This is a bad and dangerous initiative. National boards should make it plain to the ICC that Test cricket is the ICC's ultimate 'product'. The health of Test cricket is, or should be, the ICC's reason for being. It should do nothing to sponsor a contest that purports to be superior to Test match cricket. To describe a match between a World XI and a national side as a 'Super Series' Test is plainly wrong.

Since Test matches are played between national teams, no contest organized on a different principle should be given the status of a Test match. A five-wicket haul or a century in a 'Super' Test should not count towards a player's Test record, because such a contest is not a Test match. The ICC, in 2005, gave a tsunami relief match between an Australian team and a World XI official ODI status. It then moved to give Super Series contests, both one-day and five-day matches, ODI and Test status. Bill Frindall and other statisticians sensibly argued that ODI and Test match records should not be diluted by performances in contests that are exhibition matches without the national or—in the case of the West Indies—regional identities that give Test cricket its justification and meaning.

Test cricket *is* a dinosaur amongst modern sports. Like that living fossil fish, the coelacanth, it is an evolutionary miracle that Test cricket exists at all. There is a limit to which it can be taught 'modern' ways and too much meddling with its environment could kill it off altogether. The ICC and its marketing men seem to think they can improve upon Test cricket: they should to be told categorically that they can't. A modernizing ICC could do worse than imitate Google, that most modern of companies, whose motto, Don't Be Evil, is derived from a cardinal teaching in clinical medicine: *primum non nocere*: first do no harm.

The Super Test or a Whole New Ball Game

After actually watching the Super Test between Australia and the ICC World XI, I'm mortified that I wrote the previous chapter. The ICC believed that it had created a superior sort of contest that transcended the narrow nationalisms of Test cricket. And it had!

'Whoops!' I thought, as Sehwag flicked Warne straight into Katich's stomach at short-leg. Bad luck, I thought, out for 76, looking good for a 100 and more. Actually, to be fair to Katich, it wasn't bad luck—just a first-rate catch. And a fine piece of bowling by Warne. Yes, you had to give it to the great man, he'd out-thought Sehwag by bowling leg-and-middle, denying him the offside, cutting off the runs. I settled into my chair, tasted the coffee and carried on watching.

As I write this, Australia are leading the ICC World XI by 211 runs with nine wickets still to fall and I think it's been a fine day's play. Lots of wickets, great offside play by Sehwag and the rare sight of two excellent leg spinners, Warne and MacGill, bowling in tandem. I can't remember the last time I watched a Test match with such even-handed appreciation, thinking such fair-minded thoughts in such temperate words: 'fine', 'rare', 'excellent', even 'whoops'. When Dravid edged McGrath to Gilchrist, I left the 'wh' out, my mouth pursed itself into a silent, rueful 'oops'.

The Super Test is the kind of contest that allows you to enjoy the game for itself, it puts things in perspective and reminds you that Test cricket is only a game. This is probably how the evolved spectator watches cricket—someone like Peter Roebuck, for example, whose sharp, non-partisan writing has given me so much pleasure. At the end of a day's play that has gone badly for my team and delivered the match into the hands of the opposition, instead of feeling unsettled and upset by a dark wash of resentment and thwarted yearning, I am able to sit at my keyboard, compose my thoughts and write.

Yes, this is new, this satvik spectatorship, this non-violent engagement with the game, purged of tamasik patriotism and other base feelings. I begin to feel grateful to Malcolm Speed and the ICC: in inventing the Super Test they've spawned, unwittingly, the uber-spectator. This is a watershed in the history of Test cricket, and it supplies an end to Shaw's prescient but incomplete play, *Fan & Superfan*.

Because if I had watched a day's Test cricket in the normal way, if Sehwag and Dravid had been batting for India and not the ICC World XI, that first paragraph would have read differently.

'Fuck!' I moaned as the shite Sehwag turned the ball into Katich's stomach. Six inches lower and that grinning animal would have been clutching something else and he wouldn't be holding it up for the world to see either. Pure fluke: if someone drills the ball into your solar plexus and it sticks between your ribs, should it even count as a catch? Luck on that scale was the only way that rutting, peroxided pig was likely to take an Indian wicket. I thought of Sidhu and Tendulkar and Laxman caning Warne into submission and changed channels to ESPN which, sensibly, was showing every ball of Sehwag's triple century in Pakistan in 2004.

Fans like me, who till yesterday were middle aged Mr Hydes, trembling like tuning forks each time an Indian wicket fell, roiling our insides with profanity and frustration, carrying on like middle aged trolls parked by TV sets, had found a dignified, grown-up, non-atavistic way of enjoying the game.

I see now that my misgivings about the Super Test were silly and besides the point. Since I hadn't then experienced the way in which a Super Test can purge a fan of poisonous feeling, I believed that it was wrong to give official Test status to a contest between a World XI and a national side. A Test, I told everyone who would listen, could only happen between national sides because the one thing that kept a team stoked over five days, that kept fans simmering for that absurd, pre-industrial length of time, was the steady burn of nationalist feeling.

I used to worry that by recognizing the current contest as an official Test, the ICC was debasing its most valuable currency. While one such contest every four years or so couldn't by itself harm Test cricket, the danger was that this was a precedent that men like Jagmohan Dalmiya and Malcolm Speed would use to dignify all sorts of matches. Already Dalmiya had organized a farcical intercontinental one-day international. Before that, Speed and the ICC had given official status to the ODI between a Rest of the World Side and the Australian XI held to raise money for tsunami relief. How long before one of them or someone like them decided to organize a Commonwealth versus Mother Country match with official Test status? Or White Commonwealth versus Chocolate All-Sorts?

Those fears were baseless, as newspapers tend to say. In a globalizing world, cricket needs to find new solidarities that can transcend the limiting and increasingly unreal category of the nation. The Super Test is a first step, a baby step, in the right direction. A suppler, more flexible approach to team making for Test matches would keep cricket relevant. For example, England and Australia could put together a team to represent the Coalition of the Willing, while India and Pakistan could pool players to champion a related tendency, Allies for a Shilling. The ICC could in a daring, ironic sort of way organize Tests between teams based on blood types: the Ponting B Positives versus Youhana's Universal Donors. And so on.

But in extending the scope of Test cricket, the ICC must be careful not to organize teams that might stoke any form of collective feeling or, for that matter, any kind of feeling. The Super Test was a master stroke that not only destroyed the monopoly of Test cricket but, more positively, opened the door to a proper appreciation of the game's formal perfection. By purging cricket of rage and primitive solidarities, it allows spectators (as it allowed me: see above) to understand its essence in the way that G.H. Hardy once did. C.P. Snow reported that Hardy said he loved cricket because as a mathematician, the angles that cricketers made on the field put him in mind of eternal geometric forms. If Hardy had had the misfortune of attending the philistine college I went to in Delhi, he would have suffered for that statement. Coarse hearties would have shouted, 'Pseud!', and I might have joined them.

But the ICC has helped me see that the future of cricket lies in its progressive etherealization. Michael Frayn once wrote a novel called *The Tin Men* in which a computer programmer realizes that the ultimate purpose of all sport is not spectacle but data; the production of statistics that fans can consume. So he writes a program that generates football scores without the preliminary fuss of actual football matches. Once cricket fans are weaned from the gross feelings induced by nationalism and spectacle, the ICC can help them make the transition from corporeal cricket (i.e., cricket played by live bodies) to virtual cricket (played by reliable machines).

And once in a very long while, in the wake of some calamitous act of god, the ICC could revive, for the sake of charity, the old style country versus country Test match. Its rarity and years of dammed-up passion would raise billions of dollars in gate receipts and television revenues. All of us, old and young, would bay once again with primitive feeling. Purged, we'd return to the silent appreciation characteristic of the evolved fan of the new era that began with the Super Test in Sydney in October 2005.

The Modern Game

At some point in my career as a spectator, I noticed that the words used by commentators didn't match the action on the ground. The game had changed and the commentariat took a while to take the changes on board. If I had to put a date to it, I'd say the change occurred in the nineties, when the game outgrew its vocabulary.

Television punditry consists of variations on a single text: the MCC coaching manual. It isn't a coincidence that experts are sometimes called pundits; in cricket, as in other things, expertise amounts to a dogmatic and fluent recitation of orthodoxy. Nowhere are the dogmas and recipes of orthodoxy more enshrined than in cricket's commentary boxes. This is ironic given that Packer's revolution killed off the armchair professional broadcaster (Harsha Bhogle and Tony Cozier are the last of an endangered species) and replaced him with the ex-Test cricketer who might have been expected to describe the game from lived experience But the player turned commentator turned out to be as susceptible to the textbook cliché as the hack broadcasters who preceded him.

Cricket commentators equate orthodoxy with science and unorthodox play with instinct. So Sanath Jayasuriya is all flair and 'eye' while Mark Waugh is cultured elegance, thus delicately suggesting that the former is good while he lasts but the latter lasts because he's good. Experts are good at explaining how an eccentric backlift gets players out, or how a grip too close to the bottom of the handle can get you into trouble, or how an angled bat can induce an inner edge onto the stumps; they're much less inclined to explain why eccentricities work for players, why despite them they get lots of wickets or tons of runs. 'The ball snuck between bat and pad and bowled him because he was playing away from his body.' What really happened was that the ball moved more than the batsman expected, or he was too slow. But had he kept bat and pad together, the slowness or movement wouldn't have mattered. This is true, but had he blocked everything in the approved fashion, he might never have got off the mark.

Cricket is a game that is played side-on. Bat and pad close together. Foot to the pitch of the ball. The trouble with cricket punditry today is that the maxims of orthodoxy no longer fit the modern game. Contemporary commentators seem inadequate when confronted with Sanath Jayasuriya or Lance Klusener or Waqar Younis because they haven't (with one of two honourable exceptions) allowed for the revolution that modern bats, subcontinental ingenuity and the limited-overs game have wrought in Test cricket. Shaun Pollock has a lovely high-arm action. So what? Younis has a lovely low-arm action and he's done very well for himself. Lasith Malinga, the Sri Lankan fast bowler, has an action so low it would have been legal in the early nineteenth century when over-arm bowling wasn't allowed: his arm never rises above the level of his shoulder. Conventional cricketing wisdom today is at the same stage that tennis commentary passed through in the seventies, when the side-on address and the low, flat forehand were considered the foundation of good play. Well, Borg played the high, top-spun forehand chest-on like a table tennis player and won Wimbledon from the baseline. He had to do this five times before tennis pundits realized that the game had changed.

Batting

Over the last decade Jayasuriya has been the most significant batsman in contemporary cricket, more important than Tendulkar, Lara, Waugh or De Silva. He is a hugely successful heretic, the Martin Luther of modern cricket. He has made the rules of orthodox batsmanship (getting to the pitch, getting in line, playing along the ground and that holiest of holies, playing with a straight bat) seem overstated and dogmatic. Jayasuriya needs to play away from his body because he routinely hits the balls wide of him on the up; he plays with his bat at an angle of forty-five degrees because he is not trying to show the whole face to the ball, he intends to hit it with an angled blade, and in common with some young batsmen today, he uses eye, timing and hugely powerful forearms to get elevation and power. What's more, he has done this in Test cricket, with a triple century against India in Colombo in 1997 and that magnificent double century against England at the Oval in 1998 which, as much as Muralitharan's bowling, won them the Test match. It was probably the greatest attacking innings played in the last ten years, played as it was to force a result in limited time.

Is Jayasuriya exceptional? Not really. Take Shahid Afridi or Adam Gilchrist: they got their starts in the one-day game which defined their methods, but they already have Test centuries to their credit. Both of them can hit straight, but they often do this with horizontal bats, they drive through cover by swinging straight but with an angled face, and Afridi plays short-pitched balls by squaring up and angling the bat so acutely that the ball slides through slips. This freedom of the air that one-day cricket has brought, and the resulting willingness to loft the ball, has changed the pull shot. More and more pull shots are hit, not on the back foot with the ball taken at the top of its bounce, but off the front foot without the batsman going back and across. Batsmen will routinely pull balls that are barely short of a length and they aim the shot at midwicket or straighter rather than square leg. Bats with more carry, that help batsmen clear the infield, are responsible for the change. The tendency in recent years to bring in the boundary ropes in Test grounds the world over has also made the lofted stroke a percentage shot: shorter boundaries mean more sixes where once the same heave would have had you caught in the deep.

The three fastest double centuries in the history of Test cricket were hit inside the space of two weeks in March 2002. Adam Gilchrist started the avalanche with his double century in the first Test against the South Africans in South Africa, Graham Thorpe overtook the record a week later in New Zealand in England's first Test against the Kiwis and then Nathan Astle bludgeoned the English senseless in the last innings of the same match as he hit up his double in a little over a hundred and fifty deliveries. Something had changed.

The classical batting stance (side-on, feet six inches apart) is no longer the rule. Batsmen like Jayasuriya, Kallis and Klusener stand with their feet a yard apart. They don't so much go forward or back as shift weight, rocking onto the back foot for the cut and the pull, or crooking their front leg to drive, flick or pull on the up. As Boycott acutely observed, they play like batters in baseball: if the ball is in the zone, if it's there or thereabouts, it has to go.

And then there's Virender Sehwag, whose stance is orthodox but whose footwork isn't. Sehwag is a modern minimalist in that he barely moves his feet when he plays fast bowling. Cricket lore has it that Majid Khan, the Pakistani batsman, once showed his teammates in Glamorgan how he could play every stroke in the book without moving his feet. Well, take Majid Khan, put him on steroids, root his feet in the ground and you have Sehwag. In just over fifty Test matches, Sehwag averages 52 runs or thereabouts per innings and has a strike rate of over 75 runs per hundred balls. He makes Michael Hayden look sedate. Such ferocity and consistency in a batsman who disdains footwork should occasion some rethinking of the orthodox view of the ideal opening batsman and his shot making repertoire.

It could be my imagination, but batsmen don't drive on the half-volley the way they used to. Batsmen like Ganguly prefer to take the ball higher in its bounce when they leave the crease because they're aiming for elevation and power, rather than the safety of hitting a carpet shot. And the reason they're aiming for a six is that modern bats make it more likely that a lofted shot will go the distance. Observe Tendulkar and Ganguly drive along the ground: they virtually always drive on the up. Watching S.S. Das drive in his first few innings of Test match cricket was like a page from the past. He got right to the pitch to stifle the bounce and ironed the ball onto the floor. Right along the carpet, as the old commentators used to say. Even the leg side flick doesn't seem to be played on the half-volley as Gavaskar used to play it. Nowadays the ball is whipped off the pads at knee height instead of being flicked off the toes. Either bowlers pitch it up less, or, more likely, the change has to do with the power of modern bats and the size of their sweet spots.

In the evolution of contemporary batting, the introduction of the helmet has been even more important than powerful bats and the influence of the one-day game. The helmet, by removing the risk of death and unbearable pain, has decisively shifted the balance of power in favour of the batsman and in doing so, has changed the nature of modern batsmanship. Mohinder Amarnath was commonly acknowledged as one of the bravest and best players of fast bowling in his time. Imran Khan, who bowled fearsomely fast to Mohinder, has gone on record to praise his courage and ability. Had it not been for the helmet, which became standard equipment midway through Mohinder's long career, we would not remember him in this way. We would remember instead a demoralized batsman shambling up to the crease in a sola topi and then collapsing on his stumps as he tried to evade a short ball. This is no reflection on Mohinder's heart; just an illustration of the difference the helmet made to his batting. Azharuddin, for example, lovely player though he was, was vulnerable to short-pitched bowling, and he wouldn't have lasted for as long as he did in Test cricket without a helmet. Conversely, Brijesh Patel would have gone on for much longer.

But more than the difference it made to the careers of individual players, the helmet changed the attitude of batsmen as a class to fast bowling. The likes of Klusener, Jayasuriya, Gilchrist, Afridi and Astle will often hook firm footed or off the front foot without going back or across. They do this because the old spit-drying fear of mortal injury that was hard-wired into the heads of an earlier generation has vanished from the consciousness of contemporary batsmen. They will drive on the up and hook off the front foot because with the helmet on, the risk of being maimed is low enough to be disregarded. Test match totals are now built at a great rate (resulting in more wins and losses and fewer draws) because with the helmet on, batsmen have a go at the fast men in a way they didn't before, even tail-enders like Shane Warne and Brett Lee. The helmet is a great equalizer. Paradoxically, one reason why fast men with suspect actions like Shoaib

Akhtar and Brett Lee aren't driven out of the game as they would have been earlier is that fast bowling isn't seen as a threat to the batsman's life any more.

If, as a spectator, I have not felt that vicarious fear in nearly twenty years, think of how much better the batsmen must feel. I have seen Tendulkar get pinged by Donald and the ball ricocheting off the helmet, leaving Tendulkar unhurt. Fast bowlers can still intimidate, but they cannot inspire mortal fear. Batsmen now take guard knowing they can be hurt but not killed. That simple truth has liberated them. There are no Brijesh Patels in modern cricket and if there are, they put on helmets and become Mohammad Azharuddins. Armed with great new bats, fitter than before, protected by the helmet and coddled by the bouncer rule, batsmen who would once have chosen discretion, now affect valour.

Bowling

The conventions of fast bowling have been stood on their heads in recent years. The menace of the new ball has given way to the paradoxes of reverse swing in the middle overs. Donald came in first change in the limited-overs game, as did Waqar Younis; Imran routinely said that the new ball was wasted on Waqar. Where Lindwall was a great exception, now Pakistani fast bowlers routinely bowl with a low arm to inswing their yorkers. The bouncer has been legislated into relative unimportance and reverse inswing has some of the glamour that was reserved for the outswinger in the days of Botham and Kapil Dev.

During an e-mail question-and-answer session on Channel 9, Mark Taylor was asked why McGrath was designated a fast bowler while Damien Fleming was only granted a fast-medium tag. Was it speed, a minimum miles per hour benchmark? The question was asked because the speedometer had timed Fleming as generally faster than McGrath in the first Test against Pakistan. Astonishingly, Taylor said that being fast was more about method than speed. Bowlers like Fleming, according to Taylor, depended on movement or 'shape' for wickets, whereas men like McGrath concentrated on line, bounce and aggression. The first part of Taylor's answer, that fast bowlers aren't mainly defined by their speed, is one of those involuntarily daft things that all TV pundits end up saying. What he meant was that most fast bowlers do not depend mainly on movement for wickets: men like Holding and Marshall bowled straight and fast a lot of the time. So did Donald. These were great fast bowlers. But the Pakistanis have been trying to redefine fast bowling. Men like Waqar, Imran, Shoaib Akhtar and Wasim Akram have swung the old ball at tremendous speed. Oddly for fast bowlers, they didn't depend on bounce for wickets: more often than not, they trapped batsmen in front or bowled them. And their ball of choice was the banana inswinger.

Heresy of heresies, the great mantras of spin bowling as exemplified by Bedi—flight and a teasing good length—have yielded to the blacker arts of the unreadable delivery and enormous turn. Warne, not a great flighter of the ball, relies on his flipper and the obscene turn he gets from the rough. Kumble: well, who knows why he gets wickets? Apart from the fact that he turns his wrist over, it's hard to see how he is a spinner at all. Saqlain, while slower, depends mainly on his unreadable floater for wickets, Muralitharan on prodigious turn, Mushtaq on his googly, Paul Adams on the novelty of his eccentric action.

There are no Nadkarnis in modern cricket and, tragically, no Bedis either. The foot down the wicket and the bludgeoning cross-bat swipe has accounted for flighted good-length bowling. The best left-arm orthodox spinner in the world today is . . . Daniel Vettori! The two off spinners to command respect depend on a deformed, double-jointed arm and the mysterious equivalent of an off spinner's googly. Spinners who toss the ball up without being big turners of the ball get murdered by quite ordinary batsmen. The classic example was Cronje, whose target area used to be midwicket and whose mainstay was the cowswipe or jhadu shot played on one knee. Protected from real pace by the helmet and the limitations on bouncers, mediocre batsmen like Cronje terrorized conventional medium pace and spin bowling with cross-bat shots.

The Changing Game

The straight bat, the long innings of attrition or in defence, surviving the new ball, setting out your stall and playing forever, genuine slow bowlers wheeling their way through dozens of overs, none of these things will disappear from the game, but they are ceasing to define Test cricket, and as a result, the game is changing. It is rather like the decline of 'serve and volley' tennis: it will not become extinct and there will always be the stray Stephen Edberg, but where once first 'serve and into the net' used to be the staple of the men's tour, now the game is defined by ground strokes. Modern racquets give baseliners such power that rushing the net has become a low percentage ploy.

It is not a coincidence that there are more results in Test matches of late. This is partly because batsmen carry their one-day idiom into the longer game, partly because their defensive techniques have deteriorated through neglect, partly as a result of much improved fielding (more catches taken, more run outs effected), partly because glory now decisively belongs to the swashbuckler and the solid anchor is likely to be seen as a stolid barnacle. Cricket, even Test cricket, is now played to force a result, not to effect a successful holding action. The strategic draw is becoming obsolete.

Three countries are responsible for transforming modern cricket and conveniently enough, each one has specialized in one of the three aspects of the game. The Sri Lankans led by Jayasuriya have remade modern batsmanship, the Pakistanis through Imran, Wasim and Waqar have extended the range of the fast bowler's art and the South Africans led by Rhodes have invented a new orthodoxy for fielding: the sliding, curving stop, the lightning recovery from proneness, the javelin over-arm throw from the deep, the elevation of point to the pivotal status once enjoyed by cover.

The exemplary modern cricketers are Jayasuriya, Waqar Younis, Shane Warne, Muralitharan and Jonty Rhodes. Ricky Ponting, Donald, Tendulkar, Brian Lara are great players but they aren't revolutionaries, they haven't changed cricket; they have, as great players do, taken what suits them from the innovations of the modern game. The foundation of Tendulkar's game may be Bombay's grounding in the basics, but the front-foot pull, the up and over shot that deposits the ball beyond midwicket's ropes, and most of all, that one-side skip as he makes room to pulp the ball with the inside-out drive are tributes to modern bat making, the demands of one-day cricket and his genius, not necessarily in that order.

Innovation has not uprooted orthodoxy; innovation never does. It is a tincture that colours the game, subtly changing its momentum and its rhythm. The most successful team in contemporary cricket is Australia and it is, in many ways, a very old-fashioned team. McGrath is all line and length and bounce, Fleming is a regulation outswing bowler and the batsmen, even the young ones like Ponting, cut, pull and drive out of the textbook. The Aussies are a good example of how well the old verities can be made to work by a bunch of tough, professional cricketers. But Australia have Warne, the most revolutionary slow bowler of the last quarter-century and they have Gilchrist, whose style and success owe everything to the precedent blazed by Jayasuriya and the Sri Lankan transformation of batsmanship. Change is everywhere: another five years and even commentators might trade their cliches in for new ones.

Boxwallahs and Brahmins: Cricket As a Living in Madras

Till I read Ramachandra Guha's masterly history of Indian cricket, A Corner of a Foreign Field, *I knew nothing about the history of the first-class game in India. Like many fans, my enthusiasm for cricket began and ended with Test matches. Decades later, thanks to a newspaper commission, I spent a few days in Madras talking to veterans of the first-class game to understand what sort of livelihood domestic cricket provided before television revenues enriched the game. Much as I enjoyed talking to them, these were sobering conversations because they bore witness to the precarious, ad hoc patronage on which fine cricketers built their lives.*

Late January 2002. The surfeit of cricket on television had made me nostalgic for the game at the ground and I had followed the Indian team to Madras to watch the third one-day international against England. The first two matches had been split between the sides and I was present at the ground to bring us luck. My last time in Chepauk had been nearly a year ago when I helped India win the decider against Waugh's Australians. The venue was even better than I remembered it: there was a giant replay screen and scoreboard opposite us at the other end of the ground and though the Tamil Nadu Cricket Association (TNCA) stand was sibilant with Chinese whispers about the six crore rupees it had cost despite being second-hand, I thought it gave the stadium a wonderfully up to date air. It looked even more glamorous under lights, which came on after the English finished their innings.

Around the time the lights took hold, a thuggish man and his unkempt friends, in seats not far from mine, began hammering out a tattoo using Bisleri empties. When he wasn't drumming, he was pulling faces at television cameras and shaking his body in suggestive ways. 'Can't be a member,' said my neighbour disapprovingly, for we were sitting in the members' stand where the seats had the names of individual members pasted on them. I had to agree. 'The police must have let him in,' said someone else, because there were more people than seats in the stand and many of them didn't look genteel enough to be members of the TNCA. In Madras, where a middle class commitment to civic order is still discernible, the yob's inconsiderateness and the policeman's complicity heralded anarchy.

The outsider who didn't belong became a kind of theme over the three days that I spent in Chennai after the ODI, interviewing cricketers in a bid to understand the culture of cricket in Chennai.

I spoke to the great leg break bowler V.V. Kumar who, but for Chandrasekhar, would have played regularly for India, the distinguished C.D. Gopinath, who batted for India in eight Test matches in the 1950s, and that fine off spinner V. Ramnarayan, who had the misfortune of reaching his prime for Hyderabad in the 1970s when all the spinning slots in the Indian team were taken. What I gathered from my conversations with them would fill a short book; here I want to focus on what I learnt from them about cricket as a livelihood in Madras from the 1940s to the present time.

I was curious to know how cricketers had traditionally

made a living, playing cricket in India in general and in Madras in particular. The English categories of amateur and professional didn't seem to fit the Indian context. In English county or league cricket, you were paid for playing if you were a professional, while you played for nothing if you were an amateur. In colonial India, the only amateurs in the English sense of the word were princes like the Nawab of Pataudi or the Maharaja of Patiala or, more rarely, men like Vijay Merchant with a private family income. Everybody else, middle class or otherwise, needed financial help. The trouble was that, for the most part, there wasn't a structure of professional club cricket that could employ the talented cricketer and pay him for his services. Ruling princes like those of Patiala and Udaipur sometimes employed whole teams of cricketers, but this was not the rule.

To a degree that is difficult to imagine, Indian cricket was sustained by arbitrary, sporadic and unorganized patronage. In Madras, there was a flourishing system of league cricket in place by the 1940s. There were a dozen first-division teams, nearly a hundred clubs in all and over a thousand people playing league cricket. This system was supported by enthusiasm and benevolence; the enthusiasm of players like V.V. Kumar and the benevolence of patrons like C.R. Pattabhiraman, barrister, Balu Alaganan, planter, J.P. Thomas of A.V. Thomas & Co., M.A. Chidambaram, C.P. Johnstone of Burmah Shell and many others.

'Livelihood wasn't an issue,' said Kumar. What he meant was that no one in his time went into cricket thinking of it as a career. But money was an issue. How could it not be, when an autographed bat cost Rs 150? He could remember players having to beg and cringe for patronage. M.J. Gopalan, the great double international, who represented India in hockey and cricket, had a lowly job in Burmah Shell, courtesy

C.P. Johnstone, a Cambridge blue who was somebody in Shell besides being the captain of the Madras Presidency cricket team. So Gopalan cycled from petrol station to petrol station and one of his duties was measuring how full or empty their tanks were with a dipstick.

Burmah Shell, Philips, Parrys and some other companies pioneered the practice of commercial firms giving cricketers jobs and salaries but, in colonial Madras, such patronage wasn't company policy; it was a function of the enthusiasm of individual managers. After independence, public sector enterprises like the State Bank of India in the 1960s began employing cricketers on a large scale. Their example was followed by enterprises like India Cements and from the early 1980s, private sector companies began paying players impressive salaries. Contemporary cricket in Chennai is largely underwritten by firms such as India Cements, TVS, MRF, Chemplast and others. Not only do they field teams in inter-company tournaments, they also sponsor first-division clubs in league cricket and effectively take them over.

Gopinath disapproved of the corporate takeover of league cricket. He thought it was unhealthy because companies had begun to recruit cricketers from outside Madras and Tamil Nadu to help them win league tournaments. Kumar reckoned that of the twelve first-division teams, eleven were, for all intents and purposes, company teams. Club loyalties and the enthusiasm of neighbourhood cricket were being corroded by corporate money. The Madras Cricket Club, for example, competed in the third division of the league. The Madras Cricket Club is Gopinath's club and he attributed its decline as a cricket power in Madras to its inability to compete with the large corporates who could buy their talent.

This distaste for the corporate habit of importing players on fat contracts, for the explicit commercialization of cricket, is partly generational and partly rooted in a colonial preference for white collar work. The good thing about patronage in the old days was that the fiction of employment outside cricket allowed the cricketer the respectability of amateur status on the field and the reassurance of a salary off it. Had the cricketer been playing for wages as players like Vinoo Mankad did in the English league cricket, cricket would have been his job and his wages would have begun to seem remarkably like money for manual, skilled labour, but labour nonetheless. Given the upper-caste profile of Madras cricket historically, it's not surprising that there should be nostalgia for the middle class gentility that shamateur sport made possible.

I tentatively suggested to Ramnarayan that a possible solution to the problems of league and first-class cricket was more professionalization, not less. The way to do this, I suggested, was to radically reorganize the game so that clubs became commercial entities attentive to the menace of the bottomline. This would mean doing away with the territorial principle altogether and freely allowing the import of players as professional league soccer did all over the world. He was properly sceptical about the financial viability of such a league, given the fact that no one seemed to watch league or first-class cricket any more, but he welcomed the idea in principle. As a player who had migrated from Tamil Nadu to Hyderabad to find opportunities to play first-class cricket, he recognized the importance of a league that would create a market for talent and replace patronage with professional employment.

Paradoxically, it is because Madras has an old and lively sporting culture rooted in clubs and gymkhanas that its middle class sporting establishment resists the idea that money should be used to buy talent. That a club should enroll professional players as members simply to win tournaments seems distasteful when clubs have traditionally chosen teams of gentlemen from within the existing membership. The fear often is that the sporting yob, once enrolled, will lower the tone of the club. It is an unworthy fear: not so long ago, white colonials who founded many of these clubs fretted in the same way about the social consequences of admitting Indians.

Franchising First-class Cricket

Empty concrete terraces make domestic first-class cricket a game without a public. The Ranji Trophy and the Duleep Trophy have no competitive reason for being. Nobody cares who wins them any more apart from the players themselves. These tournaments have become prolonged auditions for the international stage. Even fourth-rate football between Mohun Bagan and East Bengal sells tickets; why doesn't first-class cricket? Every fan has a watertight, money-back scheme which he believes will improve the game he loves, this is mine.

Successful modern sports, team or individual, have two things in common: they try to turn a profit at every level and the sport is so organized that the individual player, if he's good enough, has the world as his stage. So Bhaichung Bhutia signs a contract to play for Bury despite his origins in the footballing backwater of Sikkim; Paes and Bhupathi seek their fortunes in major doubles tournaments the world over and desperate Serbs find glory in the basketball leagues of North America.

Since it is the nature of cricket that we're trying to understand, it is probably most appropriate to compare it with soccer because they're both team sports and they both achieved their modern forms in England. The difference in their contemporary conditions is vast and the difference is this: football is a business which pays its own way while cricket is a shamateur sport where there's money to be made, but mostly off the field of play.

The success of soccer (or basketball or American football) as a modern sport lies in the way it is organized. Soccer is structured around privately owned clubs. While these clubs are invariably identified with a city or town (Manchester United, Real Madrid, Bayern Munich) and their fan followings owe something to their urban histories, the teams that represent the clubs are not picked to represent a parochial idea. These clubs are professionally run companies that buy and sell players for one purpose: to win because success brings crowds, television revenues and profits. Chelsea, a great London club, recently fielded a team in the Premier Division, of which two-thirds of the players were foreign. Chelsea's fan following doesn't care where the ordnance comes from so long as they win their battles. Manchester United is a hugely successful business, a remarkable brand name that has an international clientele of fans who buy its merchandise and pack stadiums wherever the team plays.

Contrast this with cricket. First-class cricket is territorially organized: teams represent counties, states or provinces. County teams are run by clubs but unlike football clubs, these aren't companies—they are more like gymkhanas or, in American parlance, country clubs. They raise revenues through membership and gate receipts. Unlike football, their freedom to hire players is limited by territorial definitions. Some counties like Yorkshire mainly select players with a birth qualification to play for that county. English Cricket Board rules restrict the number of foreign players a county side can hire so that the first-class game in England can nurture home-grown talent.

English county cricket is the closest the first-class game comes to the cosmopolitan club culture of soccer. The first-class game in India has no foreign players and all regional teams need players to fulfil residential qualifications before they can be considered for selection. Similarly, barring the odd exception, the first-class game in all Test cricket-playing nations restricts the mobility of individual players in the name of territorial affiliation.

The justification for this geographical principle is that it harnesses territorial loyalties to competitive ends. This is a perfectly good idea in theory, but it doesn't seem to work in the real world. If territorial teams were supported by loyal crowds, the principle would be vindicated, but they aren't and it isn't. Counties have geographical boundaries that have no contemporary political or social relevance; they're nostalgic, anachronistic fictions and the people who live within their alleged boundaries don't take them seriously. If they did, county cricket clubs would be more solvent and their grounds fuller than they are. In India, first-class cricket is mainly organized to follow provincial boundaries, with exceptions made to accommodate historically significant teams like Hyderabad, Mumbai and Baroda.

All over the cricketing world, what most first-class teams have in common is a total lack of drawing power. Few people watch first-class matches at the ground and even when they are telecast, it's fair to say that their television audiences don't sell many advertising spots. First-class teams everywhere are parishes without congregations, empty churches where performances echo. Ironically, the last time first-class cricket in India drew huge crowds and filled stadiums on a regular basis, was when the competing teams were organized on the politically incorrect principle of religious and ethnic affiliation: i.e., the glory days of the Pentangular championship in colonial Bombay when Hindus, Muslims, Europeans, Parsees and the Rest battled for cricketing supremacy.

Bengalis will fill Eden Gardens for a one-day international, but they won't cross the road to watch Bengal beat Kerala in a first-class match. And yet, these same Calcuttans will scream, riot and kill for Mohammedan Sporting, Mohun Bagan and East Bengal. Like Chelsea supporters, the fan followings of these Calcutta soccer clubs are shaped by their histories (Mohammedan Sporting has traditionally had a large Muslim following), but these fans care nothing for ethnicity in the composition of their teams: they simply want them to win. To this end, they recruit players from as far afield as Kerala, Iran and Nigeria. The contrast in the fan base of Bengali cricket and Bengali football has everything to do with organization. Soccer is run by private clubs responsible to their owners and followings; provincial cricket is run by a 'board' that is controlled by honorary grandees and is accountable to no one.

The first-class cricketer in India plays for provincial sides that are meant to represent a sub-national belonging. Because the player's task is to represent a regional identity, the provincial board he plays for doesn't actually employ him. He might be paid for the matches he plays, but the match fees paid by the board don't constitute a stable livelihood because the cricket board doesn't offer negotiated, long-term contracts. His livelihood is supplied by the company that employs him as an ornament or to play club cricket for the company team. Also, what he makes as match fees has no relation to his ability, because those fees are bureaucratically fixed and are the same for all players, regardless of drawing power or talent. So the workman isn't worthy of his hire; the cricketer isn't paid what he is worth. In fact, his worth is indeterminable because there is no competition allowed for his services. We know what Beckham is worth: his transfer fees and his contract will tell us. We have no idea what

Tendulkar is worth because there isn't a proper cricketing market for his services; his talents aren't fungible. I'm not talking about sponsorship; we all know or think we know how much Tendulkar makes by that route. I'm concerned with payments generated within the game. The first-class cricketer is routinely shackled to territorial identities that share a double defect: while they create no real solidarity, they limit his livelihood.

First-class cricket in India is governed by an administrative structure that mirrors the shamateurism of its players. Presidents and secretaries of cricket boards officially offer their services gratis while using their honorary offices to make money, extend patronage and rig elections. These boards claim to represent regional constituencies, but are actually rotten boroughs in the gift of politicians and businessmen.

Nowhere in the cricketing world does the domestic first-class game pay its way. County cricket would collapse if it weren't subsidized by the England and Wales Cricket Board from the revenues that accrue from Test and one-day cricket. Provincial cricket boards in India make both their legitimate revenues and their backhanders by staging international matches that are distributed as political largesse by the BCCI—which is why international cricket is played in places like Cuttack and Indore. Cricket's revenues are nearly wholly derived from international matches because the only territorial identity that gets people to the grounds or lined up in front of their television sets is nationhood. This is as it should be: the only time I feel unselfconsciously nationalistic is during a Test match. International matches provide catharsis; they purge their audiences of the patriotic poisons that accumulate in them unnoticed. Like laxatives, they're good for the system.

But it is unhealthy that the game is kept alive mainly, perhaps wholly, by nationalist feeling. Again, a comparison with soccer is instructive. Soccer's World Cup makes vast amounts of money and attracts the largest television audiences in the world. Latin American nations have notoriously gone to war over football matches. So patriotism is alive and well in football. But if the soccer World Cup were to disappear tomorrow, if matches between national football teams were banned for some reason, the game would survive their loss. Soccer's standing as an international professional sport would be untouched because organizationally and financially, soccer as a league sport is financially self-sufficient, independent of the revenues raised by national jousting. Competition between national teams is the jam on soccer's table, not its bread and butter.

If you take national teams out of cricket, the game will collapse because there is no other tier of competition that people will pay to watch. The reasons aren't hard to find. The free movement of talent in league soccer, the discipline imposed by the market, the excitement generated by international competition at the club level (the UEFA Cup, for example) have saved club soccer from the tedium that afflicts cricket. Because league soccer is not insular, it never seems provincial in the way that first-class cricket often does. Because the European leagues draw upon a worldwide pool of talent, because the league game rewards talent with money and stardom, soccer at this level is both glamorous and sexy; it doesn't carry the awful taint of second-rateness that first-class cricket so often does.

Someone could ask, why should cricket follow football's example? They are different games with different histories; why should the one be remade in the image of the other? It is a legitimate question; the answer is that cricket, in the jungle of world sport, is an endangered creature. It has a small base in a handful of post-colonial countries. It needs to think about its future, to take its own temperature. The present system is dangerously top heavy: the apparent economic health of the international game obscures the termite-ridden structure on which Test and one-day cricket are based.

What happens, for example, when a team's national audience loses interest in the game on account of consistent failure? This could conceivably happen to the West Indies. Cricket in the Caribbean is already losing talent to basketball leagues in America. A generation down the road, a young Curtly Ambrose might aspire to basketball scholarships in American universities instead of the economically perilous distinction of playing for Antigua. Why should a second Steve Tikolo ever represent Kenya when that country's national team can't afford basic cricket kits? Why should brilliant players from small countries be denied riches and stardom when second-raters like Kambli and Yuvraj Singh achieve both simply because they have more consuming compatriots at their backs? Unless we find rational answers to these questions, cricket will become an even more provincial game than it already is.

The only way to do this is to radically reorganize the first-class game so that clubs become commercial entities attentive to the menace of the bottomline. India, as the largest consumer of cricket and consequently the richest cricketing nation, ought to host a league that will be truly cosmopolitan, that will create careers open to talent, where Kenyan, Jamaican, Kiwi and Aussie adventurers will seek their livelihoods, their fortunes even. The English county game is the only first-class system that comes within shouting distance of this fantasy, but cricket is too small a game in England for the revolution to begin there.

As a consumer of cricket, as a spectator, I envy the football fan who watches great foreign players strut their stuff in his domestic leagues. I envy the Chelsea supporter who urges Carlo Cudacini on with the partisan passion essential to spectatorship, but a passion that allows him to claim foreign talent as his own. I dream of a cosmopolitan cricket league where the Mumbaikars (led by Ricky Ponting) take on the Kolkata Tigers (owned by J. Dalmiya) at the Eden Gardens in the finals of the Infosys Cup. The umpires would be neutral by default.

Reclaiming Cricket Lite: ODIs Reconsidered

In a book about Test cricket, I thought there was room for a piece on the one-day game, one that argues the need to make limited-overs cricket more like Test cricket, by purging it of the special laws that disfigure it.

The rules for one-day cricket are different from those for Test cricket and the differences allegedly exist to stop fielding sides from becoming too defensive. Trevor Chappell bowling under-arm with every fielder on the boundary line might be an extreme example of such defensiveness, but it will serve as an illustration of what one-day cricket should not be. Similarly, I can remember Bishen Bedi bowling yards wide of the stumps to Imran Khan during the Test series in Pakistan in 1978. I was reminded of that passage of play while reading an interview with Bedi in a magazine, where Bedi was being lofty about Ashley Giles's line against Tendulkar in an interview. Giles bowled rather closer to the stumps than Bedi did on that occasion—the other difference was that Giles' version of leg theory paid off, Bedi's line didn't: Pakistan won the match.

One-day rules put an end to cynical defensive play of this sort by defining the wide ball more strictly, and we are all grateful for that. It is a modification that could be usefully incorporated into Test cricket; not quite so rigorously perhaps (attacking bowlers like Warne need some leeway outside the leg stump), but the latitude that the present law gives to bowlers is ridiculous. Of the many innovations made in the laws to make limited-overs cricket a more exciting game, this seems to be the only sensible one. The effect of the other changes has been to rig the game in favour of batsmen. These specialized rules aren't just unnecessary, they actually damage the credibility of one-day cricket by upsetting the equilibrium between batsmen and bowlers. The reason one-day matches are forgettable is that bowling and fielding restrictions impose a formulaic pattern upon every innings. The average innings consists of a sprint for runs in the opening and closing overs with a steady jog in between. We need to do something about the predictability of the shorter game, its lack of nuance, its strategic crudeness. The way to do it is to deregulate bowling and fielding in one-day cricket.

Under the present regime, the credibility of the game suffers for two reasons. One, the rules arbitrarily prevent a bowler from imposing himself on a match in the way a batsman can. Tendulkar can, if he wishes, bat fifty overs and score a double hundred, but McGrath can only bowl ten. Tendulkar has the scope to script the whole innings, to display patience, guile, aggression, to master the bowling attack. McGrath, regardless of how well he is bowling, must stop after his quota of sixty balls. The spearhead of the attack can seldom bowl his quota of ten overs continuously because he has to be saved up for the end of the innings, so even his meagre allotment has to be divided into spells. One consequence of this is that middle-order batsmen in limited-overs cricket rarely face an extended spell from the best or most hostile pace bowlers. A batsman like Bevan who can't find a place in Australia's Test team, can shelter in the middle order in the one-day game, and rack up the highest career average in the game. Bevan is in some ways a great advertisement for one-day cricket: his running between wickets and his ability to pace an innings are exemplary. But he is fatally uncertain against fast, short-pitched bowling and the rules that help him camouflage his vulnerability are bad rules that should be changed. Substitute Ganguly's name for Bevan's and you can see why he continued to open the batting for India in limited-overs cricket long after his weakness against the short ball was exposed.

Which brings us to the other chronic problem with one-day cricket. Not only do the rules prevent great bowlers from fully expressing themselves, they allow second-rate batsmen to flourish. Protected till recently by the no-bouncer rule, middle-order batsmen have been refurbished and converted into openers. Secure in the knowledge that they can wait out spells by good bowlers like Murali and Harbhajan, they feast on the bits-and-pieces bowlers that litter the one-day game. This can't be right. The point of any kind of cricket should be to allow excellence free rein. This can only be done by not fiddling too much with the equilibrium between bowlers and batsmen, which the laws of the longer game allow. The present laws for the one-day game have upset this balance completely.

It is possible to argue that cricket has always been a game weighted in favour of the batsmen, so if the one-day game goes a little further down that road in the interest of excitement, why should that be wrong? It's wrong because the cliché is a lie: Test cricket isn't a batsman's game. The only real evidence that's ever adduced is the axiom that in the matter of dismissals, the umpire always gives the batsman the benefit of the doubt. But to claim that this makes cricket partial to batsmen is rather like saying that the law favours criminals because it holds that defendants are innocent until they are proved guilty. Cricket simply follows the rules of natural justice.

Where one-day cricket has gone wrong is in rigging the rules so that it has become harder and harder for the plaintiff (the bowler) to make his best case. The bowler is hamstrung by arbitrary restrictions on field placement, by the bouncer rule and by over quotas, all of which help the batsman to get off scot-free more often than not. It isn't a proper trial any more. To hear commentators praise feather-bed tracks as first-class one-day wickets is to know how far the rot has gone. When cricket becomes merely an occasion for spectacular slogging against defanged bowling, you know it's time to call a halt.

One-day cricket is crying out to be deregulated. Currently it's a kind of licence Raj where inefficient batsmen flourish because the rules forbid proper competition. Cricket needs laissez-faire reform. Just as economists know that all economies, even successful capitalist ones, need some regulation, cricket's lawmakers need to understand that Test cricket has, barring a tweak or two, all the laws that one-day cricket needs. We should review every special one-day law and unless there is a compelling reason for retaining them, they should be scrapped.

The rule of thumb used in this scrutiny should not be the question, does it make one-day cricket more exciting? Excitement isn't a measure; there are people who find WWE wrestling exciting. In cricket we should start with the assumption that the bowler can bowl any kind of ball to any sort of field so long as he doesn't chuck. This freedom should be regulated only to ensure that the batsman has the opportunity to play a cricket shot, that is, a conventional stroke, at every ball the bowler bowls. The changing of the wide rule passes this test because Test cricket's rule for wides allows bowlers to bowl deliveries against which batsmen can't play a reasonable shot. Similarly, the restrictions in Test cricket on the number of fielders on the leg side are reasonable because leg theory makes it impossible to score without taking unreasonable risks.

Using this criterion, let's examine one-day cricket's restriction on the number of overs a bowler is allowed. The quota system fails the test because there's no reason McGrath shouldn't bowl twenty-five overs on the trot if he possesses the skill, consistency and energy to bowl a marathon spell. Just as there are no artificial restrictions on the number of balls a batsman can face, there should be none on how many a bowler can bowl. I think it's unlikely that captains will keep bowlers on for so long, but I can't see why they shouldn't have the freedom to choose. The only objection I can think of is the fear that teams might pack their sides with batsmen. Though I can't see it happening, because a batsman's freedom to bat out fifty overs hasn't exactly encouraged selectors to pack teams with bowlers. If Muralitharan wants to bowl right through the match because he's the best bowler in the Sri Lankan team, he should be allowed to because the point of the game is for batsmen to find ways of playing the best bowling the other team has to offer. So there should be no restrictions on the number of overs an individual bowler is allowed.

And fielding restrictions? Using our rule of thumb, the answer is only slightly less categorical. There have to be restrictions on packing one side of the wicket, clearly, but these restrictions already exist in Test cricket and are common to both forms of the game. This brings us to the fielding restrictions peculiar to one-day cricket: which determine the number of fielders and catchers a bowling team must employ within the circle and outside it at different times of the game. These are intended to curb defensive fields and promote a more attacking and exciting game. This is a peculiar justification for a form of cricket which has elevated the sharp single into an art form. Given what Bevan and Rhodes did to spread out fields simply by running hard between wickets, why should anyone assume that defensive field placements will lead to dull low scoring matches?

Like all forms of well-meant interference, fielding restrictions do more harm than good. In Test cricket, all batsmen bat under similar conditions. You can compare the achievements of individual players because they play on a level playing field. This is not true in one-day cricket under the present rules. Opening batsmen have a huge advantage because of the aggressive fields that must be employed against them. Unequal playing conditions should be anathema to any sport. Perfect equality is impossible to achieve, but cricket's lawmakers should make sure that no rule they frame aggravates or creates inequality. Anyone who follows the shorter game has felt uneasy about player records because unlike Test cricket, the numbers aren't comparable, and such unease corrodes the credibility of the game.

The perfect example of the good that deregulation can do is the change in the bouncer rule. Earlier, when every bouncer was a no-ball, batsmen were routinely on the front foot, sometimes pulling fast bowlers in front of square simply because the rules had given them a guarantee that they wouldn't be bounced. Now that one bouncer is allowed every over, there's uncertainty in the batsman's mind and the prospect of excitement and aggression each time the short ball actually arrives. Good fast bowlers have the chance to sort out bouncer-shy batsmen and the Michael Bevans of this world can't affect a front-foot valour that they don't feel. There's a good case for bringing the rule in line with the Test match rule which allows two bouncers per over so long as the umpires are strict about no-balling steepling bouncers cynically intended to prevent scoring.

The one-day game in its present form is formulaic, predictable, monotonous and wholly forgettable because a thicket of unnecessary rules writes the script of every match before play begins. It promotes and protects second-rate players, treats bowlers like extras and coddles batsmen. The excitement it creates is a kind of feverishness and the statistics it generates are an unreliable guide to ability or achievement— a dangerous thing for a game like cricket, where figures are vital to a fan's pleasure in the game. We need to reform the laws of one-day cricket and we need to start with the assumption that the shorter and longer game should, as far as possible, be exactly the same. This also means that any changes in the law for the one-day game (like the wide rule) should be implemented in Test cricket, all other things being equal. This way we shall create two authentic forms of the same game, instead of what we have currently: Cricket Lite and The Real Thing.

Gents on Top: Honorary Officials

I remember as a child wondering who Wankhede was, why Test cricket in Bangalore was played in the Chidambaram stadium. Now that I know, I still wonder why stadia that should have been named after the game's greats are named to aggrandize the administrators who built them. I have no difficulty with businessmen and politicians administering cricket: what bothers me is the hubris that allows them to build memorials to themselves and the cricketing culture that lets them do it. I think it has to do with their 'honorary', unpaid status and the self-image they carry around of themselves as patrons of the game.

The spectacle of Jagmohan Dalmiya—then president of the BCCI—the ICC and the players squabbling over contracts, sponsors and even participation on the eve of a World Cup should have driven home an important truth about modern cricket: Kerry Packer left his job half done. Everyone now recognizes that Packer transformed the game for the better, indeed, helped it survive by making it more inventive, more lucrative and more accessible through a new style of television coverage. What is less obvious is that the old regime, the gents who ran the Australian Cricket Board (ACB), the Test and County Cricket Board (TCCB) and the MCC, sidestepped revolution by buying Packer off with television rights. Then, with the deftness and discretion of long practice, the Anglo-Australian establishment made its peace with business by setting up shop itself.

This profited the old guard, not just in England and Australia, but everywhere international cricket was played. In India, businessmen like Dalmiya, politicians like Salve and bureaucrats like Bindra made careers out of administering cricket. These positions were (and in India they still are) honorary, but the powers of patronage and the scope for deal making that come with them have made thousands of cricket functionaries over the years very happy. The money in cricket administration comes from the vast sums television channels are willing to spend to buy telecast rights. All of this money is handled by unpaid gentlemen out of their love for the game. The ICC has, in recent years, begun to pay its top officials, but these professional managers still preside over a worldwide pyramid of amateur administrators.

Leaving aside for a moment the question of how efficiently or honestly international cricket is run, the prior question is this: what function do national cricket boards perform in modern cricket? They are, essentially, middlemen signing contracts on behalf of national sides. Once, when the game, like its administrators, was largely amateur, or at least before international cricket began to generate significant amounts of money, the cricket boards were honourable intermediaries: they provided the arenas for cricket's public to watch their heroes. They organized the contests, arranged the stadiums, and paid for the transport, the boarding and lodging and also the pittance that great players were paid till recently. Till the game was amateur, till the business of cricket was a matter of stipends and gate money, the members of cricket boards were patrons; once the game became thoroughly commercial, they became parasites.

Their uselessness is perfectly illustrated by the dispute over contracts before the 2003 World Cup. The ICC, without asking the men who matter, the players, consulted with its constituent parts, the national cricket boards, and with their consent, signed a set of agreements with the companies officially sponsoring the World Cup in South Africa. These terms committed all the players participating in the tournament to exclusively advertise the logos and products of the official sponsors before, during and after the tournament. Dalmiya, for all his subsequent posturing, agreed to the terms proposed without demur and was party to the contracts. By agreeing with the ICC, the national cricket boards, as the owners of international cricket, promised to deliver their employees, the national cricket teams. This Dalmiya and the BCCI did without showing the players the contracts they were meant to sign.

Such absurd high-handedness might have worked twenty years ago, when the boards owned international cricket, but by 2002 it had become clear to Indian players that the BCCI was not their only, or even their most important, patron and they refused to be taken for granted. Their real employers, of course, were their sponsors, with whom they had lucrative prior contracts that the board had committed them to breach without so much as a by your leave!

Packer's real project, whether he knew it or not, was to teach cricket boards that they were irrelevant to the game. He demonstrated that cricket's future health lay in marketing players to a television audience and milking the telecasts for all they were worth in a way that made television ratings go up, made the players rich and kept audiences happy. The effect of this lesson ought to have been the downsizing of cricket boards. From being patrons of the game, they ought to have been reformed into post offices for players' associations.

The reason more such players associations don't exist is that after Packer, cricketers began to earn money so far beyond their modest expectations that they didn't feel the need to create a union or a guild to protect their interests. Also, the culture of cricket is so irradiated with deference that the idea of collective bargaining didn't catch on. After the World Cup imbroglio, players have become more mindful of their interests. Stand-offs between boards and players like the one in 2005 between the West Indies Cricket Board and some star West Indian players when the rights of team sponsors collided with the contracts of individual players, are likely to become more common.

It's true that if the BCCI president didn't exist, no one would need to invent him. Given that the post exists, it should be filled by an election based on an electoral college dominated by players' associations. The chief of the BCCI shouldn't be an 'honorary' grandee: he should be a paid employee answerable to players, a servant of Indian cricket. And the chiefs of all cricket councils, whether national or international, should be headed by secretaries, not chairmen or presidents: postmen should have titles commensurate with their functions.

Requiem for the Ref

Rereading this piece immediately after the stand-off between Australian umpire Darrell Hair and the Pakistani team captained by Inzamam-ul-Haq led to the forfeiture of the fourth Test by the Pakistanis in August 2006, I was struck once again by the total uselessness of the match referee. If ever there was an opportunity for the referee to play a supervisory, problem-solving role, this was it. Yet, Mike Proctor, the match referee, could do nothing because cricket's laws make it clear that the umpires in the middle are in charge of the conduct of the game. Darrell Hair might have made the wrong call on ball tampering, but he was right in insisting that once he ruled Pakistan had forfeited the match, it would stay forfeited. Those who think that Hair's actions justify the transfer of these powers to the match referee might want to remind themselves of the dodgy history of this IIC-invented office.

When the history of cricket in the early twenty-first century is written, the Mike Denness affair will get a decent sized footnote. Not because it represents a decisive moment in the development of the ICC's control over the world game—it doesn't. With luck, it will be remembered as the controversy that spurred the ICC to abolish the position of the match referee, to enlarge the regulatory role of the slow motion television replay and to return to the umpires their once sovereign control over the game. If the ICC has any sense, 2002 should see the end of the improvised, arbitrary relationship between television technology and the umpires in the middle. The present arrangement manages to demoralize umpires, provoke players and infuriate spectators. In its place we ought to have a system that joins the near omniscience of the camera to the traditional authority of the umpires.

On 20 November 2001, during the second Test between India and South Africa at Port Elizabeth, Mike Denness, in his capacity as match referee, punished six Indian players, including Sachin Tendulkar and Virender Sehwag. Sehwag was banned for one match for excessive appealing while Tendulkar was fined 75 per cent of his match fee and given a suspended one-match ban for cleaning the seam of the ball without the permission of the umpires. Jagmohan Dalmiya, then president of the BCCI, called for Denness to be replaced for the third Test. The South African board went along with Dalmiya. The ICC responded by refusing to recognize the third Test of the series as an official Test match. After some brinkmanship from Dalmiya, the ICC prevailed and the BCCI agreed to drop Sehwag from the first match of the subsequent Test series against England. The ICC's sop to Dalmiya was a time-tested fudge: it agreed to set up a commission to examine Denness's decision. It would have made considerably more sense to establish a commission to review the whole institution of the match referee.

Denness's critics argued that his decisions were opaque, harsh and arbitrary. Denness, however, wasn't the problem. The problem was his office. Denis Lindsay, the South African nominated to referee the subsequent India–England series, went out of his way to show that all referees weren't cowboys on a hair-trigger. Virender Sehwag, he said generously, wasn't a criminal and oughtn't to be treated like one.

This is ironical because in the matter of draconian punishment, Denis Lindsay is the Roger Bannister of match refereedom. When he suspended Ridley Jacobs, the West Indian wicketkeeper, for three matches for cheating and bringing the game into disrepute, Lindsay rewrote the record books. Other referees might, in the future, hand out three-match suspensions, but Lindsay got there first. He also got it wrong and set a terrible precedent.

Jacobs's suspension illustrates graphically the real problem in supervising contemporary cricket: the ad hoc relationship between the umpires and the television camera. In passing, it also makes the useful point that match referees are worse than useless.

A three-match suspension is drastic punishment. Suspensions are normally given to batsmen who show dissent on being given out. Inzamam-ul-Haq was once punished for lingering at the crease after Peter Willey had given him out lbw and he only got a two-match suspension.

Jacobs's fault was that, playing against India, he 'stumped' Sehwag by breaking the stumps with the glove that wasn't holding the ball. Jacobs, the referee decided, had acted in bad faith because his hands were so far apart that he must have known at the time that he was using the wrong hand.

The reason the umpire hadn't caught Jacobs out was that the slow motion replay wasn't properly used to determine the legitimacy of the stumping. The umpiring was made to look bad by a careless match referee but instead of punishing the umpire, the match referee punished the West Indian keeper.

Didn't Jacobs deserve his punishment? To answer that, you have to look at the way cricket deals with players who mislead umpires. Every batsman who nicks the ball stands his ground and waits for the umpire to give him out, caught. The batsman knows he is out, but I've never heard of a match referee suspending a batsman for not walking. Morally, I can see no difference between a batsman who chooses to stay, knowing that he is out, and a fielder who appeals against a batsman knowing he isn't.

The twist in Jacobs's tale is that he *didn't* appeal. His teammates did. Jacobs remained silent. He was guilty, not of active perjury, but perjury by association. But Lindsay decided that Jacobs was guilty of a breach of the Players and Officials Code of Conduct. The wicketkeeper had violated the 'Spirit of Cricket', as set out in the preamble to the laws of cricket. Lindsay indicated that Jacobs should have recalled Sehwag, who had wrongly been given out as a consequence of the 'stumping'.

There are intellectually respectable ways of justifying the punishment given to Jacobs, but they don't really explain why he was so harshly dealt with. Yes, Jacobs was cheating, in the same way as batsmen cheat when they stand their ground after edging a ball to slip. The question to ask is this: if the umpire at square leg had referred the appeal to the replay, as he was entitled to do, and if the third umpire had spotted Jacobs's sleight of hand and ruled the batsman not out, would Jacobs have been punished? My guess is no, just as nothing happens to appealing fielders when the replay shows that the 'catch' had been taken on the bounce.

You could argue that such catches are close calls and that the catcher himself doesn't know if he has taken it cleanly, whereas Jacobs's hands were so far apart that he must have known he was cheating. This is a reasonable argument, but it takes umpiring into the murk of motivation. Jacobs could retort that stumpings are instantaneous acts where it is impossible for a keeper to know what he has done. Breaking the stumps is an instinct with keepers, not a considered decision.

This is not to claim that Jacobs wasn't cheating; it is to argue that the keeper should have been given the benefit of doubt that Michael Slater received when he appealed for a catch against Rahul Dravid during the first Test of the 2001 series in Bombay. The appeal was referred to the third umpire, who turned it down. Nothing happened to Slater. Unlike Slater, Jacobs did not appeal to the umpire. His fault was that he didn't set the umpire right. Had the umpire used the available technology to decide the matter, Jacobs's silent concurrence would have had no cricketing consequences. That a batsman was wrongly given out was due to the square leg umpire's incompetence, not Jacobs's doing. For the match referee to have punished Jacobs for it was an act of judicial pique, not retrospective justice.

The trouble with cricket is that it has moved from a system of supervision based on an acceptance of human (read umpiring) error and the alleged honour of the gentleman cricketer, to an umpiring regime dependent on (and second-guessed by) the all-seeing camera. Cricket's administrators have put technology at the disposal of the on-field umpires (in a limited way), to be used at their discretion. Having been given this discretion, professional umpires must be held accountable for the way in which they exercise it. Umpires and referees should be told that their job is to make the right decisions during the match, not to hold court martials afterwards. The fact that the wicketkeeper didn't appeal should have alerted an international umpire.

Match referees were created partly to make the umpire's job easy by punishing insubordination. Players become mutinous when they think the umpire is wrong. Umpires have always made mistakes and players have always felt hard done by but now, thanks to television replay, there's evidence of the umpire's fallibility. His authority has suffered and players have sometimes become openly insubordinate.

The invention of the match referee has done nothing to fix this. Football's punishments are handed out during the course of play; the match referee in cricket acts in retrospect. Red cards and yellow cards flashed by a referee policing a football match have authority because the referee is present in the thick of things. The match referee in cricket is a bureaucrat, remote from the action. Worse, his decisions are shrouded in the opaque authority of a military tribunal, immune to appeal. In the Jacobs case, Denis Lindsay obligingly illustrated the incompetence and uselessness of his office by suspending Jacobs from three one-day matches that he hadn't been picked to play. That Jacobs was not going to tour Kenya had been announced well before the incident by the West Indies selectors, but Lindsay went ahead and suspended him anyway. Later, he revoked this absurd non-punishment and suspended him from a Test match against Zimbabwe instead.

What does the match referee bring to the table that umpires don't? The answer is, nothing. Umpires pass exams, they specialize in the laws of cricket, they serve arduous apprenticeships; referees are ex-cricketers looking to improve their pension plans. If the match referee's function is to glean information from television coverage that the umpires can't see (e.g., Sachin Tendulkar using his nail on the seam), then surely that's a job better done by the third umpire. The match referee is no more than a couch potato with a big stick that he is meant to swing to defend the umpire's authority. That authority, however, has been eroded by the camera and it can only be restored by clarifying the relationship between the two, not by further diffusing the umpire's authority by installing this big brother, eternally watching.

The root-and-branch way of clarifying the camera–umpire relationship is by eliminating the third umpire and the slow motion replay and banning the use of giant screens on the ground. This solution would eliminate the match referee by giving umpires real disciplinary powers that would extend to removing serious offenders from the field of play. Having been given complete control, an umpire's performance would be reviewed using (ironically) the evidence of the television cameras and his job opportunities would depend on his performance. Both umpires would come from neutral countries. This is the soccer model of supervision, where refereeing errors are accepted as an occupational hazard. It would have the advantage of consistency unlike the present system where some decisions are referred to the camera and others aren't.

The problem with this route is that it's blocked. In cricket the slow motion replay has become part of the cricket fan's common sense. For him, seeing something on television is believing, and there's no going back.

If this is true, the alternative solution is to achieve consistency by allowing umpires to call for replays for anything they choose. This would help on the discipline front because players tend to intimidate umpires over decisions that can't be double-checked with the camera: bat-pad catches, lbw judgements, faint edges. The present convention which decrees that a catch can only be referred to a replay to discover if it was taken cleanly, but not to confirm if the ball hit the bat, is absurd and ought to be junked. The umpires in the middle should have complete access to the testimony of the camera but the decision, in every case, should be theirs to make.

The third umpire should be an auxiliary to the men on the field. He shouldn't flash a light to convey his decision because the decision shouldn't be his to make. His task should be to relay the evidence of the camera and his opinion of it, to the umpire on the field. This is the method used to determine photo-finish boundaries, and there is no reason why it can't be used for dismissals. The other function of the third umpire could be to dial up the men in the middle, should he happen to see on television Mike Atherton sanding the ball or Tendulkar buffing his nails on the seam. It would be the job of the two umpires to advise Tendulkar that he ought to use a nail file instead, or to inspect the ball for signs of damage, or to decide during the course of play if he deserves summary punishment.

This is the way to go because it makes of the television camera a reliable eyewitness that umpires can call upon, not an electronic big brother whose inhuman omniscience shoves the umpires into the margins of credibility, diminished in the eyes of the players they supervise and derided by the audiences that watch them on television. It would keep the umpires in charge as they traditionally were, and always should remain. It would also (and this would be the priceless bonus) drive into extinction that sinecure-hunting carpetbagger, the match referee.

The Fifteen Degree Solution

In 1995, on Boxing Day, Darrell Hair called Muthiah Muralitharan for throwing during a Test match at the MCG. Nobody knew it then, but Hair had written the first chapter of a story that was to end in a fundamental rewriting of cricket's rule book. Bodyline had forced a change in the rules about field settings on the leg side, but the chucking controversy led to a more basic change: a redefinition of what constitutes a legal delivery. What started as the questioning of one slow bowler's freakish action—Muralitharan's—snowballed into an investigation of bowling actions generally. The camera technology and the advances made by sports medicine that had been used to test the legality of Muralitharan's action were used to survey and scrutinize modern bowling actions of all kinds. The results of these surveys were so startling that they forced the ICC to rewrite, some would say, compromise, the earlier, stricter definition.

1

Hardware and software in perfect alliance
The Council's got chucking down to a science

The row over chucking and the problem of defining and policing illegal actions is a dispute between science and subjectivity, between the infallibility of computers and the errors of men. In the human corner we have umpires whose job it has been to call bowlers who throw. In the computer's corner we have technologists and computer scientists (all, mysteriously, natives of a single university in Australia) with their all-seeing machines and software.

When cricket was plagued by an epidemic of dodgy actions a few years ago, the ICC effectively sub-contracted the task of confirming if a bowler threw to the machine men. Umpires lost their magisterial function: they were reduced to snitching on the suspect player and waiting for the honorary prefects in the said Australian university to test the action via laboratory simulations and sophisticated cameras, and pronounce on its legality.

The reason for this innovation was that television cameras had begun providing ever clearer views of bowlers in their delivery arc, which highlighted kinks that might otherwise have blushed unseen. The need for a definitive view endorsed by the hardware and authority of science became more urgent because of the way in which Muralitharan's action was called into question by Australian umpires. Murali had a substantial international career behind him when he was first called and while he had one of the oddest actions seen on a spinner in the game's history, it was embarrassing for the ICC to have a famous bowler called for the first time so far into his career. The umpires who called him, variously abrasive and excitable (one of them even called Murali's leg breaks), helped light the fire which became a conflagration in the hands of the toughest, canniest captain of modern times, Arjuna Ranatunga, who stared down offending officials in defence of his star bowler. Murali was tested by the boffins, cleared and then indicted again for his doosra, setting the stage for ICC's later flounderings.

2

The most sinned-against hero since Vyas' Karan
The one, the only, M. Muralitharan

When the scientists first announced that Murali's action only seemed illegal because of the illusion created by a congenitally bent elbow, cricketers and officials were sceptical because they trusted the evidence of their eyes. The subsequent outlawing of Murali's doosra seemed to vindicate the doubters. And when it was announced that he straightened his arm over fourteen degrees while bowling it, cricket's wiseacres sniffed harder.

Bedi and Atherton publicly, and many players and umpires off the record, continued to believe that he chucked. Even a film made of Murali bowling in a rigid brace didn't convince the doubters. When the inaugural ICC award for bowler of the year was given to Warne over Murali, it was rumoured that several jurors, Holding and Botham amongst them, refused to reward a bowler who they believed threw more than he bowled. Certainly, cricket fans had to suffer Benaud and Holding being evasive in print and on television about the reasons for their choice.

The ICC's decision to appeal to the authority of science was good policy made bad by ad hoc implementation. When close scientific scrutiny showed that most bowlers straightened their arms, the ICC parked its brains and pressed the accelerator. It invented discriminatory guidelines for umpires: fast bowlers were to be allowed the most leeway in straightening their arms, with declining allowances for medium-pacers and spinners.

3

Chuckers are bowlers, they said in the end
(Not that they chuck, they just hyperextend).

There were three problems with this 'solution', each one
of them formidable enough to make angels back off. One,
the unequal allowances were unfair to slow bowlers. Two,
they were impossible to implement. Three, the scientists on
whose research these guidelines were allegedly based disagreed
with them. For example, the unequal chucking allowances
were justified by the involuntary straightening caused by the
stress of bowling at higher speeds. One of the scientists
objected, saying that Murali's arm speed equalled that of
many fast bowlers. He also went on to recommend a common
standard: all bowlers, he recommended, should be allowed
to straighten their arms over fifteen degrees. Clearly, different
strokes for different folks was a plausible motto for a
commune, but a bad prescription for cricket.

Suddenly, that's where we are now. The scientists have spoken
to an ICC committee that has accepted their recommendations
and abruptly, the same players, commentators and journalists
who had pilloried Murali as a blot on the game, its history
and its statistics, are lining up to endorse this more liberal
licence to bend and straighten the bowling arm.

What revelation wrought this miracle? What new scientific
insight goosed the ICC into preparing to abandon its
painfully recent chucking guidelines? The clincher, it turns
out, was the news that a study of the bowlers in the ICC
Champions Trophy revealed that 99 per cent of them
chucked. This isn't so different from earlier declarations that
90 per cent of all bowlers throw, so the turnabout must have
to do with the names named rather than the general
conclusion. It turns out that under the current definition of

a legitimate delivery, such pillars of the bowling establishment like McGrath, Pollock, Gillespie (and in the past, paragons like Holding) chucked. They straightened their arms in excess of the current ten degree allowance for fast bowlers.

Abruptly the world's cricketing establishments (and sanctimonious ex-cricketers and pundits) were brought face to face with the alarming reality that the records of their heroes were as thoroughly derived from their dart-board skills as Muralitharan's. More so, if anything, because it was only Murali's doosra that was outlawed: his customary deliveries were deemed to come in under the five degree limit for spinners. In contrast, Australia's fast bowling firm, Messrs McGrath, Gillespie & Lee soared above the ten degree limit with routine deliveries.

4

Before close of play, a final hurrah,
For 'Dodgy' Gillespie and 'Chucker' McGrath.

When Murali pointed this out later, the spokesperson for Cricket Australia, deaf to irony, huffed on about the complex science behind the findings and the unfairness of accusing great bowlers of chucking! There's never been a more emphatic vindication of a player in the history of cricket and after years of being singled out and persecuted, Murali was entitled to say so. He and Ranatunga stood out as resolute, principled men; most of their critics look like ambushed opportunists. Since he had called Murali a chucker in 2004, it would have been reasonable to expect the Australian Prime Minister, John 'Loose Lips' Howard, to either denounce McGrath and Gillespie as chuckers or apologize to Murali for being an ignorant politician on a hair trigger. I haven't heard a peep out of him. Nor have any of us heard or read a mea culpa from Michael Holding.

This silence, this lack of public self-criticism, should make us wary of embracing the ICC's new enthusiasm for a fifteen degree limit for everyone. After the fiasco of the previous guidelines, the last thing cricket needs is another drunken lurch at reform. Where's the hurry, now that the ICC believes that everyone chucks? We should talk this one out.

Just to illustrate the need for discussion: why fifteen degrees? It can't be because McGrath and Gillespie wouldn't fit the smaller size, surely? Boycott thinks the limit has been raised and extended to slow bowlers to include Murali. This is so wrong, it's perverse. Murali doesn't need fifteen degrees: after remedial work, his arm only straightens in the region of ten degrees while bowling the doosra. A cynical Sri Lankan could more plausibly argue that the ICC stretched the rules to fit the fast men in and then tossed a bone to the others by giving them equal latitude.

So, to return to the question, why fifteen? The ICC's answer seems to be that up to fifteen degrees, a straightening arm is invisible to the naked eye. The ICC is trying to reassure us; given its recent record, this should make us very afraid. The new rule, the ICC is saying, changes nothing practically: the spectator won't even notice the difference. The new rule will be aimed at the egregiously illegal bowling action, visible to the umpire's eye. Inquiries will only be initiated into actions that seem illegal to the umpires in the middle.

For those of us who want the law on chucking to err on the side of strictness, there are two problems with the ICC's explanation. It's not clear that arm straightening up to fifteen degrees is invisible. If we are to believe that Lee, Akhtar, Harbhajan and McGrath straighten their arm less than fifteen degrees, then it is clear to most of us that sub-fifteen degree straightening is visible. At the risk of sounding insufferable, I should add that I've long believed that McGrath straightens his arm visibly and wrote as much in an article in a magazine in June 2004, some months before the scientists reported to the ICC committee. So, if the object of the law is to prevent visible chucking, the limit should be pegged lower. If the object is something else, the ICC should tell us what it is and the cricketing world can debate the issue.

Second, the idea that umpires in future will only call bowlers on the basis of what they can see from square leg or from behind the stumps at the bowler's end in a state of technological ignorance, is daft. Such chasteness isn't possible. The TV camera in the stadium is the snake in Eden—once it's there, you can only affect innocence, you can't live it. Every umpire will continue to second guess his intuition by studying television footage and slow motion replays; he'd be stupid not to. Which brings us back to the original question: why fifteen degrees?

Why, for example, shouldn't the ICC take a figure from the *low* end of the research findings on flexion, say three degrees, and demand that every bowler come in at or under this minimum deviation. It should make it clear that as the apex body of the game, its main concern is with making all bowlers conform to the law rather than stretching the law to fit some bowlers. Any fast bowlers who find it impossible to bowl at ninety-eight miles an hour without exceeding the three degree cutoff will be welcome to decelerate till their bowling arcs fit the ICC template. Any spinners whose 'doosras' (or for that matter, 'pehlas') require a suspension of disbelief greater than three degrees (or four, or five, so long as the limit is low and general to all bowling species) will be sentenced to long hours in solitary, watching corrective videos of Bishen Bedi in his delivery stride from every angle that the archives can supply. If the scientists are to be believed, many bowlers won't make the cut, but the integrity of a game like cricket was never going to come cheap. So why fifteen degrees?

We don't need to answer that question in a hurry. We can take our time about it. The ICC needs to collate and publish its findings, complete with names and numbers. If they can measure actions from the televised past, so much the better. Instead of making Murali the lightning rod for the controversy over chucking, why not test all contemporary bowlers who represent their countries in Tests or ODIs and publish the degree to which they straighten their arms? If, for example, it was revealed that respectable fast bowlers—say, Glenn McGrath, Darren Gough or Makhaya Ntini—straighten their arms regularly, the outrage about Murali's bowling records might be set in context. It might become more difficult to demand ringingly that Murali's 'ill-gotten' figures be erased from the record books, if his fast bowling contemporaries are shown to be chucking their way to statistical heaven.

Let everyone involved with the game compare one bowler's 'bit of flexion' (McGrath's mealy-mouthed description of his twelve degree chuck) with another's. Let us argue over methodology, about comparisons, about the omniscience of science and the fallibility of men for the next year if we must. Let us calculate average degrees of straightening for fast bowlers and finger-spinners and medium-pacers and wrist-spinners before we settle on the appropriate level of permitted 'flexion'. Above all, let us not take the opinion of the ICC or its committee as holy writ. Cricket needs conservative physicians to tend it at this uncertain hour: these men are barber surgeons.

The Game Elsewhere

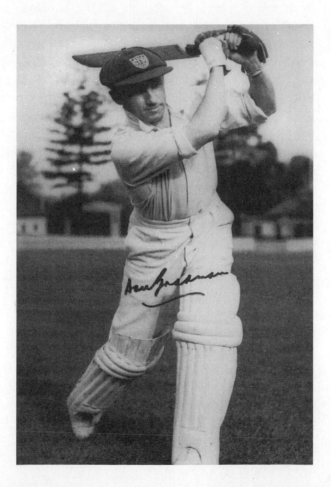

The West Indies

I've never been to the West Indies. Neither have you. You might have visited Barbados or Jamaica or the Leeward Islands, but that just tells me that you've been a tourist in the Caribbean. The West Indies . . . that's a country only fans can visit because it's a figment of Test cricket's imagination. It assembles itself when eleven men walk down pavilion steps to play a Test match. For Indian boys growing up in the sixties and seventies, it was cricket's highest heaven. Fittingly, India's ambassador to the game's Middle Kingdom through those glory years was our greatest player, Sunil Manohar Gavaskar.

Something has gone, and ink and print
Will never bring it back;
I long for the great days again,
When the Kings, in white, were black.

After 'The Bookworm' by Walter de la Mare

When I was in school, there was a country called the West Indies which was and always would be the undisputed champion of the cricket-playing world. Like Atlantis or Macondo, this country had no coordinates; it was an exotic land, proximate to nothing—its cricketers were gods.

Except one or two who weren't. There were West Indians like Roy Gilchrist and Charlie Griffith who chucked. Ken Barrington used up a chapter of his autobiography, *Playing It Straight*, to show that Griffith threw his bouncer. He had a photo of Griffith in his delivery stride with his arm cocked like a javelin thrower about to spear the air. Charlie wasn't a god; he was a demon, a rakshasa, who had broken Nari Contractor's head with a bouncer that didn't bounce. Nobody in my class knew much about Contractor. He was an old cricketer, not a working model, a captain with a queer name who had been retired by a demon bowler. Our captain was the Nawab of Pataudi. We didn't think of him as the current captain because we didn't think we'd need another one. He was young and whole—except for one eye which didn't hold him back; it made him an epic hero.

This didn't mean he could beat the West Indies. No one could, on account of them being gods. The captain of the West Indies, Frank Worrell, visited my school in Delhi. I didn't meet him; it was after class hours or something, but the cricket team got to shake his hand. Then, a year later, he was dead. Leukaemia. We knew what leukaemia was; it was blood cancer. Dying of it took time, so he must have had it the day he came to visit. The thought of Worrell dying on his feet even as he shook our hands made us solemn. His death was a tragedy, a public tragedy, something that I remembered for years, something that I knew my classmates wouldn't forget, like the death of Martin Luther King. That's how important the West Indies team was for boys who followed cricket. This meant nearly everyone in my class, except a boy who was fat and played tennis. He claimed he didn't know who Worrell was.

Wesley Hall, the better half of the fast bowling firm Hall & Griffith, was as godlike as his fast-bowling partner was wicked. Hall had bowled the last over of a tied Test and kept the Aussies from winning. His run-up began where the sight screen ended. His gold cross bounced off his enormous chest as he ran in, hypnotizing frightened batsmen. There was no television then, but we had a picture of him in our heads, put there by commentators like V.M. Chakrapani and Pearson Surita, who presided over a little golden age of Indian cricket broadcasting before Suresh Saraiya filled the airwaves with syntax-free noise.

They beat us, somewhere in the mid-sixties, then they beat us again, and when we finally beat them in 1971 in the West Indies, we were wildly happy, but deep within we knew that we had beaten an ageing team. Hall and Kanhai were done; Sobers had one great innings left in him. There was Lloyd to whom the flame had been passed, but for a year or four, West Indian supremacy, the cornerstone of Test cricket as I knew it, wobbled. Defeating the West Indies was unsettling because we liked having the West Indies in charge of world cricket. They were brilliant to watch and we didn't want England or Australia on top. We knew we weren't good enough to be the world's best team; till we were, we wanted the Windies to rule.

*

Why did West Indian supremacy seem part of the natural order of cricket for Indian boys? We knew nothing about the Caribbean outside of cricket, being too young for Derek Walcott or C.L.R. James or rum. That the West Indians were black made no difference to us: twelve-year-old boys, even post-colonial boys, don't run to political correctness. Given how keen Indians are on being light-skinned, in the matter of cricket we were completely colour blind. (It is an interesting sidelight that the two foreign cricket heroes Indian actresses went out with were both West Indian and black: Garfield Sobers (Anju Mahendru) and Vivian Richards (Neena Gupta). We disliked English teams for their dullness, admired the Australians from a distance because they didn't tour India much, knew nothing about the South Africans or the Pakistanis because we didn't play them, but we worshipped the West Indians.

We worshipped them because they were larger than life. Everything they did was idiosyncratic, stylish, and gilded with their pleasure in playing. Style in the Indian fan's vocabulary was synonymous with flourish; we loved the West Indian cricketing manner because it confirmed our understanding of style: extravagant backlifts, Kanhai's falling hook, Lloyd's improbable speed at cover, Richards slapping Chandrasekhar one-handed for four, Marshall sprinting through his bowling action without pausing to leap, Kallicharan's left-handed loveliness, the furious exertions of fast bowling made ethereal by Holding's lethal grace. Even as we rooted for India, and even as the West Indies inevitably beat us, we recognized that the specialness of their play had as much to do with self-expression as competitiveness.

To put this in comparative perspective, the antithesis of the West Indies for us was England. With the exception of Gower, Botham, Knott and Snow, English cricket for forty years was staffed by joyless journeymen. Since Barrington retired in 1968, England hasn't produced a single great batsman. Boycott was what Gavaskar would have been without the genius. Gooch and Cowdrey have their admirers, but their mothers wouldn't claim greatness for them. Then there were the Southern African imports, Robin Smith and Allan Lamb, who played seam bowling like well made wind-up toys but never came within reaching distance of the first rank. Gower was wonderful: a left-handed waif from Neverland, bat in hand he was a maestro who made bowling sides do his bidding like docile orchestras. But he was never the fulcrum of his side, nor dominant enough to qualify as an immortal; he remains, as Christopher Isherwood once said of himself, in the front row of the second rank.

Interestingly, English teams have always amounted to more than the sum of their parts: the glue of a grey professionalism made them harder to beat than their meagre talent suggested. They had a certain life denying skill (best illustrated in recent times by the decision of Nasser Hussain to make Ashley Giles bowl left-arm over the wicket, wide of the leg stump, to thwart Tendulkar), a low-grade canniness, that compensated for a near-complete absence of flair. Among the many things the West Indies gave to world cricket, being not-England was an important gift.

*

Since you have to take sides if you're listening to or watching a Test match, our rule of thumb, the rule of thumb all Indian cricket fans followed, was this: if India wasn't playing, we rooted for the West Indies. It was an odd business, this referred loyalty. I remember the West Indies tour of Australia in 1975–76. Lloyd, in a pre-tour press conference, was a happy man. His team was stuffed to bursting with once in a generation young talent. The West Indies had discovered Gordon Greenidge and Viv Richards the year before in the course of their tour of India, they had Roberts, then the most fearsome new ball bowler in the world and now they had found a young Michael Holding. Then there was Lloyd himself and that pocket berserker, Roy Fredericks. If they give us fast pitches, said Lloyd, we'll deal with them. It was a six-Test series—the West Indies lost 5–1. I was devastated. India had been well beaten by Lloyd's men; that we could deal with. We were Indian fans, used to losing, but having our conquerors routed was demoralizing; it devalued our defeats.

Switching our 'if India isn't playing loyalty' to Australia wasn't an option; the West Indies were irreplaceable in that role because they managed to be formidable and likeable at once. If the alleged gentlemanliness of cricket was ever embodied, if there ever were any cricketing gents, they played for the West Indies. Think of McGrath, Warne, Ponting, Waugh, Hayden, pretty much the whole Australian team that's ruled the world these past ten years and the spitting and sledging and effing that's been their theme song and then think of the West Indies in its pomp: Sobers, Lloyd, Richards, Marshall, Holding, Roberts, Ambrose, Walsh, champions who didn't need 'mental disintegration' as a verbal strategy, who menaced opponents with genius or a speaking look. Having the good guys in charge was a comfortable feeling; now we're ruled by enforcers.

When I read Lara on Tendulkar, I find nothing but generosity, the recognition of a great contemporary. Similarly, asked to comment on the likelihood of Ponting overhauling his records, Tendulkar talked of playing Ponting in the nineties when he showed early signs of his special talent. In contrast, my main memories of Australians commenting on their peers is Ponting's characterization of Lara as a selfish batsman after Lara had established a new Test record with 400 runs, of putting personal glory before the interests of the West Indies team (implicitly congratulating himself as a team player), or Warne trashing Murali's record as one inflated by cheap wickets against weak sides. It isn't hard for the neutral fan to spot the difference between men who let their work speak for itself and players spinning for posterity before their careers are done.

*

The historical reason no other team can fill the special place that the West Indies held in the imagination of Indian fans is that Indian cricket came of age during the high noon of West Indian dominance. There were other great triumphs, most notably the Chandrasekhar-led victory against England at the Oval in 1971, but the big story of modern Indian cricket is, as Raju Bharatan might have put it, our duet with the West Indies. Starting with Gavaskar in 1971 and ending with Gavaskar in 1983–84, India made its bones against the West Indies. And because the world champions had such mystique, India's occasional but spectacular successes against them in this period were limned with a special radiance. Gavaskar's debut series—774 runs in four Tests, a double century and a century in the same match and all in the cause of a series win away from home—would have been sensational in any context, but against the West Indies, in their backyard, it became the stuff of legend. An obscure calypso writer, Lord Relator, composed a verse in praise of Gavaskar so sublimely awful that it passed as naively good and helped transport Gavaskar's achievement to the realm of knightly lore. On a smaller scale, the menace of Roberts and company in Madras in 1974–75 made Viswanath's 97 *the* Indian innings against real pace on a fast pitch. West Indian greatness was such a given that anything achieved against them seemed larger than life, colossal.

The next landmark in this narrative of Indian heroism was the time the team chased down 403 runs in the fourth innings in 1976 at Port of Spain (again starring Gavaskar with Amarnath, Viswanath and Brijesh Patel in supporting roles), which nudged Lloyd towards the four-pronged pace attack that underwrote West Indian dominance for years

afterwards. Then came that storied conquest of the World
Champions at Lord's, winners of the first two World Cups,
vanquished, against all the odds, by Kapil's devils in the finals
of the 1983 World Cup. Finally, as a coda, we might end
with the savage ninety-four ball hundred struck by Gavaskar
against a rampant Marshall in the Delhi Test of 1983. India
had a special relationship with the West Indies: Caribbean
greatness was the stern context for individual heroics and
epic (if occasional) team triumphs.

Now Australia rules the world and has done so for nearly
ten years now and it can be reasonably argued that Australian
dominance is the arena for Indian derring-do. Warne and
McGrath have a decent claim to being the greatest slow and
fast bowlers in the history of Test cricket, and Steve Waugh,
Adam Gilchrist, Matthew Hayden and Ricky Ponting are or
once were, among the batting greats of the modern game.
We have had the rousing spectacle of Tendulkar (and Laxman
and Sidhu) dismantling Warne from the late nineties onwards,
Harbhajan's single-handed destruction of Australia's batting
juggernaut over a three-Test series, Dravid's match winning
centuries in Kolkata and Adelaide and above all, the greatest
innings ever played by an Indian batsman, Laxman's 281 at
the Eden Gardens that reversed the momentum of a follow-
on, broke Australia's winning run and set up a series win
for India.

But glorious and satisfying as these achievements are, the
vacuum left in world cricket and in our imaginations by the
wretched decline of the West Indies hasn't been, and can't
be, filled by Australia, any more than Germany could hope
to replace Brazil in the affections of the world's football fans.
Brazil is more than a national team: it is proof that competitive
professional football can be a thing of beauty and pleasure
and delight. Pele, Garrincha, Socrates were great individual

players, geniuses even, but there have been great players elsewhere: Beckenbauer, Eusebio, Cruyff, Maradona. What makes the Brazilians different is that when they play together, they make magic, they offer the most chauvinist fan passages of transcendence, in earthbound stadiums they conjure up football's heaven. When good footballers die, they go to Rio.

Not Munich.

The Germans are a formidable football machine: at their best they generate awe, at worst, fear and loathing, but never have they inspired reverence or affection or love in anyone who isn't German. Their victories breed resentment because of the manner in which they are won: I can remember the German goalkeeper hospitalizing a French forward with a frighteningly cynical tackle in a World Cup match. Their defeats are cues for Schadenfreude.

Australia is contemporary cricket's Germany. Hayden and Ponting and McGrath are the Teutons of the modern game, superbly fit, their regimens based on the latest sporting science, their talent organized and marshalled in academies, their sporting campaigns preceded by calculated campaigns of intimidation. Australia's supremacy, hard-earned and deserved though it is, highlights how little the cricket world can afford to do without a West Indian side strong enough to demonstrate that cricket needn't be graceless to be competitive.

The West Indies could be less than nice: four fast bowlers bowling twelve overs an hour didn't always make for pretty cricket and Indians my age remember Bedi declaring the innings closed with five wickets left to fall, in Sabina Park, 1976, because the remaining batsmen were either injured or tail-enders who couldn't cope with the diet of short-pitched balls Lloyd's bowlers were serving up. And, as we noted in the beginning, there was Charlie Griffith and Contractor's broken head. But on the whole (as fair-minded pedants like to say), West Indian cricketers gave my generation of spectators more pleasure than any three cricketing nations put together; more, their brilliance and grace helped us see that the game at its very best was bigger than nationalist feeling.

So I hope the Indian team plays wonderfully the next time it plays the West Indies. But if the men from Macondo play better and take the series, somewhere inside me, a boy's ghost will stir . . . and grin and cheer as cricket's world turns right side up again.

The Bradman Class

The thing about a game with history, a game that's been written about and argued over is that it gives you metaphors for describing the world and sporting achievements that can be used as shorthand for greatness. But, in the history of sport, there is one man whose prowess is too much of a good thing, whose record is so staggering that it's hard to find anyone in any other walk of life who might measure up. Who can we call Bradmanesque?

G.H. Hardy, the Cambridge mathematician who mentored Ramanujan, used to rank mathematicians in cricketing terms. The best were in the Hobbs class, named after the great English opening batsman. Then along came the boy from Bowral and Hardy, reluctantly but fairly, demoted his countryman and created a new category, the Bradman class. The rightness of naming the summit of achievement after Bradman is obvious, but it does raise a question: having created the category, who on earth could Hardy have found to fill it?

We who follow cricket know that Bradman is one of a kind. Cricket is the one game in the world where every debutant for the last fifty years has known with complete certainty that he will never get within shouting distance of the records set by a man who retired in the middle of the twentieth century. If you wanted to bet that Rod Laver's achievement in completing two tennis Grand Slams wouldn't be surpassed in the next fifty years, a long-lived bookmaker might take your wager. If, with the Tiger on the prowl, you wanted to put money down on the invincibility of Jack Nicklaus's tally of major championships, he'd grab your money. But no bookie in his right mind will bet against Bradman. With an average of 99.94, Bradman lives alone on Olympus. Tendulkar, the best batsman today, with an average hovering around 57, labours in the foothills.

The singularity of Bradman's record doesn't simply lie in the distance between him and the next man; what makes it unique is that the gap shows no sign of closing. Think of another sport, of some extraordinary breakthrough that took the world's breath away when it occurred. Take Bob Beamon's monster long jump in the Mexico Olympics. While the rest of the field was aiming at a record twenty-eight feet, Beamon cleared twenty-nine. The record lasted a while, then the world closed in and it was overhauled. In a comparable sport like baseball, Babe Ruth's home run record stood for decades and was then broken in one season by two players. In the fifty-eight years since Bradman's retirement, no batsman who has played twenty Test matches has come within 30 runs of his average. Sometimes, sports writers argue that earlier players shouldn't be compared with later ones. They argue that the sport has changed so much over time because of better technology and greater athleticism that players today play it at a higher level. By this reckoning, Laver's record can't be usefully compared with, say, Sampras's because tennis now is a faster, more competitive game. It's not an argument that works with cricket.

The changes in cricket's laws and the improvements in its technology have favoured batsmen. Contemporary batsmen play with more powerful bats and better protective equipment; they're coddled by restrictions on bouncers and supplied with pitches where the bounce is true. The helmet, by removing the risk of death and unbearable pain, decisively shifted the balance of power in favour of the batsman. Sir Donald played Larwood and leg theory in a cloth cap, he played nearly half his cricket in England where pitches were left uncovered and overnight rain made the ball skid and turn, and he still managed to score his mountain of runs at a rate which would do credit to a one-day batsman.

Bradman knew when he retired that he was cricket's solitary immortal and for the rest of his life he tended his flame. He had a distinguished career as a cricket administrator and stockbroker so it wasn't as if he hoarded his aura by becoming a recluse. Till the end he spent more than three hours a day replying to the hundreds of letters he received. He accepted the honours and distinctions that came his way, the knighthood, the fan mail, the worship of his countrymen. What he resisted were the seductions of celebrity, the ribbon cutting retirement that champions too often wallow in as they try to revisit the limelight or make a living. Kapil Dev, Azhar and the rest show us every day that celebrity can be milked; Bradman knew instinctively that immortality must be guarded.

But to return to the Bradman Class. That Bradman is the twentieth century's greatest sportsman is true but banal; the real question is, who, from any field of human endeavour, could live in Hardy's category alongside Bradman? Einstein? No, because any candidate must, in his field, be a nonpareil and in physics Newton ranks as Einstein's peer. I challenged a friend to find me a name; he thought for a second and said, Shakespeare? The Bard and Brad? Yes, I think we can live with that.

Bradman's List

Inventing best-ever cricket teams is something fans do. Ramachandra Guha wrote a lovely book organized around made-up cricket teams, Wickets in the East. *It was nice to learn after Bradman died that he wasn't above this useless but essential pastime. As with everything the great man did, his all-time greatest cricket team has lessons for us. He probably played book cricket too.*

The responses to the team of all-time greats allegedly put together by Bradman and published after his death, were fascinating. Sunil Gavaskar made a statement saying that he didn't believe Bradman had chosen such a team because, in Gavaskar's opinion, a man who had shunned controversy in life would scarcely have wanted to stir it up posthumously. Everyone, from the Indian press to the curator of the Bradman museum in Australia assumed that Gavaskar was sore at being left out. Gavaskar explained that he had made that comment before the final eleven was announced, so it wasn't pique, just an honest opinion.

Whether Gavaskar's reading of Bradman's character was right or wrong and whether the list was genuinely Bradman's or not, it's worth remembering that when the text of a letter, purportedly written by Bradman criticizing Australian umpires for no-balling Muralitharan, had been made public,

Bradman's family had protested, saying that these posthumous revelations were unauthorized. Knowing this, it was a fair assumption on Gavaskar's part that the new revelation from the grave was as dodgy as the first one, probably a marketing ploy to sell a book.

The idea that Gavaskar would react like this out of pique is daft. Not because Gavaskar is above petty competitiveness or any reason as lofty as that. Gavaskar was a great batsman and suffers as little from false humility as Bradman did. But like Bradman, Gavaskar tends his aura vigilantly. Had Gavaskar felt badly about being left out of the final eleven, he would have done everything possible to mask that reaction because to betray heartburn would be to diminish himself in the public eye. Gavaskar is circumspect in his public utterances; it's a characteristic which makes him a bland, even boring television commentator. Even when he offers provocation, it's carefully premeditated. For example, on India's last tour of Australia, Gavaskar was doing commentary as part of the Channel 9 team. Channel 9's commentary was telecast all over Australia and the rest of the world but at the end of the day Gavaskar did special telecasts beamed only to India. His criticisms of Australian umpiring (which was atrocious) were vigorous, but typically they were voiced only on the special broadcasts to India, never in the course of Channel 9 commentary.

When Gavaskar declared that he was reacting to the long list, not the final team, I believed him. If he had known about Bradman's final eleven, my guess would be that he wouldn't have said anything at all, because Tendulkar is something of a protégé and Gavaskar wouldn't want to be seen raining on his parade.

There was another great opening batsman, a contemporary of Gavaskar's, who was tip-toeing with delight after

Bradman's team was announced. Barry Richards was on television commentating on the India–Sri Lanka Test series, when he was asked how he felt about being named by Bradman as one of his two opening batsman. It was lovely to see how delighted this grizzled veteran was; it was also poignant because to be picked by Bradman as one of his immortals was some compensation for all the Tests he had never played.

My guess is that the team was, in fact, chosen by Bradman because I can't imagine a forger putting together such a lopsided and idiosyncratic side. Anyone faking a Bradman XI would have put together a more plausible one. I mean, which faker would have the nerve to choose a side with four specialist batsmen (one of whom had played all of four Tests) and a wicketkeeper averaging under 20 runs an innings! It would take the absolute self-assurance of Bradman to assemble a side based, so far as anyone can see, on just two principles: familiarity (all the Australians he chose had played in teams he had captained) and, in the case of Tendulkar, similarity; that is, Bradman's conviction that Tendulkar's style and technique resembled his own.

What was interesting about our reaction to Bradman's team was the conviction that he got it wrong, that he should have had Gavaskar or Weekes or Headley or Hobbs in the team. This makes sense only if we assume that Bradman was doing a selection based on a god's eye view of Test cricket since its inception. He wasn't; he was making a selection from the players he knew best, players he had watched a lot of, players he had an opinion about, players who had strummed some chord of delight in his cricketing soul. Think of his team as you would think of a literary anthology. All anthologies make a token attempt to be representative and all anthologies (all the good ones, anyway) represent, in the end, the tastes of the anthologist. This is as it should be, because the reason we attend to Bradman's team is because we admire Bradman and are interested in his opinions. If we wanted a team based on a dozen parameters of fairness (like the list of the hundred best Test centuries in the history of the game), we'd feed the statistics into a machine and print out the results instead of badgering Bradman for his opinions.

What Bradman's team teaches us is the importance of respecting our own experience. If Gavaskar was asked to name an eleven, he would, of course, survey the history of Test cricket, but I'd like to think that he would trust his feelings, his prejudices if you like, and pick eleven players who had thrilled him. Bradman would be one of them (there are some statistics no one can ignore) but, inevitably, most of them would be his peers, men he had played with or against, men whose talents he had admired from close up, men who had stocked his mind with first-hand memories.

Bradman's team is important because it teaches us the virtues of nostalgia and memory. In its partiality and subjectiveness, it reminds us that people who weigh their memories of cricket against some imaginary consensus, some abstract yardstick of fairness, some computer generated model of the complete cricketer, would be better off watching baseball. For what it's worth, my all-time team would certainly have Gavaskar opening the innings and, if I felt opinionated enough that day, Viswanath would waddle in two wickets down.

The Jones Affair

*After Jones was caught calling Amla a terrorist, the
desis I spoke to didn't know what the fuss was about.
Upwardly mobile Indians are so keen to be sensible
and professional and global that they can't tell a slur
when it's served up to them on an amplifier. Anxious
to be good fellows, they mistake casual bigotry for
bluff Anglo humour. Insensitivity of this sort is bad
enough if you're white and Antipodean; it's sad and
self-hating if you're Indian. Perhaps the tendency to
take a 'robust' view of the Jones incident might have
had something to do with the fact that the Indians I
spoke to were neither bearded nor Muslim.*

When Hashem Amla, a bearded South African Muslim
of Indian descent, took a catch in a Test against Sri
Lanka in August 2006, Dean Jones, ex-Australian international
and match commentator said: 'The terrorist has got another
wicket.' Jones thought he was making a private comment to
his fellow commentators, but the microphone was switched
on and it carried his words, live, to a television public.

Jones was sacked by Ten Sports, the Dubai-based television
channel that had hired him. He expressed regret for his
indiscretion, indicated that he got on with Muslims (he was
great friends, he said, with the Pakistani team which was
mainly made up of Muslims) and said sorry personally to

Amla. In the days that followed the incident, Jones's defenders made arguments in mitigation. Allan Border claimed that calling Amla a terrorist wasn't so bad because he knew for a fact that Amla's teammates called him that to his face. Except that they didn't. Gordon Templeton, the South African team's media manager, bluntly described Border's claim as nonsense; Border, he said, was trying to shield Jones: no South African team member had ever used 'terrorist' as a nickname for Amla.

Peter Roebuck, in the pages of *The Hindu* (Saturday, 12 August 2006), forsook defence and went on the attack. Jones's critics, he wrote, '. . . hiss and snarl like cornered canines.' They were slavering dogs because they were using up stores of indignation that might be better used denouncing ethnic cleansing, grinding poverty and the bombing of the innocent. Right. Just as Roebuck might be better employed digging up landmines in Lebanon or tending lepers in India instead of hacking out copy for the sports pages.

But we get the point. Border and Roebuck are saying that Jones is *basically* a good guy and that given the scale of evil in the world, his offence was trivial. He was stupid, idiotic, foolish and insensitive in saying what he did, but not bigoted.

Harsha Bhogle's reaction to the incident was along the same lines: 'It was a throwaway line that people would have used at workplaces and factories all the time. Sitting under a tree with a cup of coffee we can say what we like, we can get away with it, but with a "live" microphone he has let the world know what he thought. He's been a bit stupid but, knowing Deano, he'll be the first to put his hand up and say that.' Bhogle is saying that Dean Jones was unprofessional and indiscreet and 'a bit stupid'.

Roebuck nudged us towards the reasonable conclusion. 'Does anyone suppose, though, that his comment betrayed the secrets of his soul? Has any rancour been detected therein?'

If you're not used to Roebuck's high-purple, sub-biblical style, this means Jones didn't mean it, *couldn't* have meant it, because everyone knows that Jones isn't a bigot or a racist.

This was the same defence that Darren Lehmann mounted when he called the Sri Lankans 'black cunts'. It was also the defence used by Jewish friends of Mel Gibson (another man who has spent some growing up time in Australia) after his anti-Semitic outburst. Mel, they said, isn't like that.

Isn't like what? What does a man's track record have to be before a bigoted comment made by him qualifies as bigotry? It's unlikely that a television commentator would have prior form or known links with the National Front or the Vishwa Hindu Parishad or a pro-apartheid party. But why should we need more than the evidence of our ears?

Let's try to set this in a 'western' perspective because Jones's defenders seem to be having trouble appreciating the vileness of what Jones said in the context of cricket in Sri Lanka. Here's a hypothetical circumstance. Tiger Woods is playing golf at the US Open. He sinks a putt, there's a pause and the commentator, thinking he's in a commercial break, says to his colleague with the microphones on, 'The nigger's holed another one.' How long do you think that commentator would last on prime time? How many golf correspondents and commentators would characterize his comment as a 'bit stupid'? And how many people would buy the line that, 'Some of my best friends are . . .?'

The truth is that no American commentator working for a major TV channel would use kike or nigger or faggot with their colleagues around even if they thought the mikes were switched off because political correctness, in the best sense of that term, has made these words unsayable. To use these words in polite society is to court ostracism.

Dean Jones said what he did because he thought his

colleagues in the box would be amused, because he didn't think the words he used were taboo. Jones assumed that a remark tossed off like that would pass without challenge or reproach. That's the real significance of this incident, not the fact that he got caught with the microphones on. 'The terrorist has got another wicket,' is the casual bigotry of the locker room which assumes that the guys will go along. It is bigotry founded on an assumption of shared prejudice because you can bet Dean Jones's last Australian dollar that he wouldn't have said what he did with Rameez Raja and Imran Khan in the room.

That's why the eagerly forgiving attitude of his peers is disappointing. They responded like members of a guild, not as professional men looking out for cricket or broadcasting. Revealingly, not once in Roebuck's article is there any mention of Hashem Amla, let alone any sympathy for a young sportsman who finds that the suspicion his beard provokes in everyday life has followed him onto the cricket field thanks to a commentator who mistakes bigotry for cleverness.

The reason kike, faggot and nigger are taboo today is because public opinion backed up by social sanctions has made them unsayable. If an Indian commentator was caught calling a Muslim player a katua, or a Dalit player a chamar, he would never work again. Roebuck and Border and cricket's commentariat seem to think calling a bearded Muslim a terrorist doesn't belong in the same category of proscribed words. Well, it's up to us to persuade them that it does, through a policy of zero tolerance.

It was unsubtly suggested in the press that Jones was sacked from Ten Sports because his employers were Muslim. I hope that isn't true. I'd like to think that ESPN and Star Sports and Zee Sports, regardless of the religious beliefs of their owners, would have done the same thing. India is a secular, pluralist nation and sports channels that work out of this country need to make sure that the people they employ respect those ideals.

Meanwhile, Border and Roebuck, when they're done with special pleading, could do worse than take their cue from an Australian colleague writing about the same incident:

'From Lehmann to Justin Harrison to Lleyton Hewitt—and the numerous controversies surrounding many Aboriginal athletes—our reputation as a fair and tolerant sporting nation has taken a battering in recent years. Yet the biggest problem is not how we are perceived outside our borders but rather how we perceive ourselves. If, after the Jones controversy, we tolerate the outburst and roll our collective eyes at the whistleblower, we have a problem far more serious than mere overseas perception.'
(Alex Brown, *Sydney Morning Herald*, 9 August 2006)

Southern Manhood

When I listen hard enough, I can tell the difference between those strange flat vowels that characterize South African and Australian English accents. They play cricket very differently too. A reminder that not all white settler colonies produce the same sort of sporting culture.

When Rod Marsh and Dennis Lillee were caught betting against their team, the Australian board did nearly nothing. It went without saying that Marsh and Lillee were competitors incapable of betraying the baggy green cap; as for the wager, well, every grown-up Australian was a betting man. Offered odds of 500 to 1 against an English victory, which red-blooded punter could refuse? Australia understood.

Australia understood again when Shane Warne and Mark Waugh were found out. This time it wasn't actually a bet, but how could a regular guy like Waugh who went to the races any time he could, pass up the chance of taking money off a bookie? Australian cricketers are Australian men, Crocodile Dundees in whites and floppy hats, Fosters drinking, flat-vowelled mavericks, good blokes every one . . . and if the odd one's caught making a little on the side, what's the point of getting hysterical? They're men, not Boy Scouts.

South African cricketers on the other hand *are* Boy Scouts. When Hansie Cronje was caught making up to a bookie, the

South African cricket establishment and sporting public reacted with indignation, denial and appalled disbelief. An Australian doesn't mind thinking of his cricket team as a well-drilled band of highwaymen, pulling off one heist after another. South Africans are more likely to think of the Springboks as a team of wardens flushing out poachers. So when the tape found Cronje on the take, Boers in Bloemfontein, Calvinists in Cape Town, voortrekkers in the veld reacted as if a Troop Leader had been caught buggering a Tenderfoot. The horror, as someone once said (having lodged himself in a dark, moist place), the horror.

Ricky Ponting, sitting out the one-day series between Australia and South Africa, made a common mistake. Commenting on television, he said that the two teams played in essentially the same way—they played hard and they played to win. Both thought themselves the best; clearly, for Ponting, the South Africans were kindred spirits in a cricketing world filled with whingeing Poms and wimpish Indians. Superficially, the two teams resemble each other: both sides come of white settler stock, both sledge mightily and both have a markedly inbred look. And since cricket today is dominated by these two southern hemisphere countries, it is tempting to collapse the two into one flowering of white southern manhood. But skin deep is where the similarity ends. The macho romance of two tough sides doing battle on the field and being mates off it, swearing at each other on the pitch but meeting for a drink at the end of the day, stops well short of the end of the day, because Ponting's South African counterpart is likely to be teetotal, non-smoking and a born-again Christian.

This has something to do with origins. Cronje springs from exiled virtue, Ponting from expelled vice. White settlement in South Africa began in the seventeenth century. The early footholds established by the Dutch East India Company were settled by Boers, which is the Dutch word for husbandsman or farmer. Boers were mainly of Dutch extraction, but there were German and French Huguenot lines as well. What they had in common was that they were low-church Protestants fleeing inhospitable mother countries. The self-image of the Boer is based on the idea of a virtuous community besieged. First it was Catholic bigotry in Europe, then the bullying interference of the British Empire in the white colonies which sent the Boers trekking into the interior of South Africa in search of self-government and finally, the sea of blackness that lapped at the edges of their hard-won white dominion.

The similarities with white settlement in America are uncanny. The Pilgrim Fathers were close cousins to the Boers in the matter of religious belief, and self-righteousness played an important part in building white America. The British Empire didn't last long enough in the American colonies for cricket to take root, but it is worth remembering that baseball was played in segregated leagues till well into the twentieth century.

The difference in the historical evolution of the two countries wasn't apartheid—there was plenty of separate 'development' in the USA—it was the American Civil War. The defeat of the Confederacy didn't destroy racism, but it levelled the white laagers that the southern states wanted to preserve. There was a civil war in South Africa at roughly the same time as the War between the States, but crucially the British triumph was less conclusive than Lincoln's and the Boers emerged with two states of their own in southern Africa: the South African Republic and the Orange Free State. It was as if the American Civil War had ended inconclusively with Texas and Georgia becoming independent.

The Boer or Afrikaner dominated white South Africa and brought to its sport a sense of white tribal solidarity. When white South Africans, emerging from denial, shrilled that Cronje had let the side down, they weren't talking about the cricket team. The Australians dealt with Marsh and Lillee and Waugh and Warne in a more relaxed way because the virtue of white Australia wasn't riding on their actions. Being white in Australia is normal. Having dealt satisfactorily with their natives (less numerous to start with) by stealing their children, robbing them of their ancestral lands, and helping them along the high road to alcoholism, Australians were free to be quirky, rugged individualists in an infinitely large country. If Warne and Waugh represent anything, it is the Australian ideal of blokedom and given that the Australian myth of origin centres on convict ships, Australians are unlikely to be shaken to their foundations because a few dollars changed hands off the cricket pitch.

Many members of contemporary South African sides have been avowedly Christian: two former captains, Hansie Cronje and Shaun Pollock, their most famous player, Jonty Rhodes, and many others. It isn't simply that they are believing Christians; it is also a part of their public identity. Being publicly pious in South Africa is a good thing because religion makes you a good man.

Some years ago, Jonty Rhodes took an amazing catch off a Tendulkar square cut at point. He flew in the air and caught the ball parallel to the ground. But there was some doubt about whether the ball touched the ground when he landed. Geoff Boycott, expert commentator, thought it had, but the umpire disagreed and India's finest had to go. Watching it on television, the catch looked good to me and I forgot about it. The next day, there was an interview with the umpire where he was asked about that decision and I can remember my astonishment when he said that Jonty would never claim a catch that wasn't fairly taken because he was Christian and since Rhodes had appealed, that was good enough for him, he didn't need slow motion replays.

When Cronje was first photographed after his confession, he had his pastor with him for insurance. Interestingly, he made not one, but three confessions: one to Ali Bacher, one to his pastor and a third to Sports Minister Balfour: white establishment, church and state, the trinity that has always defined Boer manhood. The state, unfortunately, is now black, but it's the only one there is to run to in a crisis and old habits die hard. It's hard to imagine Warne or Waugh turning up with their priests in tow; blokes don't do that . . . they'd be laughed into the Tasman Sea. If they did bring anyone along, it would be their lawyers.

There isn't much to be said for either, but I prefer the Australian model of manhood because it isn't a sick-making mixture of piousness and hypocrisy. The scandal certainly made the South Africans more entertaining. Earlier, fielding apart, they were a robotic, boring bunch of players. After Cronje revealed unsuspected depths, their on-field presence was excitingly edged with squalor. Cronje (who always looked a bit off-white to me) was replaced by Shaun Pollock, son of Peter, nephew of the great Graeme. He, like his predecessor, was a cricketing Christian. Watching him run up to the crease, red-haired, freckled, clean-cut and god-fearing, the original South African Adam, I thought of temptation and wondered what excitement lay in store.

A Clean Breast

Captain. Christian. Crook. The fourth word beginning with C that brings those three words together is the proper noun, Cronje. The denial, the hypocrisy and the sad scramble for extenuating circumstances that marked the outing of Cronje as a match fixing, bribe taking liar were instructive. They reminded us how closely assumptions of integrity are tied to skin colour in countries like England, Australia and South Africa. For admirers of Edward Said, the Cronje affair provided a textbook example of Orientalism in action.

Hansie Cronje was a serial confessor and he never repeated himself. He made a clean breast of his dealings with Indian bookies to that Svengali of South African cricket, Dr Ali Bacher. Then he made another clean breast of it to the South African sports minister, Ngconde Balfour. This must have been a different breast because afterwards, Bacher was categorical that Hansie had owned up to payments from bookies while the breast bared to the sports minister was not just clean, it was Boer white, unmarked by the taint of money.

So Cronje had negotiated bookie payments without actually taking them; he had spoken of roping other players in without actually talking to them; he had conspired with bookies but had never actually fixed a match. Cronje wasn't owning to the squalid South Asian habit of taking bribes. His sin, if he had sinned at all, was a more rarefied kind of wrongdoing, not a crime in law but an infringement of honour. Cronje did the clean breast routine with his pastor too because he was, as South Africans are quick to tell us, a good Christian. We don't know if this third confession matched the version according to Bacher or the version according to Sports Minister Balfour or if it was one more variation played by the versatile Cronje on his mea culpa theme. Perhaps what he owned up to was succumbing to temptation on a cellular phone, of talking the talk without doing the deed. A virtual sin if you like, not to be confused with the real thing.

Cronje, as his countrymen clearly saw, was not a cheat. Allan Donald thought he was set up. Bob Woolmer thought he was set up. Barry Richards thought he was naïve and stupid. Ninety-four per cent of the respondents to a South African radio poll wanted Cronje to play again. Ali Bacher, while relaying Hansie's contrition, made it a point to say that Hansie was harassed by Indian bookies right through the Indian tour. A South African cricket official of Indian descent was beaten up by laager louts who knew—like Woolmer and Donald—that Cronje had had sin thrust upon him by desis.

Cronje, naïve? This was the man who threatened to desert the South African team for a fat county salary unless the board offered him a more lucrative contract . . . and got his way. Cronje had two homes, the captaincy of a sports mad nation's cricket team, adulation and lots of money. He wanted more money and didn't mind how he got it. That made him greedy and cynical, not naïve and stupid. Ambushed by the Delhi police's tapes, he lied to everyone; confronted with the evidence, he confessed to everyone . . . and then dissembled about his confessions. That made him greedy, cynical, dishonest and manipulative. Cronje confessed to

Bacher that he had taken money from a bookie during the tri-nation series in South Africa before the Indian tour. A man who had signalled that he was open to suggestion when the price was right wasn't in the best position to turn around and claim to have been harassed by bookies. If you're selling, buyers will call to get their bids in.

The good Dr Bacher was keen on context. The Indian subcontinent, he pointed out in his statement, was the problem. *Outlook*, the magazine that first broke the match-fixing story years ago, praised Bacher's acuteness in diagnosing the root of the ailment. It hadn't occurred to the crusaders in that magazine that it was curious that this insight came to Bacher *after* the Cronje scandal broke. Had Bacher made a public statement about match-fixing before, it would have been an act of statesmanship, the intervention of a man concerned for the health of the game. Once Cronje was discovered, it looked remarkably like damage limitation in Bacher's backyard.

Suddenly, everyone in the cricketing world—players, umpires, cricket administrators—had a bookie story to tell. Cyril Mitchley, the South African umpire, surfaced to tell of the times he was offered money by bookies. Why hadn't we heard from him before? Why didn't the match referees— allegedly informed of these offers—tell the ICC? Chris Lewis, the English all-rounder, sold a story to the *News of the World* telling of English Test players in the pay of Indian bookies. He first went to the English cricket authorities with the story but nothing happened. The official investigating his complaint didn't even ask for the names of the three players that Lewis claimed were involved in throwing matches.

Bacher's statement to the press after the scandal broke would have done a tabloid proud: it was stuffed with sensational allegations—about match-fixing during the World Cup, about the Pakistan team throwing the fixture against

Bangladesh, about the likely involvement of Pakistani umpire Javed Akhtar. Bacher explicitly charged Akhtar with fixing a Test match between England and South Africa by gifting the English a series of lbw decisions. This was a career-ending charge against a Test umpire: so had Bacher learnt something about Akhtar that he didn't know earlier? If he had known at the time that umpires were fixing Test matches, why didn't he say so then and why was he singing so long after the event?

The answer was simple: the men administering the game knew there was match-fixing going on, but national honour in every case demanded that the truth be suppressed, that inconvenient witnesses be fobbed off with token enquiries. Cricket relies on chauvinism for its television money and gate receipts—no country was about to admit to its black sheep first. The perfect example of this attitude was the furtive, hole-in-corner way in which the Australian authorities dealt with Shane Warne and Mark Waugh when they were discovered taking money from bookies. The incident was suppressed and Mark Waugh had the gall to journey to Pakistan to testify in a match-fixing enquiry conducted by the Pakistanis. When the scandal broke afterwards, Warne and Waugh claimed they had been paid for information about the pitch and the weather! They got away with a slap on the wrist and a fine.

Unhappily for Bacher, Cronje was on tape and the Delhi police kept serializing his story. Cronje tried the Australian defence (I sold information not matches) but it didn't seem to work, so we had Dr Bacher down in the dirt, shovelling, hoping to spread the manure around. This was Plan B or the Warren Hastings defence.

It went like this. The subcontinent was a swamp of Oriental corruption. The usually upright Cronje (or any other Occidental) didn't stand a chance: he was sucked into the slime. It was nearly involuntary and not really his fault. Cronje's little payoffs, Warne's indiscretions (like Hastings's East India fortune) were symptoms of an *Indian* disease. So if the Indians and Pakistanis reformed their bookies, made betting legal and generally stopped being corrupt, seduced white men could go back to being honest again.

It was a decent defence and two hundred years ago it worked; Warren Hastings, then captain of the English side, was acquitted. Legalized betting might largely replace shady bookies with respectable bookmakers and genuine punters, but it won't stop players making money on the side. Rodney Marsh and Dennis Lillee bet on England winning a match against an Australian team of which they were key members—at odds of 500 to 1—and collected because Australia lost against the odds. Exemplary punishment might make players think twice about extra-curricular earnings, but nothing in the Australian record suggests an enthusiasm for punishment: Rodney Marsh ran the Australian Cricket Board's cricket academy for years and Shane Warne (only half-jokingly) said he was looking forward to his knighthood.

Instead of waiting for Indians to lead them not into temptation (and deliver them from evil), Dr Bacher might have tried to teach his South African charges a lesson they ought to have learnt in Calvinist Bible classes: the ethic of individual responsibility. He could have had them coached on how to turn down bookies without hurting their feelings. And the BCCI in India could have helped by supplying him (and the Australians) a list of Indian synonyms for 'no'.

Local Heroes

Larger than Life: Mansur Ali Khan Pataudi

I met the Nawab of Pataudi over dinner once, in Abbas Ali Baig's house. The other name I can drop is Sunil Gavaskar's. I was an undergraduate when I shook hands with him as he stepped out of a lift in a hotel in Delhi. Gavaskar was unarguably the greater player, but meeting Pataudi ranked higher. Gavaskar wasn't a nawab, he had two eyes, he wasn't married to Sharmila Tagore, hadn't been to Oxford and didn't talk posh. If you're an Indian cricket fan, these things matter.

Growing up in the sixties, the Nawab of Pataudi, Jr., was more than my favourite cricketer, he was my hero. He was the captain of India in 1964 when the MCC toured with a second-rate team led by M.J.K. Smith. That was the first cricket series that I actively followed with the help of running commentary on All India Radio and the pictures published in *Sport & Pastime*. Pataudi did nothing noteworthy either as captain or player. All five Tests were drawn and the Nawab's contribution as a batsman was one double century and several ducks.

But it didn't matter. I knew about Pataudi before I began to follow Test cricket, in the same way as I knew of Dara Singh and Milkha Singh. India was a brand new country in 1957, the year I was born, and in its enthusiasm for mascots, it fashioned heroes out of some pretty eccentric material. I knew, for example, that Dara Singh was India's first world champion and he had got there by wrestling King Kong to the ground. This was a fact; the older boys I played gully cricket with had told me. Just as they had told me that Pataudi had just one eye.

Looking back, it's hard to believe the hours we spent debating the state of Pataudi's eye. There was a colour picture of him in the souvenir album that Esso published in 1964 to mark the MCC tour. It was a spiral-bound album and each player had a page to himself, with space for a picture and a short biography on the right. You bought the album from the petrol pump and then each time your parents filled up, you collected some photos and stuck them in the marked spaces. As a marketing ploy, it was brilliant: no Burmah Shell pump sold my parents a drop of petrol till I had filled in the whole album.

As a result, I knew more about Jim Parks and Phil Sharpe than anyone needed to know, but Pataudi's bio was frustrating because it didn't settle the matter of his eye. Was it a glass eye or a normal one that didn't work? It was hard to tell from the photo. Still, it was a dashing picture with Pataudi looking vaguely rakish, as a nawab should. The bio let you know that he had captained Oxford and played for Sussex, which didn't hurt the image. Forty years ago, these things mattered.

A part of his mystique was the romance of him being a nawab multiplied by the improbable fact that he was the son of another nawab of Pataudi who had also captained India. To complete the fairy tale for seven-year-old fans like me, just two years before the MCC tour he had become, at twenty-one, the youngest captain in the world, when he was given the job in the West Indies after Charlie Griffith broke

Nari Contractor's head. And there was more: he wasn't just the Nawab of Pataudi—he was Tiger. For us, it wasn't just a name, it was an attitude. I remember him fielding in the covers against the New Zealanders in the Feroz Shah Kotla stadium in Delhi, chasing balls down, well, tigerishly. I think the reason we worshipped him was that at a time when Indian Test teams ranged from mediocre to terrible, he still managed to lead them boldly, with panache and without deference. It didn't hurt that he was born and raised in privilege; ironically, the citizens of republican India were delighted to be led by a debonair prince.

So did his batting matter? Of course it did. There were the two fifties he made against Simpson's Australians that helped India win the Bombay Test in the three-Test series played immediately after the MCC tour. There were the fifty and hundred in a losing cause in Headingley in 1967. India lost every Test in that series, but listening to *Test Match Special* on the BBC's World Service, I was content that my hero had top scored in the first innings, then hit a wonderful century, 148 out of a total of 510 to avoid a follow-on (India lost respectably by six wickets). Listening to Arlott and Johnston speculate about the batting heights Pataudi might have scaled with two good eyes, I forgave him all the innings when he scored nothing and hadn't seemed to care. Best of all, there were the two fifties he hit against the Australians in the Melbourne Test where, literally hamstrung, he hit 75 and 85, 'with one good eye and on one good leg . . .' (Mihir Bose, *A History of Indian Cricket*). India still lost by an innings, but I was used to finding individual consolation in collective failure and the thought of Pataudi, hobbled but heroic, hooking and pulling his way to gallant defeat was enough.

I didn't actually see him play that many innings. There was his top score of 203 in Delhi in that dull dead rubber against Smith's MCC and the hundred against the New Zealanders the following year which, for once, was in a winning cause. But I can't really remember his stroke play, in the way I can for Gavaskar or Azhar or Laxman, or any batsman made familiar by live telecasts. I saw more of him after he retired and turned up on television as an expert than I did when he was a player. He was the best expert commentator I've ever heard: sharp, sardonic and rude, but I'm glad he didn't make it a living because it left my memories of him intact. I didn't have to watch him age into a professional hack. Looking at Richie Benaud on Channel 9 peddling trashy memorabilia, it's impossible to believe he ever played cricket. Pataudi was my hero from a time before television, through a childhood where I followed cricket by hearing it described, in a golden age where I didn't have to see to believe.

Money in the Bank: Sunil Gavaskar

Those hundreds he made against the West Indies? He made them in a sun hat. Every bouncer could have helped him star in a rerun of Nari Contractor's nightmare. As a Delhi boy, I watched him play Imran Khan and Malcolm Marshall at Feroz Shah Kotla. Watching from the pavilion stand over the bowler's arm, without the two-dimensional foreshortening that makes cricket on television a defanged, video game version of the real thing, I flinched at the ferocity of the bowling and worshipped, as fans will, the fearless classicism with which each ball was played. He was the best batsman ever to play for India and the best batsman of his time, bar nobody: not Viv Richards, nor Greg Chappell.

The mid-sixties were a barren time for Indian batsmanship. The great stars of the past, Vijay Manjrekar, Vijay Hazare, Polly Umrigar, Chandu Borde, were gone or fading, and the new decade threw up no worthy replacements till it was nearly spent. So if you began following cricket in the mid-sixties, you had no batting heroes. There was Pataudi, of course, and I saw him strike a century against the New Zealanders at Feroz Shah Kotla in Delhi, but I can also remember the string of noughts and low scores he regularly produced. Had he had both eyes . . . who knows, but as things stood, he was a romantic hero for us, not a great, dominant batsman. Actually, the sixties were a terrible time for Indian batting. The cupboard was so bare that Budhi Kunderan, our wicketkeeper, was the hero of the 1964 series against M.J.K. Smith's MCC team. Filling in for Farokh Engineer, he had the top score for the series (192 in the Madras Test) as well as another century. Jaisimha, Pataudi, Sardesai, Hanumant Singh, Ajit Wadekar, Rusi Surti, Durrani, Engineer, Kunderan, all had their moments, but even their mothers would have baulked at describing any combination of these players as a formidable or even an adequate batting line-up.

Over the past thirty years Indians have come to take individual batting genius in the Indian team for granted. We may not win many Tests, but for three decades now, the batting has been anchored by at least one great batsman supported by a couple of very good ones. Tendulkar and Dravid; Tendulkar, Manjrekar and Azharuddin; Azharuddin and Gavaskar; Gavaskar, Mohinder Amarnath and Vengsarkar; and at the start of this run we have Gavaskar and that other mighty mite, G.R. Viswanath.

It all began with Viswanath and the debut century he produced against Bill Lawry's Australians in Kanpur in that closely contested series played through the winter of 1969–70. He scored a duck in the first innings of the Kanpur match and a century in the second. Then, in the Delhi Test that India won, Viswanath was at the crease, in the company of Ajit Wadekar, when the winning runs were scored. All India celebrated, not just the victory but also the arrival of a genuine batting hero, the first since the heyday of Umrigar and Manjrekar. More importantly, he was the first Indian batsman in a long while to face fast bowling not just bravely or gallantly (Pataudi and Jaisimha and Engineer did that) but soundly.

Gundappa Viswanath will always have his admirers. They

don't make up a fan club; they constitute a cult. I know, because like many young boys who watched him play those early innings, I am a member of that cult. There was an improbable quality about Vishy's batting that touched him with magic. He looked like a sawn-off dacoit and played like a wristy angel. Think of someone who looks like Graham Gooch and plays like David Gower, then cut him in half, and you have Viswanath. Sitting in Kotla on that wonderful winning day, every spectator knew that the Era of Viswanath in the annals of Indian batsmanship was about to begin, but it never came to pass. After the long drought of the sixties, Indian cricket was to be blessed by not just one, but two wonderful batsmen: G.R. Viswanath and S.M. Gavaskar. They were the same height, they became brothers-in-law and together, they served India wonderfully well for many years, but only one of them, at the end of his career, entered a claim to greatness . . . and it wasn't Vishy. Viswanath was a watershed. The modern era in Indian batsmanship begins with him, but his debut is the curtain raiser. The main act on this bill was the long and incomparable career of Sunil Manohar Gavaskar, the greatest Indian batsman ever, barring nobody.

Nearly half our memories of Gavaskar are radio memories. Months after his earth-shattering debut in the West Indies, Doordarshan showed us a few minutes of footage of a five-Test series. Likewise, his epic 220 at the Oval and his fall within touching distance of victory, came to us over the ether, courtesy the fruity voices and old-world charm of BBC's *Test Match Special*. But I watched Gavaskar play a lone hand against Imran and Sarfaraz in Pakistan in 1978, I saw that flame-thrower assault he led on Malcolm Marshall and the West Indian pace battery at the Feroz Shah Kotla in 1983, where he got to a century in under a hundred balls, and I watched that great valedictory knock where he fell within sight of a hundred after a masterly exhibition against Pakistan's spinners on a breaking wicket on which the ball was turning square. Like the thousands of others who had the luck to watch genius, live and in the flesh, I too can say, 'Mine eyes have seen.'

But is he greater than Tendulkar? That's the question, isn't it? Any assessment of Gavaskar's place in Indian cricket written after Tendulkar's debut must make that comparison. There's no question that Tendulkar will erase all or most of Gavaskar's records by the time he retires. There's also no argument that he is by some distance the better one-day batsman. But is Tendulkar the better Test match batsman?

The answer must be no. I could cite the standard arguments and they have force. One, Gavaskar helped India win abroad more often. Two, he scored his runs as an opening batsman against fast bowlers at their freshest. And three, he was more dependable. But I think all of them miss the point. And the point is this: Gavaskar played out a whole Test career without getting seriously hit by the rising ball. In contrast, I have personally seen Tendulkar being pinged on the helmet several times. That's the difference that sets them apart. Despite the lack of a helmet, Gavaskar looked more secure at the wicket than Tendulkar does. That's an extraordinary compliment. Protective gear, especially the helmet, is so integral to batting these days that it is hard to imagine the continuous, contagious and spit-drying fear that fast bowlers inspired before its adoption. We used to pray that Chandrasekhar would fall quickly lest he be maimed. We watched helplessly as promising careers were blighted by the fear of injury and death that Test-quality fast bowling inspired. Brijesh Patel with a helmet on could have been a proto-Azharuddin. Conversely, one of contemporary cricket's most celebrated figures, a man known for his will, endurance and courage, Steve Waugh, might have had a shorter career without a helmet. Even with it on, Waugh jumped about enough to give fast bowlers hope.

In contrast, Gavaskar played Roberts, Holding, Snow, Lillee, Thompson, Marshall, Imran, faultlessly without the insurance of a helmet. In Delhi he played six short-pitched balls from a lethally quick Imran, one-handed, down into the ground. How good is that? Better than Tendulkar would have been, I suggest, once he had been struck on the head a few times without the benefit of protection.

Some will dismiss this by arguing you can't hold the helmet against the contemporary batsman because it isn't his fault that the game's protective gear has changed. It's a fair point but it errs in not allowing that a batsman's skill and comfort level against fast bowling can still be gauged by how often he is involuntarily hit. The perfect test case is Mohinder Amarnath, a stout-hearted batsman whose career would have been cut short by his weakness against the short-pitched ball had it not been for the arrival of the helmet. Once he pulled the helmet on, he became one of India's bravest and best batsmen against quick bowling.

There are those who whisper that Gavaskar's Test record is inflated because he played for some years against teams depleted by Packer's marauding and filled his boots. And it is true that Gavaskar did very well against Bobby Simpson's fledglings in Australia and against second-string West Indian teams filling in for Packer's pirates. But it is also true that he didn't have the opportunities the current Indian side has for fattening averages at the expense of novice sides like Zimbabwe and Bangladesh, nor did he play a West Indies team in dire decline.

Gavaskar was the greatest batsman I've ever watched play. I am perfectly willing to concede that there might have been batsmen nearly as good. Viv Richards comes to mind, so does Gordon Greenidge. Greg Chappell has his supporters as does, of course, Tendulkar. Nobody else makes the cut. But even amongst this short list of contenders, what makes Gavaskar unique is that his batting, his presence at the wicket was all of a piece: it was great natural ability married to an orthodox classicism. Cricket journalism tends to equate classical play with long, limber batsmen: Gavaskar adapted orthodoxy to the needs of shorter men, he made classicism crisper and more compact. It is that pared down perfection, that absence of flourish, that certain, inevitable, clockwork response to a bowler's challenge that was his true claim to greatness.

Gavaskar is remembered for the perfection of his defence, his invulnerability. This was a boon to an Indian team notorious for its fragility against fast bowling. Gavaskar supplied Indian batting with backbone. But this achievement obscures what to me is Gavaskar's greatest quality: the beauty and perfection of his stroke play. There was no batsman who approached the precision of his footwork or the classical rightness of his technique. Never did he look clumsy or crude as Tendulkar so often does when he plays that front-foot pull-swipe or the down-the-wicket hoick. Had Gavaskar played for England or Australia, we wouldn't have to read those endless articles celebrating and mourning Barry Richards's peerless talent. That a batsman with four Tests to his credit is constantly spoken of in the same breath as Gavaskar—whose reputation as the greatest opening batsman of modern times was built over sixteen years of awesome batsmanship—tells us more about the white Commonwealth and its nostalgias than it does about cricket.

There were no disfiguring mannerisms. Unlike Tendulkar, he didn't adjust his guard in public. His kit was immaculate: the two-strap pads custom-made for him; the arm guard, and, towards the end, the little skullcap with its drooping ears. The broad-brimmed hat he borrowed from the Pakistanis who pioneered it, but the elephant hair bracelet was an eccentric touch of his own. Before the bowler ran in there would be that quick glance around and he'd settle into his stance, first one foot in its appointed place, then the other. He was the one batsman Indians watched without fear. You knew that when he went, it would be on account of a very good ball, not fear, or ineptitude or fickleness. He was money in the bank. For the length of his career, he underwrote Indian cricket. He made us feel solvent. We shall never, as old-fashioned cricket writers used to say, see his like again.

Adventure and Hope: Kapil Dev

He was a great bowler, but people came to watch Kapil Dev bat. Those four consecutive sixes off Eddie Hemmings to save a follow-on: not since Salim Durrani had anyone had the nerve to try anything like that, and not even Durrani had Kapil's ball-striking genius. A provincial player from a state with no cricket pedigree, he played for India when he was nineteen, was captain of India at age twenty-three and then won the World Cup as captain by the time he was twenty-four! I can still picture him catching Viv Richards off Madan Lal in that World Cup final: he loped off after the ball and collected it over his shoulder. It was a tough catch at a tense time in the biggest arena in cricket, but he made it look simple with his easy athleticism and Br'er Rabbit smile.

I remember Kapil Dev's debut in Pakistan. The memory has a period feel to it because it unspools in black and white. It was 1978, a time when Doordarshan made television programmes, Weston made television sets and only real life happened in colour. But we weren't complaining as we watched young Kapil bound in to bowl: for a generation that had grown up listening to the BBC's *Test Match Special* on shortwave frequencies that mooed and whistled, watching a Test match telecast live from another country (especially

Pakistan) was a modern miracle.

We hadn't played a Test against Pakistan since the early sixties and when we played them at hockey, we generally lost. The only time we had beaten them comprehensively was Dacca, 1971. Bangladesh wasn't a Test-playing country then; it wasn't, come to think of it, a country. Which was why we were touring in 1971, and our captain, General Jagjit Singh Arora (unaccountably missing from *Wisden*'s archives) had been given considerably more than eleven men. The violent contest ensured that seven years later, the 1978 series was more than a cricketing contest.

Pakistan had a very, very powerful team; Mushtaq Mohammad was captain, and to back him up was a glittering array of Packer's pirates: Zaheer Abbas, Javed Miandad, Asif Iqbal, Intikhab Alam, Wasim Bari, Imran Khan, Sarfaraz Nawaz . . . If we hoped to do well, it was because we had Gavaskar (like Lord Krishna, worth whole armies) and the great spinners: Bedi, Prasanna and Chandrasekhar, who had had a very good series just before the Pakistan tour.

Well, we got hammered. Zaheer and Miandad sent the spin trio into early retirement and Gavaskar played a lone hand against Pakistan's rampaging pace attack. We lost the three-match series 2–0 and that score line flatters us. We was killed.

Kapil Dev was the silver lining. This loose-limbed gawky Jat bowled fast and batted furiously. He didn't get many wickets and he didn't score a ton of runs, but he hit Sadiq Mohammad on the helmet with a bouncer before he had time to react and he faced Pakistan's fast men with the sort of uninhibited aggression that no Indian of my generation had seen before. Think of Yuvraj Singh pumped up to the power of ten and you have some idea of what that debut meant to Indian cricket, to us.

If Kapil hadn't happened along we'd have had to invent him. For a start, he was big. At a time when most Indian Test cricketers, with the exception of Tendulkar or Sehwag hover around the six-foot mark, that sounds unremarkable, but in the seventies, when Indian cricketers came in three physical types, puny, portly and passable, size mattered. The best batsmen, Viswanath and Gavaskar, were five and a half feet standing on their toes. Our 'fast' bowlers, Solkar, Abid Ali and Madan Lal had twelve-valve hearts in Standard Herald bodies. Bedi and Prasanna, great bowlers both, were pear shaped for most of their playing lives. And such tall ones as there were, men like Mohinder Amarnath and Vengsarkar, were battlers without the physical presence and simple self-assurance that this big rookie had been born with.

I can remember a famous picture of Kapil hooking Botham during the 1981 tour of England. The camera had caught him at the end of his one-legged pivot and something about the pose suggested that he had really creamed that ball. You could see Botham at the top of the frame looking up at the end of his follow through—their big boy against ours. We lost that series comprehensively and Botham's figures were better than Kapil's, but he was our best bowler and an 80 he struck was the most violent innings I'd ever seen in Test cricket. During that series he was asked in a television interview on the BBC about the comparisons that were being made with Botham. He thought for a second and said in that Rapidex drawl that he was to make famous in the course of an amazing career: 'Ah play mah way.' He certainly did.

He was a gust of fresh, provincial air that blew away the stifling prudence of middle class cricket. And this isn't sentimental hindsight: I was a student in England when India toured in 1981 and the magic about watching Kapil play was the dizzy thought that anything was possible. After years of trench warfare dominated by defensive foot-soldiers, India had found a cavalryman eager to lead the charge. A lot of the time, the team was mown down, but there were some famous victories, none finer than the World Cup in 1983.

The winning of the World Cup in England was Kapil's finest hour, not only because we won but because the manner of the victory showcased Kapil's particular talents. First there was the berserker 175 against Zimbabwe at Tunbridge Wells where he single-handedly won the match for India. Then there was that marvellous catch running backwards to dismiss Viv Richards in the finals, but most of all it was his achievement in making a bunch of military medium losers (Madan Lal, Roger Binny, Mohinder Amarnath, Balwinder Singh Sandhu) believe they made up a bowling attack that could win cricket's greatest prize. Only an inspirational cricketer like Kapil could have helped this middling bunch play so far above their abilities.

But it is in the nature of inspiration that it comes and goes and not even Kapil could turn it on at will. He wasn't a particularly good captain: he captained India in thirty-four Tests of which he won four and lost seven. By way of comparison, Gavaskar captained India in forty-seven, won nine and lost eight. But there was one last achievement as captain after the World Cup. Restored to the captaincy three years later, he led India to a comprehensive series victory against the old enemy, England.

That's the reason why Kapil has a fair claim to be India's cricketer of the century: not because he is representative of the traditional strengths of Indian cricket, but precisely because he is not. On the strength of his enormous talent and his willingness to lead by example, he helped the Indian team crawl out of its bunker and go over the top. There had been aggressive and dominant Indian cricketers before him:

C.K. Nayudu, of course, is the great example. But he, despite his talent and charisma, falls victim to the Barry Richards Syndrome: he just didn't play enough Test cricket to be a serious contender. Then there were men like Mushtaq Ali, Lala Amarnath, Salim Durrani, Farokh Engineer, cavaliers all, who lightened the lives of careworn Indian fans, but none of them had the discipline to sustain their talent and daredevilry over a long career.

Kapil Dev, it bears repeating, took 434 wickets at under 30 runs per wicket, scored more than 5000 runs (eight centuries and twenty-seven fifties amongst them) at an average of over 30 runs per innings, played more Test matches (131) than any other Indian cricketer bar Tendulkar and over a sixteen-year career, never missed a Test because of injury. To be a top class outswing bowler for as long as that specially when you're not fearsomely fast, requires unwavering discipline and commitment. When you think of the punishment his body took as a fast bowling all-rounder who played more than half his cricket on dead Indian wickets, the awesomeness of his achievement becomes apparent. Mushtaq Ali et al. were comets to Kapil's constant star.

But how does Kapil stack up against other great all rounders? To weigh the historical achievement of an Indian cricketer, we should compare him not only to his compatriots but also his contemporaries and rivals from other Test-playing countries. Someone championing Gavaskar's cause as India's greatest cricketer can legitimately argue that he was the greatest opening batsman of his time. The only serious contender is Gordon Greenidge. There are those like Christopher Martin-Jenkins who will argue Barry Richards's cause, but it's time we stopped strumming cricket's might-have-beens. By this logic, Lawrence Rowe was arguably the greatest top-order batsman who never was: the man had a triple century and a

double century to his name in Test matches before eye trouble
ended his career. We don't know how good Barry Richards
might have been over a long Test career because he didn't
have a long Test career. Period. Had Graeme Hick not been
cruelly exposed in the Test arena, white nostalgists would
now be telling us that but for cruel fate he would have been
the equal of Viv Richards! But Kapil played in the same era
as Imran Khan and Ian Botham (I shan't include Richard
Hadlee, who was arguably the greatest bowler of the four,
but not good enough as a batsman to qualify as an all-
rounder of their class) and a powerful case can be made that
they were Kapil's betters. If we were to pick Kapil as the
greatest Indian player of the twentieth century, do we really
want our Indian champion to have been the third best player
of his kind amongst his contemporaries? More parochially,
if Imran Khan is Pakistan's greatest-ever player (which he is)
and Kapil is ours, do we want Their greatest to be self-
evidently greater than Our greatest? Unless we can make a
case to the contrary, maybe we should choose Gavaskar over
Kapil Dev.

So is there a case to be made? I think there is. There's
really nothing to choose between Kapil and Botham as
bowlers. As a batsman, Botham has a definite edge and the
record to prove it. Botham was a fine fieldsman close to the
wicket, Kapil was brilliant in the outfield. As a captain Kapil
has a World Cup to show for his efforts, while Botham has
nothing comparable.

The comparison with Imran is harder to sustain. Imran
was the scarier fast bowler though Kapil has the larger tally of
wickets. Imran was also one of the pioneers of the dark art of
reverse swing. He was incomparably better as a captain. Kapil
was probably the better fielder and much the more talented
batsman, though Imran husbanded his batting talent better

than the prodigal Indian. My own feeling is that Imran is ahead of Kapil by a nose but it's not a clear-cut thing. And it can be said in Kapil's defence that unlike Imran, he would never have been narcissistic enough to forget his teammates in victory.

Only one comparison remains. How does Kapil measure up against Tendulkar and Gavaskar? You can make the list of contenders as long as you like, but the contest for the greatest Indian cricketer of the twentieth century is basically a three-horse race. If standalone talent was the only criterion, Tendulkar would probably get most people's votes, but it isn't. Tendulkar has made no difference to India's fortunes abroad and that's a terrible indictment, while Kapil and Gavaskar have won us matches more than once in epic offshore struggles. So it has to be between the two of them. I'm an old partisan of Gavaskar, but Kapil gave us all so much pleasure that I can't see even Gavaskar's fans minding too much if the jury awarded the palm to Kapil.

Even today, when India does badly, I ward off depression by thinking of a particular photo of his. It's an early picture and the photographer has caught the young Kapil gathering himself in his pre-delivery leap, exaggeratedly side-on, head flung back, eyes gleaming with passion and purpose. Kapil deserves to be our cricketer of the last century because he was a talisman: once upon a time, he stood for both adventure and hope.

Cricket's Talat Mahmood: Mohammad Azharuddin

I was commissioned by a magazine to interview Azharuddin in the late nineties during a low point in his career as an international cricketer. I flew into Hyderabad, feeling like a high-powered journalist. The feeling didn't last; I learnt that a journalist trying to interview a Test cricketer is a supplicant in a whimsical darbar. I disliked every second of the interview because Azhar in civvies wasn't the thrilling batsman my son and I admired; he came across as a sporting starlet. Writing up the interview afterwards helped clear up the bad taste in my mouth: he was a celebrity and I was a journalist, using him as material. Perhaps he was right to be wary.

Since he became a fixture on our television sets some years ago, Azharuddin's shape has changed. He began public life as a stick figure, so thin that the only substance to him was the bulk of his protective gear. The things you noticed about him were the square amulet he wore round his neck and the way his lip curled lopsidedly over large incisors. He looked like Goofy padded up. In the middle years of his career, through his long tenure as skipper, he thickened. Azhar was never obviously overweight, but that whippet leanness disappeared as he grew into physical maturity. Two or three years ago he began to pare himself down again, but nothing I had seen on television prepared me for the way he looked in real life.

In black dress trousers and a slick black T-shirt that clung to him like Spandex, Azhar (or his body) looked eighteen years old: his torso arrowed down to a tiny waist, his arms were taut with tubular muscle and if the point of the costume was to convince the world that he wasn't too old for Tests at thirty-seven (he had just been dropped from the tour of Australia), I was convinced.

The interview was blighted before it began. Azhar was moving house the day I was scheduled to meet him. From a mid-morning rendezvous, it got pushed further and further back and by the time we met, it was seven in the evening and dark. I had been told to call before setting off to his new bungalow in Banjara Hills to check if he was home; when I did, he came to the phone and demanded in surly tones why I wasn't there already. I left in a hurry.

We talked sitting on two plastic chairs in the front yard of his house. There was a silver Mercedes Benz parked in a corner and up-ended packaging marked Fragile. His bathroom's geyser wasn't working and the electrician was late. There was no table to rest the cassette player so Azhar offered to hold it through the interview. He switched it off when his cellphone rang, which it did a lot, and on one of those occasions, forgot to push the record button on again. I found out when I got home after the interview and sat up till midnight transcribing it from memory. Every cricketer is two persons: one is his cricketing persona and the other is how the public imagines him in civvies, when he is not playing cricket. When he started his Test career, Azharuddin, the cricketer, was a wristy, consistent, one-paced batsman who worked the ball around, kept it safely on the ground and ran like a deer. Azharuddin, the man, was by common consent an unsophisticated, lower middle class, family-loving lad from Himayat Nagar in Hyderabad and a devout, observant Muslim. When TV audiences saw him raise his head heavenward after getting to a hundred they nodded and looked knowing. Unspoilt he was.

In those days, there were two ways of being a Hyderabadi Muslim cricketer in India. You could be an aristocratic stylist in the manner of Abbas Ali Baig or, more famously, the Nawab of Pataudi. For this you needed a family tree, an Oxbridge degree and reasonable amounts of money. You also needed to be from elsewhere: neither Baig nor Pataudi were natives. Or you could go the anonymous middle class way of Abid Ali and Arshad Ayub. For Azhar, there wasn't a choice. He attended the same school that Abid Ali had been to, a St. Something. It was a convent, Azhar impressed upon me. English medium.

English medium or not, the early Azhar was famously inarticulate and universally liked. His good nature left him nicely positioned to be the compromise candidate when Srikkanth was sacked as skipper after a blameless tour of Pakistan. Up to this point in his career, Azhar was Mr Nice Guy. The nineties saw his image going into free fall. This is a summary of the media version of his decline and fall: Azhar, after becoming captain, was spoilt by adulation. He became the flashy, aggressive, brilliant batsman that we're now familiar with: a sparkling blue jagger with one flaw, a weakness against fast bowling. Instead of bidding for greatness, he indulged his genius and fell short of immortality. (Christopher Isherwood, the English novelist, said of himself that he was a writer of the second rank . . . but the front row of the second rank. This would be, for many cricket watchers, an appropriate summary of Azhar's place in the game.) In the mid-nineties, the story went, he developed a new persona:

he became the shades-wearing, Pepsi-selling, starlet struck, B-List celebrity that he now is.

This is an old story and it is easy to tell. Because real life is seldom touched with originality or imagination, it is often depressingly true. Was it true about Azhar? I didn't want it to be true when I went to Hyderabad to interview him, because once upon a time I had imagined that there would be an era in Indian batsmanship that we would remember by his name; one that would succeed Gavaskar's. Mohinder Amarnath and Dilip Vengsarkar were splendid batsmen, but they had the misfortune to play much of their cricket in Gavaskar's shadow. They were batsmen of character and Gavaskar had enough character for ten.

Azhar was different. He was extravagant, flourishing, light years from the orthodoxy of Bombay. People groped for precedents; some, desperately, came up with Viswanath. This was absurdly wrong because Vishy was compact and close to the ground while Azhar was all gangling elegance. It was only after a while that people saw Azhar as an original: untutored, therefore wholly himself—Suleiman the Magnificent with a light willow blade in hand instead of a scimitar. The loops and flourishes it described were so far removed from the disciplined arcs of Gavaskar's bat that Azhar's batting seemed scroll work—ornate, occasionally overwrought.

Gavaskar retired in 1987; soon afterwards, Azhar succeeded to the captaincy. Vengsarkar and Mohinder bowed out, leaving him the major batsman in the side. He was a young man in his mid-twenties; captain of India and its best batsman. Greatness was within his grasp . . . but sadly for him (though he didn't know it then), Gavaskar's flame had already passed into the keeping of a rookie in Azhar's squad, in every way his opposite: a Maharashtrian Hindu, an orthodox bat, squat where he was slender, all strength to

Azhar's grace. There never would be an era of Azharuddin; the baton of Indian batting passed from Gavaskar to Tendulkar. Azhar should have been the Mohammad Rafi of Indian batsmanship, but he ended up as its Talat Mahmood.

What changed? You could argue that Azhar, like that other artist, Zaheer Abbas, was pipped at the greatness post by an incurable defect: a weakness against quick bowling. Those of us who had the misfortune to watch the 1978 series against Pakistan on black and white television, saw Zaheer Abbas at his flat-track best, make Gavaskar look like Barrington, a grim accumulator of runs. Zaheer in that series was unstoppable. He pulled, drove and cut our attack to ribbons. But no one will seriously suggest that he was, over an entire career, the equal of Gavaskar. Zaheer didn't make the cut against real pace. This is, in the subcontinent, a terrible judgement. In Australia, Doug Walters was suspect against the fast men, yet he retained a substantial reputation. Mark Waugh for some years has been dodgy against the bouncer, but you don't hear commentators suggesting he's a coward or a wimp.

But in India, being suspect against fast bowling isn't just a weakness; it is a moral defect, a stigma. Umrigar's place in India's cricketing pantheon has been unfairly diminished by this awful whisper. Contrariwise, Vijay Manjrekar and Vijay Hazare are worshipped though their career figures aren't better than Umrigar's, because they faced fast bowling without flinching. Viswanath, whose career stats are effortlessly surpassed by Azharuddin's, will always have a shinier halo in Indian cricket's special heaven because of that 90 he hit against Andy Roberts on a fast Chepauk pitch. You should have seen him.

I prefer to believe that Azhar pursued flamboyance not because reliability was beyond his abilities, but because he chose to. At some point, he decided to live life in the fast lane. As a man this meant changes in his personal life that this essay has no interest in; as a batsman this meant abandoning the purist's patience in selecting the right ball to hit: Azhar just hit more and more deliveries, disregarding the percentages. When his methods worked, he produced passages of such withering magic that bowlers like Klusener wilted.

Azhar and Tendulkar have been India's best batsmen over the last decade. Tendulkar is the one with a real claim to 'greatness'. And this is true; but there is something we lose in this comparison. Tendulkar's assault on Warne and the Australians in 1998 was more consistently devastating over a series than anything Azhar had ever managed. Tendulkar's knocks had everything: he sorted out one of the greatest spinners cricket has ever seen and he did it via a combination of orthodox shots and improvised aggression. They were masterly, breathtaking innings; but they weren't bewildering or magical. Tendulkar's genius is wholly rational: even his novelties, those inside-out cover drives or those paddle sweeps, are considered solutions to bowling problems.

In contrast, Azhar's century against South Africa at Eden Gardens in 1996, his hundred against the Proteas in South Africa in partnership with Tendulkar that same year, his century between lunch and tea against the Australians in 1991–92, his 121 in 111 balls with twenty-two fours against England in reply to Gooch's bludgeoning triple century, induce in us a sense of wonder; they are magical because his methods are so unlikely, so contrary, so absurdly out of tune with the orthodoxy of the straight bat. Klusener, after being caned by Azharuddin, said ruefully that bowling at him was like bowling at a revolving door. Azhar plays with an angled blade; he whips his wrists through even the straight-lofted drive, he is never back and across, his back lift wastes so much time. If we are to find a parallel for him, we have to look outside

India, to that troubled West Indian genius, Brian Lara.

Azharuddin is best understood as a right-handed Lara. Neither is orthodox in any recognizable sense, though Azharuddin's shots are more idiosyncratic than Lara's. Both have extravagant backlifts, the same visceral aggression, the same difficulty with the very fast short-pitched ball (think of Lara's travails against McGrath) and superficially similar problems with their public image, though to be fair to Azhar, nothing he has said to the press has ever rivalled Lara's famously offensive outbursts. Both of them are different from Tendulkar in precisely the same way: where Tendulkar has the full repertoire of orthodoxy, Lara and Azhar know one kind of music and they need to make the opposition's bowlers dance to that tune. When they succeed they're likely to change the course of a match in a couple of hours; when they fail they look reckless, irresponsible, and silly. The cliche is true: brilliance is brittle; when Tendulkar isn't timing the ball, he can change gears and bat himself into form; Lara and Azhar don't have that option: for them, it is all or nothing.

When I asked Azhar about his best innings, he mentioned his lightning century against the Australians in Adelaide in 1991. His account of it is interesting. It had been a bad series for him till then. He had got into a front foot habit during the English season, and his first move was forward. In Australia he kept getting out in the slips. He got out early in the first innings at Adelaide. But the second innings was different. He hit just about everything. There were twenty boundaries in his century. Typically, Azhar offered no explanation of what he did right the second time round; he just hit everything.

I asked him about his big century against Gooch's men in England, hoping he would explain just why he played so well. I was in very good nick, he said simply. I scored runs that whole tour. Only once did he offer a comment on technique. Zaheer Abbas, he said, helped him with his batting at a low point in his career and helped turn him into an attacking player from the steady batsman he had been till then. His grip was wrong: his hand didn't go far enough around the handle, with the result that his right hand was coming off when he played on-side shots. That adjustment, together with the hectic pace of one-day cricket, made him a dasher.

A maternal uncle introduced Azhar to the game. He remembered being fascinated by the shape of a cricket bat. He was mad about the game: he would go and stand for hours watching senior boys play till they asked him why he was hanging around. He seldom said anything to them, because he didn't want to impose. I was shy, he said. He began playing with a hard ball around the age of eight. The first Test match he ever watched was in 1969, in Hyderabad. He used to listen to radio commentary; he can remember Lindsay Hassett and Alan Mcgilrae doing commentary on Radio Australia for the 1976 series. His heroes were all men who had turned out for Hyderabad: Ghulam Ahmed, Pataudi, Jaisimha.

His first Ranji season was less than great. He got one fifty. But in his second season, he got a hundred in his first innings, then a double century in a Duleep Trophy match against Central Zone. That was his breakthrough game. Hanumant Singh, who was a Test selector then, was watching. Azhar was twelfth man in the first two Tests against England before he was picked for the third when Kapil Dev and Sandip Patil were dropped as punishment for playing poor shots. By the time he made his debut, he had played every grade of cricket there was. He was emphatic that it was too easy these days for young cricketers—they got opportunities without consistently demonstrating their worth. There was a certain poignance to that; this wonderful cricketer consigned to the margins while young pretenders like Hrishikesh Kanitkar and Martin, without a smidgen of his ability, took his place on the Australian tour.

It was hard drawing him out about the current game. It wasn't the ordinary caution a player would show while speaking of his contemporaries—he just seemed deeply wary of journalists. It got to a point that when I asked him to name the best Indian batsman he had played alongside, he hesitated so long that I qualified the question: excluding the present bunch of players. He thought for a while; Gavaskar, he said finally. And Mohinder Amarnath. The best fast bowler? There was no hesitation on this one. Wasim Akram, for his amazing variety; he could do anything. The toughest team to play was the Australians: they never stopped coming at you. Best umpires? Dicky Bird, David Shepherd and Venkatraghavan.

I could have got this for the price of a postage stamp on a printed questionnaire, I thought in quiet despair. Then he began to talk about his seasons with Derbyshire and became more animated. He played for Derby in 1991 and 1994. Kim Barnet was his captain and he loved it there. The start of his first season wasn't great, but things improved and he scored 2000 runs. Everyone went out of their way to be friendly: the committee, his teammates, everyone. He loved the long bus journeys to away matches; he liked touring. Derby town was two hours from London and it didn't worry him that it was a small provincial town. Hyderabad was like that too.

The one subject on which he was really forthcoming through that entire conversation was his weight. And I was curious. How did a man of thirty-seven arrive at a handspan waist? Between 1988 and 1994, he said, the dates tripping off his tongue, he had become very overweight because he was eating just anything and drinking aerated drinks. But the main reason he ballooned was that he was taking cortisone for a groin injury and the steroid speeded his metabolism up, so he ate a lot. It didn't affect his batting, though it slowed him down in the field a bit. Then, in 1994, he began eating carefully. He cut out red meat and soft drinks, did sit-ups, played lots of squash and became fit again. It sounded simple.

He was willing to talk about the way he had been dropped. He had read about it in the papers. They should have had the courtesy to call him, he thought. But there was symmetry to selectorial behaviour. He had read about his selection for his debut Test in the papers too. He thought it was immature of the selectors not to have told him personally. He liked 'immature'. He thought Indian crowds were immature too: they didn't understand the work, the pride, the pressure involved in playing for the country. Modern cricket spectators didn't understand the game at all; maybe 10 per cent did, the rest were there for a good time.

The interview petered out as I ran out of questions. All the while we were talking, Azhar was carrying on a parallel conversation made up of asides to the workmen who were making his new house liveable and little chats he had with friends on his cellphone. The contrast in his manner, as he alternated between these two conversations, one in Dakhni, the other in English, was striking. He was fluent in both languages, but where he was guarded and wary in English, he was bonelessly relaxed in Dakhni. When his electrician finally arrived to fix his geyser, he was reproached with a smile. Azhar spoke to all the workmen without airs, with easy charm and camaraderie. On the phone he chattered happily and I had the sense of a man wholly at home in his skin.

English is his language of business, the language he transacts Pepsi contracts in, the language he speaks to journalists in. It is in English that he stipulates that any interviews he grants should be cover stories. Don't run it at all if you're going to do it on the inside pages, he told me. If it isn't on the cover, there's nothing in it for me. In retrospect, I can see that he was within his rights to ask, but at the time it seemed vaguely repellent that someone as celebrated as Azhar should ask to have his face on a cover. Surely the point of celebrity was that it happened unbidden. He looked shuttered and assessing as he led me through his ground rules, light years from the lithe, smiling man that my son worshipped on the cricket field. Nonplussed, I said that I'd talk to the editor.

Months later, as I watched him play a brilliant comeback innings in the Test against South Africa in Bangalore, my son and I clapped for his century till our hands ached. After watching dour roundheads like Tendulkar and Dravid struggle through that disastrous series in Australia, it was wonderful to watch a cavalier bat. Meeting him had been a mistake, for the same reason that it is a mistake to watch great sportsmen on television doing commentary. They're mostly not as good talking into the camera as they were playing into it, unless they're exceptions like Boycott or Amritraj. In person, Azhar was a bit like modern Hyderabad: once provincial, but now celebrated and very nearly metropolitan. Back in whites, though, he was that singular, dashing, wholly original batsman we had all known and loved on the telly for a decade and a half—the One and Only, New and Improved, Mohammad Azizuddin Azharuddin.

Style and Azharuddin

This article was a sequel to the Azharuddin interview. It was written some months later (he was still an active international cricketer) when I was trying to find the words to explain Azhar's manner, both on the field and off it. Then it came to me: Azhar was an example, an illustration, of the Indian take on 'ishtyle'.

When I met Azharuddin for the first time, he was out of the Indian team, playing first-class cricket after a long time, he had moved into a new house in Hyderabad as a token of his commitment to the first-class game and he wanted publicity. He was open about it: he said he had consented to the interview because he had been given to believe that he would be on the cover.

The magazine ran the story as a profile and didn't put him on the cover. The photos used with the article were archive snaps because by the time it was published, Azhar was back in the team and didn't have time for a photo-op. The last time I saw him was on the cover of a newsmagazine. Cronje had just fingered him and Azhar was where he had wanted to be: on the cover of every magazine in the country.

The man who had helped arrange my interview with Azhar was an avuncular figure in Azhar's life. He remembered the Himayat Nagar lad who had broken windows (his windows, not folkloric ones!) playing cricket. He remembered the time he woke up one morning and realized Azhar was famous: that once gawky lad was sitting on the swing in the front yard of his house, all made up for filming.

For a shy man, Azhar loves the camera. He loves it like moviegoers do: in a star-struck way. Think of pictures of Azhar in civvies: shades, raised collar, generically expensive threads. When Sangeeta Bijlani figures in the pictures, she is generally snuggled up to him, but Azhar's always looking directly into the camera, straight into it, oblivious of his wife except as a celebrity accessory (like his shades), hypnotized by the stardom it represents.

The camera doesn't love him but that, ironically, is because his on-field manner is a parody of filmi swagger, his sketchy stab at ishtyle. When I met him in real life, I was struck by how *built* he was. It doesn't show on the cricket field because the litheness and grace are obscured by Azhar's patented shamble: slightly crouched, his shoulders raised, his arms dangling at distance from his sides like limp brackets, that asymmetric stiff-legged walk that looks like a limp but isn't . . . it's Hyderabadi hip, tapori chic, Himayat Nagar's take on cricketing cool. When he runs between wickets, he holds the bat halfway down the blade and when he runs in from close in to the wicket on the off-side, he picks up the ball and flips it, palm out, to the keeper. I've never seen him hit the stumps with it or even get it in quickly enough to threaten the batsman trying to make the crease; he does it because it's part of his cricketing manner, his trademark flourish.

Style's important in Indian cricket in a particular sense of that word. Style in this context doesn't mean method or manner or way of playing. When an Indian commentator, fan, journalist or spectator says a player has style, he almost always uses it in the other sense of the word: flair, dash, panache, elan.

In this use of the word, Viswanath is a stylish batsman but Gavaskar is not. Style here means flourish, that little twirl of Vishy's wrists as he magicked the ball in the arc between square-leg and midwicket, the more extravagant loop of Azhar's bat that helps massage balls from outside the off stump into vacant spaces on the leg side, style means the firm-footed cover drive Ganguly plays, leaning into the ball so he completes the stroke on one knee . . . shot, sir!

Style also means swagger, extravagance, attitude . . . Salim Durrani had style: he was attractive in a large, light-eyed way (so long as you didn't hear his startling soprano voice), but more importantly, he was an eccentrically aggressive batsman who took a disc jockey view of cricket: he gave his audiences the hits they wanted. So if you asked for a sixer when Durrani was batting, he'd oblige you with one . . . or perish trying.

Pataudi had style too: the cap raked over his eye (to cut out double vision, but who knew at the time), the nawab thing, the Oxford thing, the romance of having wooed and won Sharmila Tagore, the piratical glamour of his one-eyed batsmanship; he had enough style for the whole team. And since he played for Hyderabad and captained India and is a Muslim, it doesn't take much imagination to compare the two. But it's a bad, unfair juxtaposition because Pataudi wasn't a Hyderabadi and his wife wasn't a starlet and for Indian cricket's middle class following Tiger's career is a fairy story while Azhar's threatens to become a cautionary tale.

The only way of making sense of Azharuddin's career is to see it as a quest story with style as its holy grail. It helps explain his life choices, the changes in his batsmanship and his relationship with his diversified but cricket-centred world. It's an approach that works for other players—not all of them, but some. Take Vinod Kambli. He is the definitive example of the corrosive triumph of style over substance.

Sachin Tendulkar and Vinod Kambli, as all India knows, are both pupils of the legendary coach Ramakant Achrekar. They attended the same school and played school cricket and first-class cricket for the same teams. Sachin got to the Test team first on the strength of his prodigious talent but when Kambli followed suit, a few years later, his record in his first few Tests eclipsed Tendulkar's. He hit two double centuries in back-to-back Tests besides a one-day century in Jaipur. If Sachin is middle class in his origins, Kambli's background is more straitened. As Kambli said in the first flush of his Test success, Sachin took the elevator to the top while Kambli had to take the stairs.

Except that he never reached the top. Kambli's successes came against mediocre opposition on flat pitches. He was a decent left-hander with dodgy footwork (so what's new?) and a problem with the short-pitched ball. Gore Vidal cruelly said of Solzhenitsyn's massive novels, that they showed us how Tolstoy might have read without the genius. Kambli, you could plausibly argue, is Lara without the same. Kambli could have tightened up and become a less ambitious, more reliable middle order batsman, but he bet the house on style.

Style for Kambli meant both flourish and attitude. On the one hand, there was the extravagant shot making outside the off stump from the start of the innings, the wilful belief that idiosyncratic style could stand in for sound technique. It has worked for some: Majid Khan was a great opening batsman minus footwork and very little that Jayasuriya does has any connection with a straight bat. But it didn't work for Kambli because the hand-eye coordination that separates the Majids and Jaysuriyas from the ordinarily competent just wasn't there. Kambli needed to work on his technique and moderate his ambition, but he did neither. He worked instead, on his manner: there was the jewellery, the shaven head, the Sobers-like twirling of the bat, the over-the-top crowd pleasing on the field. It didn't work: all the style together didn't add up to runs on the board. It's a depressing truth: you can't be a stylish genius without genius.

Azhar, on the other hand, is a genius—not the master Lara is, but as good or better than Gower who, everyone agrees, is Minor Genius Grade I. Unlike Kambli, Azhar served a long apprenticeship to discipline before he committed himself to flamboyant aggression. And it worked: he sometimes got out in irresponsible ways, but the stylish fireworks came off often enough to keep his batting average in the high forties. For Azhar, in purely cricketing terms, the change of gear from being a conscientious if wristy batsman to an explosive entertainer paid off.

His problem was that he wanted to leverage this new cricketing flamboyance into a more glamorous persona. He didn't want to be the nice provincial Muslim lad any more. From the movie mannerisms young Indian men affect—the turned up collar, the walk, the haircut—Azhar made an unusual move for a cricketer: he made a bid to live the life. It is the difference between imitating the flash street-cool of the *Rangeela* character and actually wanting to be Aamir Khan. In India there's just one model for the metropolitan bon vivant: the Bollywood star, so Azhar married an actress and began living like a hero. Multiple Mercedes cars, plural plots, designer threads, platinum watches . . . this wonderfully original batsman chose to buy a derivative lifestyle, which consisted mainly of acquiring extremely expensive things.

He is probably the first Indian cricketer who could afford to try. Azhar's career, unlike the careers of earlier stars like Gavaskar and Kapil Dev, coincided with the great financial boom in Indian cricket, when advertising money poured in because of television. And he was India's best batsman for a while and then its captain for ten years. Tendulkar apart, no one benefited more than Azhar did: he became Pepsi's mascot. He is the only cricketer, besides Tendulkar, who had a Pepsi commercial all to himself. It's the one about the team photograph, where the cardboard cutouts of cricketers around Azhar keep changing but he remains constant, the eternal international, smiling and swigging Pepsi.

It's a lovely commercial, affectionate and funny, the best Azhar has ever done, and he carries off the cool durable dude with some style. But commercials aren't real life. Azhar is thirty-seven. He doesn't have that much time left at the international level and that's where the money is. The money that pays for the hero's lifestyle comes from commercials and sponsorships and both dry up when you aren't a contender.

You'd think Azhar and Sangeeta could retire on what he's made: money in the bank, lots of real estate. But you can't retire a lifestyle. How much is enough? Nothing is. Try to remember that Shah Rukh Khan dances at private parties to put money by (he says) for his son or a rainy day. So did he cross the line, this ageing athlete, in his search for sustainable style? Despite the creepy Cronje, I'm not sure that we'll ever know.

The irony is that having walked out of his marriage and risked estrangement from his natal family to reinvent himself, to make that metaphorical journey from Hyderabad to Bombay, to shed the skin of the pious provincial and morph into the big city dasher, Azhar now struggles with ghettoes in other people's minds. In the scuttlebutt collected by Manoj Prabhakar (former teammates and officials darkly imputing Gulf connections with underworld Muslims) Azhar detects sectarian prejudice. He's daft enough to say so. He immediately becomes the Muslim playing the minority card and is enthusiastically attacked by everyone from Bal Thackeray to

Javed Akhtar. He apologizes and retreats into silence.

Soon after this, the RSS house magazine accuses Shah Rukh, Aamir and Salman of being part of a Muslim conspiracy to dominate Bollywood. Gulf money and the reliable Muslim underworld are trotted out again as proofs of this large Khan design. Poor Hrithik Roshan (engaged to Suzanne Khan!) becomes the vanguard of the Hindutvawadi campaign against the dark side.

Azhar is learning what many desis have learnt before him: when push comes to shove, style's no substitute for identity. Often (mercifully, not always), who you are is what we think you are.

The Small Enforcer: Sachin Tendulkar

Had J.M. Barrie needed a cricketer for Neverland, he might have dreamt up Sachin Tendulkar. No player was more perfectly designed to be the eternal prodigy. He's so much the boy that it's hard for us to let him grow into a man. After seventeen years as a Test cricketer, after marriage and two children, when he explained his recent, more accumulative batting style as a symptom of sporting maturity, we refused to take him seriously. That light treble voice, that round-faced enthusiasm . . . how could their owner claim the alibi of age? Good reasons like injury, luck and human error are inadmissible when Tendulkar fails us. I was thirty-two to his sixteen when he made his Test debut and I still expect to live through him the brilliant youth I never had.

B atsmen aren't remembered only for their shots; you remember them for their mannerisms, their stance, their physical presence. I remember Gavaskar for the military snap with which he shouldered arms, both pads together, bat raised high. I can't recall him shaping to play and then withdrawing the bat: there was a crisp, lucid certainty to everything he did which made him the great classical batsman of our time. I remember him for the compact grace that informed his presence at the crease, from taking guard to settling into his stance.

Tendulkar is different. He's about as tall as Gavaskar is, they're both Bombay batsmen and compared to someone like Lara, Tendulkar seems correct, even orthodox, but he and Gavaskar are chalk and cheese. Tendulkar can produce the most wonderful shots, but you wouldn't call him a beautiful batsman. Graceful he is not, in any conventional reading of the term. His defining mannerism at the crease is, in the words of the writer Ruchir Joshi, the 'signature crotch yank as he adjusts his abdomen guard.' He can look oddly clumsy for a great batsman: when the ball keeps low Tendulkar will jackknife into an exaggerated half squat, like someone who has just discovered that he urgently needs to go. When he plays forward, he is correct, but always in a slightly over-produced way: his defensive play lacks the clockwork economy of Gavaskar's technique. The ratio of bat to body in Tendulkar's case makes it hard for him to look pretty: he's so small and the bat is so large that it looks more like an accomplice than an instrument. Laxman, long and languid, pulls and hooks in an easy, upright way; when Tendulkar pulls, he looks like a small enforcer with a big cosh.

Tendulkar has a claim to being the greatest batsman in the world because he is that rare thing: an original. Gavaskar at his best used to make the classical prescriptions come to life; Tendulkar's genius lies in the impossible shots he hits off perfectly good balls. Not impossible in the sense of outrageous and chancy—men like Jayasuriya own that corner of the market; no, impossible because he hits shots mortal cricketers wouldn't attempt, and because he makes those shots look safe, even plausible, when they are not.

I have in mind the range of off-drives he plays to balls pitched on a good length or short of a good length without width on offer. He seems to stand up straight without doing much with his front foot, the bat comes down in a little arc and then stops well short of a follow through. The scene ends with incredulous bowler staring at Tendulkar and cover fielder trotting off on peon duty, resigned to a game of fetch. Something similar happens with his attenuated straight drive that shaves the stumps at the bowler's end on the way to the boundary. It's not the straightness of it (straight drives, after all, are meant to be hit straight!) but the lack of obvious effort or risk which makes the shot a bowler killer. When Lara hits you straight, the bat describes such a flamboyant arc that it's like being lashed with a whip; Tendulkar's down-the-wicket shot is more like being heavily nudged by a barn door. When he hits that straight drive, his bat is at once shield and bludgeon and as the ball speeds past the blameless bowler, Tendulkar must seem both irresistible force and immovable object.

And then there are those other shots: the upper-cuff over slips and gully, the inside-out shot driven through or over cover, the paddle sweep hit so perpendicularly that it finishes as a reverse straight drive completed on one knee, the pull off the front foot hit brutally over midwicket; the trajectory-defying flick that turns the ball on the off-stump or outside, through midwicket—what these strokes have in common is that they are difficult and dangerous shots, methodically and safely played. That's why bowlers in their follow through sometimes stare at Tendulkar as if he has grown another head: he makes unlikely shots look reasonable. It's this straight-bat magic that got Graeme Hick to turn out to captain his county, Worcestershire, against India in an unimportant tour match: he said he just wanted to stand at slip and watch Tendulkar play.

Tendulkar's remarkable repertoire of shots, his style of play, grows out of a particular temperament and a peculiar talent. Tendulkar himself has often said that he is by nature an attacking batsman. This is true, but in itself it tells us little about what makes him special. Jayasuriya is an attacking batsman by instinct, as are Ponting and that cheerful murderer, Gilchrist, and they're very different from Tendulkar. Gilchrist, on present form, is the best batsman in the world. With a batting average over 60 and a strike rate that makes bowlers feel they're bowling in the highlights segment of the evening news, Gilchrist on song can make Tendulkar look low key. The difference between the two isn't one of talent—indeed, if Gilchrist can bat like this and stay at sixty-plus, he and not Tendulkar will be remembered as the great turn-of-the-century batsman. The difference is temperamental. Gilchrist bats in a wholly carefree way; coming in at six or seven in Test matches, he subjects all bowlers in every situation to his brand of assault and battery. Perhaps it has to do with the confidence of coming in low in the batting order of a great team, perhaps being a wicketkeeper batsman with more than one string to his bow frees him of the fear of failure; whatever it is, it makes his demeanour at the crease very different from Tendulkar's.

No Indian cricketer, not Tendulkar, not even the inimitable Kapil Dev, has survived cricketing glory in this country over a whole career without becoming careworn, and Tendulkar isn't a product of the Bombay school of batsmanship for nothing. However different they may be from one another, the great Bombay batsmen distrust extravagance or flourish. Like Gilchrist, Tendulkar will, most times, try to impose himself on the bowling; unlike him, he will discriminate between bowlers, change his game to suit the moment, come up with novelties like a grandmaster discovering a new wrinkle in an old gambit. In the first Test of India's tour to South Africa, Tendulkar hit one of the great hundreds in recent years. At the start of that innings, he hit Makhaya Ntini for 16 runs in an over, with three boundaries. One of these was tipped over slips simply because there was no third man. It seemed a zero-percentage play given how many slips there were, but it became the trademark shot of this particular innings. They kept bowling short outside the off stump to him and he kept cuffing the ball in the air down to third man for four. And he did this, as he does everything, in a calculated, methodical way and in so doing, he made a bizarre shot seem like business as usual. Throughout this masterful knock, Tendulkar continuously showed intent, an aggression unalloyed by doggedness or care. It was a rare moment in his recent career where we were allowed to see genius expressing itself unburdened by responsibility.

Tendulkar padded up is usually a mass of inhibitions. His face is carefully inexpressive, but through the visor you can see his eyeballs virtually disappearing into his skull, so massively concentrated is he through an innings. In the course of every long innings he plays, you can see the tension build and then find release in shot making. The weight of responsibility, the fear of letting his side and his country down will sometimes have him leaving every ball bowled an inch outside the off stump alone, as he did against McGrath in Australia, before exploding into a flurry of shots once he was set. That innings was cruelly terminated by an idiot umpire (this happens to Tendulkar a lot—not many umpires want to give genius the benefit of doubt), but most innings he plays are a bit like that one: his runs come in clusters, not in a steady stream, his innings are made up of explosive episodes. Unlike Gavaskar, inevitability isn't the hallmark of a long innings by Tendulkar. A century by him is an odd mixture of calm and storm. His greatest innings, of course, specially his hundreds in one-day matches, are simply single long violent spasms. They have become rarer, those extended bursts of berserker brilliance, because he is too much the Bombay batsman to be prodigal. So sometimes you'll see him curb his shot making, mainly in the interests of the team, but also because he wants to prove to himself and his audience that he can play with puritanical self-denial. The perfect example of such a knock was his century at Chepauk during the third Test against the Australians in 2001. It was a dour, unlovely innings, all Bombay solidity, but it won India the match.

So much for temperament. What is Tendulkar's special talent? Every bowler who has ever sent down an over to him says the same thing when asked for a sound bite on what makes Tendulkar the best batsman in the contemporary game. To a man, they say this: 'He picks up the length of the ball earlier than anyone in the modern game so he has more time than his peers to make the shot.' There is such unanimity on this that it must be true. In his prime, Tendulkar used the time that his eyes bought him in the cause of aggression. He would get into position early for that perpendicular paddle sweep, skip down the wicket for the lofted drive over straight mid-on, or advance while making room to drive a spinner inside-out over extra cover. His batting average soared and it took the combined efforts of McGrath, Australian umpiring and some wretched luck (the miraculous catch that Ponting took at Wankhede Stadium in 2001 off Tendulkar's pull after it ricocheted off short leg's back is a prime example) to bring him down to earth.

Even so, his career Test average had risen to 58 and was threatening to touch 60 when Nasser Hussain came to town. Hussain had a plan for Tendulkar, a plan of great simplicity. The way to keep Tendulkar from scoring runs was to bowl wide of him. Marx memorably said that everything in history happened twice: first as tragedy and the second time as farce. Well, in this replay of leg theory, a boy born in Madras played Jardine, a left-arm spinner stood in for Larwood and

Tendulkar, against his will, was cast as Bradman. Amazingly, the ploy sort of worked: it frustrated Tendulkar to the extent of getting him stumped for the first time in his Test career. And the reason it worked was this: Tendulkar tried to wait the bowlers out as Gavaskar might have done, but this game of patience and attrition didn't come naturally to him. At the same time, being a Bombay batsman and not being Gilchrist, he hated the thought of being forced into unorthodoxy and extravagance. It was the same story in the first Test of the 2002 Test series in England when run-saving sweeper fielders and cynically wide bowling goaded him into error. In between these two Test series with England was a run of single-digit scores during the tour of the West Indies. No permanent damage was done, as the fine 90 in the second Test in England showed, but the fact that he fell in the nineties dimmed his aura a watt or two.

Right now, Tendulkar is a great batsman who doesn't scare the opposition. It's as if the fact that he sees the ball so early has begun to work against him: he has almost too much time to play the ball and he uses it to think and fret instead of using it to attack the bowling. There is a tense premeditation to his play these days which is different from the calculated aggression we used to see earlier. Viv Richards said after his failures on the tour of the Caribbean that Tendulkar didn't seem to be enjoying his cricket. Perhaps he is right. Perhaps the master should learn from his protégé. Perhaps Tendulkar could take a leaf out of Sehwag's carefree book: he could stop being Atlas and just go with the flow.

Kumble, or the Style with No Name

Cricket's specialist vocabulary is elaborate and it grows all the time. I can think of half a dozen terms that entered the game during my career as a fan. Reverse sweep, flipper, reverse swing, doosra, silly point, paddle sweep, pinch hitter, upper cut . . . all of these were invented to describe cricketing innovations for which no terms existed. But the terms for classifying bowlers remained inflexible, which meant that originals like Chandrasekhar and Kumble, who didn't fit the available pigeon-holes, didn't get their due. In the essay below, I try to find the proper words for naming Kumble.

Five hundred wickets into his career, you might think Kumble would have cricket writers rummaging through their memories, trying to fix his place in the history of Indian cricket. Not a bit of it; what we have instead are character sketches. A loyal servant of Indian cricket (not a Master of the Universe like Tendulkar), a gentle giant off the field, a raging elephant on it, all determination, all heart, willing to bowl all day, a slow bowler with a fast bowler's aggression, a team man, the perfect senior pro, modest, never got the recognition he deserved, Old Reliable and so on, endlessly as if Kumble's career were an experiment run for sixteen years to prove that character is destiny.

This idea, that what a person does, his behaviour, his

achievements, spring from who he is, his nature, has long been a basic assumption of the realist novel. That's why book reviews so often turn on how a novel's characters are drawn, whether they are believable, vivid, rounded or not, because the plausibility of the novel and its action depends on the quality of its characterization. A version of this idea rules thinking and writing about cricket.

Since cricketers and cricket writers aren't nineteenth-century novelists, their use of this master concept is inconsistent and rudimentary. Character can mean nature, as in 'I played my natural game'. When Kapil Dev said on an early tour of England, 'Ah play mah way,' he meant that he gave free rein to his essentially aggressive nature. When a commentator says that a player played his natural game, he's almost always referring to a fast-scoring batsman, someone like Viv Richards or Virender Sehwag. Theoretically, it's possible for people to say Trevor Bailey played his natural game and scored nothing in three sessions, but they seldom do because in this usage, nature or natural means raw or wild talent untamed by coaches and their orthodoxy.

At other times, 'character' in cricket is used to mean the opposite of natural talent. Thus, when Nasser Hussain and Duncan Fletcher talk about wanting players with character in their teams, they mean that they'd rather have tough professional players with a modicum of talent who'll deliver day after day to the best of their limited ability than wayward geniuses. When cricket writers line up to praise Kumble as a man of character, they mean it in this, special sense of the word. It's a backhanded compliment because 'character' here is a consolation prize, a substitute for great talent or genius. Character in this case is what allows journeymen to maximize, occasionally transcend, their natural potential.

The tributes to Kumble after he won the Test for India at

Mohali and scaled the 500-wicket mountain, were at once sincere and patronizing. Kumble is universally admired; like his Karnataka teammate, Dravid, he seems cultivated, intelligent, poised, kind, well spoken, one of nature's gentlemen. A newspaper report called him a stalwart, another a veteran, one profile described him as 'untiring', 'resilient' and said that there was no 'harder trier' in cricket. It went on to suggest that a proper leg break would have made him the perfect bowler. Yes. He'd have been celebrating a thousand wickets with a proper leg break.

Actually, that's unfair. It's reasonable to expect a leg break bowler to bowl leg breaks. Kumble does occasionally spin the ball away, but not in the normal course. On the other hand, I can think of many wrist-spinners with a proper leg break—Narendra Hirwani, Laxman Sivaramakrishnan, Mushtaq Ahmed, even the great Abdul Qadir—who weren't conspicuously more successful than Kumble. When commentators try to address this issue—how does a wrist-spinner without a leg break get 500 wickets—the default answer is strength of character, the component parts of which are the above-mentioned resilience, effort and tirelessness.

This is a mistake; a failure of the imagination brought on by an addiction to 'character', a lazy reliance on orthodox definitions and an unwillingness to think historically.

Kumble hasn't got 500 wickets because he's a defective leg break bowler who makes up for his shortcomings with will; he's got 500 wickets because he's a supremely good fast top-spin/googly bowler in a young Indian tradition of spin bowling. The inability, the unwillingness to recognize this, is what made Kumble say, resignedly, that even after 500 wickets, commentators are sceptical about his methods, constantly counselling him to toss the ball up, slow down, achieve drift, bowl like some leg spinning archetype.

This obtuseness is understandable in cricket writers from abroad; it's unforgivable in any Indian writer who has seen Chandrasekhar bowl. Kumble and Chandrasekhar are different bowlers in the same way as Abdul Qadir and Shane Warne are different bowlers. But Kumble is exactly the same *sort* of bowler that Chandrasekhar was. Kumble has done his best to make the connection. He said in an interview that he found no help or counsel from any spin bowler except Chandrasekhar. The reason Chandrasekhar had useful advice to give was that he recognized in Kumble something of himself.

What the two of them have in common isn't 'nature' or 'character' but a technique, an art, that for want of a name is described as leg break bowling because whatever it is that they did, they did it by turning their wrists over. Chandrasekhar was genial, carefree, famously fond of Mukesh's songs and allegedly unaware of which way the ball was going to turn; Kumble is all focus, intent and grim purpose. But both made the ball bounce and shoot and made batsmen look foolish by flicking off their bails as they shouldered arms. If we learn to recognize Chandrasekhar and Kumble as pioneers, their common art can be passed on as a new genre of 'slow' bowling; if we persist in reading it as an aberrant form of the leg spinner's art, their astonishing achievement will be written off as a mutant dead end and peter out. Kumble is, as Chandrasekhar was, an original, not a wannabe leg break bowler.

Chandrasekhar, whose descendant Kumble is, was seen as a mutant, a freak. His right arm withered by polio, his style was described as a function of his disability. His temperament, conveniently for cricket writers, fitted this freakishness. So where Bedi's success was attributable to skill and guile, Chandrasekhar's was a natural phenomenon untouched by thought. Ironically, Kumble and Chandrasekhar have both been condescended to for very different reasons: Kumble because his commitment is seen to make up for his technical limitations and Chandrasekhar because his success was put down to polio! That Chandrasekhar has lived with this demeaning myth for forty years says more about cricket writing than it does about Chandrasekhar.

This slide from stereotype to patronage is a chronic part of cricket writing. We see the story playing itself out again in the context of neo-off break bowling. Saqlain Mushtaq invented the doosra and Muralitharan perfected it. You can differ about the doosra's legality (though I can't see how it can be bowled without straightening the arm), but now that the ICC has anointed it with fifteen degrees of latitude, we need to recognize that this is a new form of off break bowling because it isn't finger spun: the bowler needs to turn his wrist over. The willingness to explain novelty as aberration persists. Ironically, Murali's defenders, anxious to shield him from the charge of chucking, argue that his ability to bowl the doosra and turn the off break as much as he does has to do with freakishly flexible wrists and a congenitally bent elbow. The peculiarities of Muralitharan's arm may well have some bearing on his style, but they don't explain it, or exhaust its possibilities. If we assume that the fifteen degree rule is here to stay, then we can see from the example of Harbhajan and Saqlain (both equipped with standard issue arms) that off break bowling has been remade and this new style needs to be understood and taught on its own terms.

Part of Kumble's trouble has been that he has shared his time at the top with Warne, the leg spinner's leg spinner. Warne, thanks to his accuracy, his ability to turn the leg-break square, to use the rough, to drift the ball in and move it out, his flipper, his talent for terrifying batsmen who don't play for India, has defined the modern leg spinner's menu and Kumble doesn't offer most of the items listed there. This is because he isn't a leg spinner, but the inability to take in that fact is, of course, the problem. When writers compare him to Warne, they marvel at how much Kumble has achieved with no flight, no leg spin, no drift, no guile, just bloody-minded perseverance. They don't mean to patronize him, but an error of classification automatically leads to condescension.

Luckily Chandrasekhar took nearly 250 wickets and we're celebrating Kumble's 500. Their style of bowling will ultimately be judged by the statistics it leaves behind. Numbers aren't everything, but it's hard to patronize 10 wickets in an innings without looking silly . . . which didn't stop Warne from trying. After Kumble got all 10, Warne supplied his gloss on the achievement by observing that the other bowlers in the Indian team couldn't have been doing their jobs. It was a silly, unworthy thing to say, but it was half true, though not in the way Warne intended it. Unlike Warne, Kumble's never had a McGrath-like bowler as a siege engine, making the breach each time for him to storm through; in spite of that he's got to 500 in roughly the same number of Tests as Warne did.

Now that he's there, it's about time someone invented a name for what he does and what Chandrasekhar did before him. If it isn't right-arm leg break bowling, then what is it? Till it has a name of its own, it'll forever be mistaken for something else. I'm open to suggestions. The name should be in keeping with the vocabulary that cricket uses to name styles of bowling and it should indicate that Kumble and Chandrasekhar's methods are unconventional. Right-Arm Heterodox, perhaps?

Extravagantly Sound: Rahul Dravid

I look forward to some bilious critic attacking Rahul Dravid. It'll make for a change. The press he gets is so fawningly good; it would embarrass a North Korean despot. I set out to write a hard-nosed, unillusioned assessment of an overrated batsman . . . and look what emerged.

Rahul Dravid is a paragon, the arch-gent of modern cricket. He's urbane, modest, resolute, dependable, well spoken and he even has a decent line in self-deprecation. Asked in an interview, after a day's play during which he had completed a solid century, if he planned to go after Lara's new record, he laughed and instinctively came up with the graceful answer: 'For me to get 400,' he said, 'you would have to play a six-day Test match.'

But is he a great batsman? That's the big question, and there is a flotilla of other, more specific questions that follow it in close formation. Is he the greatest batsman ever to represent India? Does he have a claim to being the greatest batsman in the world today? If Rahul Dravid gets to an average of 60 (at 58.75 per innings, he's within a double century of it) and retires at the big Six-O, will the statistical weight of this achievement allow him to lay claim to being the greatest batsman of the last twenty-five years, greater than Tendulkar, Lara, Waugh, Gavaskar, Richards even?

Consistency at a very high level is an important part of being a great batsman: it's why V.V.S. Laxman will never be one. To play sublime innings every now and then isn't enough. On this score, Dravid is the most dependable batsman India has ever produced, statistically more reliable than Gavaskar, which is a staggering achievement. I would argue that Gavaskar faced the greater challenges: he opened the batting against better fast bowlers without a helmet, but a batsman can only play to the conditions he's given so that can't be held against Dravid. You could also argue that Tendulkar in his pomp averaged roughly what Dravid does today and he made those runs at a greater rate. Morever, to compare the figures of a completed career against one that's still a work in progress is misleading: averages taper off towards the end of a player's span and it is possible that two or three years from now Dravid's average will hover around the mid-50s as Tendulkar's does, or, if he ekes his career out too long, the early 50s, which is where Gavaskar ended his wonderful career. Still, the fact that a pessimistic career forecast has Dravid *declining* to Gavaskar's statistical level, says something about the height at which he currently stands.

On nearly every count, Dravid's record is outstanding. He has by far the best record for an Indian batsman away from home, a crucial statistic for a team that's notoriously shaky at dealing with foreign conditions. He has played a string of big decisive innings in the course of the last five years that have won Test matches for India abroad, most recently the two fifties he made in the summer of 2006 on an eccentric pitch to see India home in the West Indies.

But figures aren't everything. If they were, we wouldn't be asking the question we started with. Nobody asks it of Lara or Tendulkar any more; we know they're great batsmen. So why—despite the massive consistency of his record—do we not take Dravid's greatness for granted?

The simple answer is that Dravid has played all his cricket in the shadow of Tendulkar, regarded by many critics as the greatest batsman in the history of Indian cricket. By the time Dravid began playing Test cricket, Tendulkar was a Test star of seven years' standing. If the early nineties belonged to Lara, the second half of the decade was Tendulkar's. The seal on Tendulkar's pre-eminence was affixed by Bradman himself when he observed that Tendulkar's batsmanship resembled his own. Coming out from under Tendulkar's shadow was made even more difficult by the fact that this grizzled veteran was younger than Dravid. It is natural for a young batsman to supersede the champion of the previous generation, as Tendulkar replaced Azharuddin. But prodigies like Tendulkar upset this sequence: a year older than the great Mumbaikar, it must have sometimes seemed to Dravid that he had been sentenced to second fiddle for life.

But through the last five years, Dravid, by sheer weight of runs, has been the most valuable batsman in the Indian side. That his peak has coincided with a relative decline in Tendulkar's performance has underlined his pre-eminence. Journalists and commentators everywhere have acknowledged with respect and admiration Dravid's achievement, but there has been no rush to celebrate the arrival of a new 'great'. This is partly because Dravid, having been around for ten years, isn't a new meteor in the night sky. It is the fate of low-profile high performers to be taken for granted.

Dravid is a great defensive batsman and the label 'great' is generally applied to batsmen who dominate the bowling, whose preferred style, as with Lara and Tendulkar, is attack, not attrition. Attacking batsmen are sexier than defensive ones. The absolute truth of this can be demonstrated by a thought experiment. Sehwag opens the innings and falls early.

Dravid walks in at his usual position at number three. Then the spectators notice long hair under the helmet and realize that Chappell has promoted Dhoni. The crowd erupts, the stadium begins to fill, viewers everywhere put their lives on hold in anticipation of mayhem. And this is Dhoni, a cheerful Afridiesque brute, who makes no claim to higher batsmanship. Had Tendulkar in his pomp not walked in at his assigned position in the batting order, collective disappointment would have rustled round the arena. Not so with Dravid. Dravid will never make your pulse race; acknowledging the greatness of those who do, like Viv Richards or Tendulkar, comes more easily, more naturally.

But this can't be the whole explanation. Sunil Manohar Gavaskar played most of his innings in defensive mode and the Indian cricketing public wasted no time in hailing him as the greatest ever. This had something to do with his record-breaking debut series where he scored 776 runs in four Tests with three centuries and two half centuries. In the greatness stakes, getting off to an early start helps (as with Tendulkar) as does an explosive one (as with Gavaskar). The fact that Gavaskar was an opening batsman invested his innings with drama: there's something about an opening batsman facing down fast bowlers which is dramatic and exciting in itself. Also, Gavaskar generally closed out his centuries, unlike Dravid who through the first half of his career had the frustrating habit of getting himself out in the eighties and nineties. But even allowing for these differences, it's curious that we admire Dravid where once we stood in awe of Gavaskar.

I think the reason for this, the reason why Dravid is only just beginning to be given his due as a great batsman, has to do with his style of batsmanship. Spectators and cricket writers reserve their highest praise for batsmanship that seems effortless. The oohs that follow Tendulkar's attenuated straight drive, the high-elbow one, minus follow through, are our tributes to magic. The timing! The genius!

Dravid's batting style is the opposite of effortless. It's elaborate, flourishing and effortful and despite all that the ball doesn't rocket off his bat in the way that it does with Tendulkar or Sehwag. You seldom applaud a Dravid stroke for its power or timing. Energetic hook shots dribble over the boundary line. Drives are hit hard into the ground and nothing is ever hit on the up. Every shot is preceded by a high flourishing backlift but unlike Lara, whose backlift ends in high-risk shot making, Dravid's arabesques, more often than not, result in the ball being dropped by his feet for a single. And the man-in-a-bunker effect is exaggerated by Dravid's stance: low, dogged, sweat running off him in rivulets.

Dravid doesn't fit the categories invented by Coarse Cricket Writing to docket batsmen. Here a sound technique always implies a 'compact defence'. Well, Dravid's defence isn't compact: it's extravagant. His wrists twirl, his bat loops before the ball is disciplined into the ground. Dravid is a great batsman who can do everything: he hooks, pulls, cuts, sweeps, flicks, and drives, but his entire technique is centred on the need to make sure that the ball hits the ground first. To that end Dravid plays the ball later than any batsman in cricket; so late that more often than not the ball ricochets off an angled bat and hits the ground at a steep angle, Dravid's apparent effortfulness, his sadhu-like indifference to the sex appeal of shots hit on the up, the absence of ooh-making timing are symptoms of his decision to sacrifice power to reduce risk. The reason his shot making sometimes looks studied is because Dravid is wholly committed to the ground beneath his feet.

His methods aren't orthodox. It is important to say this if only because both critics and admirers describe him as an orthodox batsman. For example, Sambit Bal, paying tribute after Dravid had scored a series winning 270 against Pakistan in 2004 wrote: 'Dravid's batsmanship has often been taken for granted because it is so firmly rooted in orthodoxy, because it is so utterly comprehensible and so utterly lacking in mystique.'

This is well meant but wrong in every syllable. It confuses sound batsmanship with orthodox technique and it is a confusion that many commentators share. Dravid's patience, temperament, discretion in the matter of shot selection and defensive ability don't automatically add up to orthodoxy.

If orthodoxy is shorthand for the coaching manual or the prescriptions of the MCC, Dravid is the opposite of orthodox. Orthodox batsmanship is founded on economy: the straight backlift, the shortest possible arc to the point of contact. Gavaskar was, quite literally, the embodiment of orthodoxy, the coaching manual made flesh. Even the way he shouldered arms was perfect, compact, both feet together, bat raised high and out of the way.

Dravid's defensive technique, on the other hand, is extravagant. The bat describes a little scimitar loop before straightening. When he drives through extra cover off the front foot, there's an exaggerated stride to the pitch of the ball and at the end of the follow through, his wrists break, suggesting a curious bottom-handedness to the shot.

His hook is a marvel of ornateness, from the looping backlift to the almost pedantic deliberation with which he turns his wrists over the top of the ball. It's like someone acting out the coaching manual in mime. Compare his hook shot with the same stroke played by his compatriot, V.V.S. Laxman. Laxman, who is generally regarded as a lovely, wristy batsman of a distinctly 'Oriental' cast, plays the hook better than anyone in the Indian team, yet his version of the shot is economical compared to Dravid's. Dravid's wristiness, the flourish in his shot making evokes Viswanath rather than Gavaskar. He's much the taller man, so his stroke play seems less compact, but in terms of stroke production Dravid has much more in common with southern stylists like Viswanath, Laxman and Azharuddin, than he does with, say, Gavaskar or even Tendulkar. The best way of setting Dravid in the context of Indian cricket is to see him as Viswanath's technique inhabited by Gavaskar's temperament.

His technique is a genuine mystery: how does he marry these operatic methods to such orthodox ends? How does such a curlecued technique achieve such consistent results? How do these flourishing strokes come together to make him the soundest batsman in the game? I don't know. But I do know that attributing his soundness to orthodoxy misses the point and ignores the singularity of his achievement.

It's impossible for a lay viewer to know how a great player achieves his effects, but for what it is worth, I think the flourish in Dravid's batting is a way of finding balance and delaying the decision to play till the last possible second. Watching him bat is like watching the movement of an old-fashioned clock: the pendulum counting off its arcs, the gears and levers moving in perfect, elaborate accord to strike the hour when it's due and not a second earlier.

Style and idiosyncrasy in cricket is associated with attacking batsmanship. Dravid teaches us that batsmen can be defensively sound in an original way. Someone should break his technique down into its component parts so it can be taught to others at a time when defensive techniques are atrophying. Tendulkar has been hit by the ball more often than I can count and Sehwag without a helmet wouldn't last the length of a Test match. Dravid almost never gets hit by the fast men. More than any batsman playing today, Dravid can be compared with the greats of the pre-helmet epoch because you know that he owes his runs to his technical genius, not the insurance he wears on his head. Rahul Dravid is thirty-four years old; we should enjoy him while we can. When he gets to that 60 average (as he will) the world will chorus his greatness; but those of us who share a country with him, should start singing now.

Learning to Love Ganguly

Australian and English players, journalists and their cricket establishments detested Ganguly because he didn't mind winding them up: he lacked deference. Lots of Indians disliked him because they valued discretion and modesty in a player and Ganguly had mislaid his reticence gene. Because Ganguly had no ambitions in the 'good chap', 'stout fellow' department, he felt free to be his own man as a captain: unparochial, loyal to the players he thought were good, willing to back his hunches. He had neither Imran's authoritative hauteur, nor Ranatunga's smiling, beatific ruthlessness, but his talent for in-your-face insolence that served India well through his captaincy.

Each time England or Australia toured India during Ganguly's captaincy, the cricket season became the hunting season as well. Ganguly was the fox and the hacks who followed the touring cricketers about were the hunt, riding to hounds. It became something of a ritual. When Waugh's Australians toured India earlier, print and broadcast journalists in the touring party, notably Ian Chappell and Malcolm Conn, became fixated on Ganguly and his wickedness. Later, when the English toured, Nasser Hussain was cast in the role Steve Waugh had essayed earlier: Leader of Men. You had to have someone playing the archetypal leader of men if Ganguly's inadequacies were to be properly highlighted.

One English journalist wrote that given Ganguly's record of indiscipline, he was qualified to lead a brat pack, not men. Another, Michael Henderson of the *Daily Telegraph*, cited Ganguly's seven punishments at the hands of match referees and asked with ponderous irony: 'Some leader of men, eh?' The first thing to notice is how grown men go on about leaders of men without self-consciousness or embarrassment. The English are peculiarly susceptible to this Boys Own Paper idiom because the English in general and English cricket journalists in particular have a head boy view of hierarchy.

Nasser Hussain by general acclamation was a leader of men. The reason he made a good head boy while Ganguly didn't is because Hussain understood that authority was handed down from above. Speaking to Derek Pringle about the Denness affair, Hussain said: 'The way the world works is that you have your bosses and your guv'nors who run things and the ICC runs cricket. The sooner everyone realizes that the ICC runs the game as it should be run, the better. The two gentlemen who are running the ICC are doing a fine job. Everyone must understand who is running the show and everyone should adhere to what the governing body says.' Lord Maclaurin couldn't have put the case for the headmaster better. And had Hussain tugged his forelock any harder, he'd have yanked his hair out.

Within this sad, twilit, deferential world populated by guv'nors (!), bosses, head boys and fags, obedience is a kind of religion. The decisions of constituted authority demand complete submission. This is particularly true of English cricket writers. Theirs not to reason why.

Stephen Brenkley of the *Independent* defended the ICC rule that disallowed appeals against the match referee's decisions because the right to appeal would let lawyers into the game. His piece was such a perfect instance of the English cricket correspondent leaping to uphold the sacred right of the powers that be to cock-up that it cries out to be quoted at length.

'The case of Arjuna Ranatunga,' he wrote, 'taught cricket that harsh lesson. Ranatunga infamously led his players to the edge of the pitch after Muttiah Muralitharan was called (wrongly) for throwing in a one-day international between Sri Lanka and England in Adelaide in 1999. The match was eventually restarted but was played in a spirit of outright acrimony. When the match referee, Peter van der Merwe, tried to impose punishments the Sri Lankans brought in the lawyers. The upshot was that only superficial penalties were imposed. That was a bad day for the game.'

For Brenkley, the fact that Muralitharan was wrongly called for throwing by an umpire (which might have unfairly ended a great career) wasn't infamous; it was the Sri Lankan captain's spirited defence of his bowler that outraged him! Brenkley was disappointed that the Sri Lankan players couldn't be punished by the match referee for protesting against a dreadful piece of umpiring. Neither in this passage nor in the rest of his article did Brenkley address the real issue, which is, how do you deal with bad or incompetent umpiring? And he forgot to mention that the umpire who called Muralitharan for throwing on that occasion had been temporarily suspended from his day job because his employers thought that he was too stressed out to cope! Brenkley wasn't calling for the head of the person who appointed an unfit umpire or demanding that professional umpires be penalized for incompetence; no, he was worried that Ranatunga and his men got off without being caned. It shouldn't come as a surprise that his piece was called 'At long last the game gets a governor'! It would be funny if it weren't so sad.

It's important not to mistake pundits like Henderson and Brenkley for reporters. They're failed leader writers, ideologues who never made it to the edit pages. Reporters base their opinions on what they've seen; ideologues guard second-hand opinions against the corruption of experience. Henderson, for example, was eloquent about the manifest guilt of the punished Indian players at Port Elizabeth when the controversy first broke. Then, just before the first Test between England and India began in Mohali, he wrote that 'India lost in South Africa and, in losing, and no matter what people have said here on their behalf, their players behaved poorly'. How would he know? In between his condemnations of Indian conduct, he appeared on a television show on Star News and blithely announced that he hadn't actually seen the match in question or even video clips of the incidents that had provoked Mike Denness's punishments! Days after the controversy broke, a controversy that threatened to split the cricket-playing world, the *Daily Telegraph*'s cricket correspondent turned up on prime time, taking sides on the issue without taking the trouble to look at what actually happened on the playing field. The man must have the balls of a brass monkey.

In a remarkable article written on the eve of the first Test, Henderson resumed his role as Master of the Hunt. Ganguly was his quarry and the whole article read like an obscure ritual of denunciation. He told his readers that Ganguly was known to Australian cricketers as the Bengali Boor and also Lord Snooty. In a paragraph or two Henderson warmed to his task and had an anonymous Australian player say that Ganguly was, 'The biggest shit I've ever come across in the game.' Then, having hit his stride, Henderson attributed to several players collectively the bizarre view that 'Ganguly is really a "tart"!' These read like the words that Henderson himself would have used to describe Ganguly, though he was careful to fire his guns off the shoulders of anonymous informants. Craven is a word Henderson used for Ganguly in one of his many denunciations—putting abuse into inverted commas, as Henderson did, seemed reasonably craven to me. What should worry Henderson's readers is not the rudeness of 'tart' or 'shit', but the hysteria that they indicate. To join a cult is to purge yourself of individual sense the better to share in collective hysteria.

This doesn't wholly explain why Ganguly gets men like Henderson so stirred up. Why 'tart' for example? Sometimes I think of the boarding school feel to this feeding frenzy and wonder.

Still, Ganguly's standing in the eyes of India's cricket public can't be the creation of Anglo-Australian cricket writers. What explains the way in which the amiable crowd at Chepauk booed India's captain when he emerged from the pavilion for the closing ceremonies of the third Test against Australia at the end of the great 2001 home series? Chepauk spectators who had given a Pakistani team a standing ovation after it had defeated the home side in a decisive Test, the same Madras crowd that had graciously cheered Waugh's beaten Australians when they walked out for the prize giving, now booed a captain who had led the Indian team to its greatest series win in decades of Test cricket.

Some of the booing could be put down to Ganguly's awful batting in the second innings when India needed him to steady the innings after Tendulkar's dismissal. Instead, he slashed one through slips for four and then nicked the next ball and departed, almost as if he was relieved to put some distance between himself and hostile Australian close fielders. Still, through that series Ganguly had set the field for Harbhajan's heroics, changed the batting order to promote Laxman at

Kolkata and stopped the most fearsome juggernaut in cricket history, this all-conquering Australian cricket team.

Granted, his personal form with the bat as captain had been poor but there have been other captains in cricket's history with records more modest than Ganguly's who have been respected for their leadership qualities alone. Mike Brearley was one of them and in contemporary cricket, Nasser Hussain, England's captain, had a nightmare with the bat for a year before scoring a century in Sri Lanka—this didn't stop English cricket correspondents from hailing him as the country's most inspirational captain in a long time. All he did to earn these accolades was to beat Pakistan and Sri Lanka at home and while these are notable achievements, they don't compare with coming up from behind and beating Waugh's Invincibles. So why does Ganguly get such a bad press?

One simple answer is the power of Australian public relations. Modern cricket is ruled by Australia because that is where it was invented—by Kerry Packer and Channel 9. The Australian team's image machine doesn't stop with its full-time media manager; it includes, in an informal way, television commentators, Australian cricket correspondents and the great unwashed who follow the team around. Ganguly was targeted in a strategic way and everyone had a go at him: Waugh in his statements before the tour began, Ian Chappell in his columns and in his obsessive television criticism of every field placement Ganguly made (it was a miracle the Indians won a series through which everything their captain did was a mistake), print journalists like Malcolm Conn of the *Age* who took it upon himself to upbraid Ganguly for not respecting the institutions of the game and, even more bizarrely, spent many column inches ventilating the grievances of an obscure, self-appointed spokesman of a gang of Australian spectators.

The reason this campaign worked was that Ganguly was a hard man to like. He came across on the field as narcissistic, selfish and petulant and he had had an image problem since his debut tour of Australia in 1992 when it was rumoured that he thought it beneath his dignity to carry drinks onto the field. But why was that worse than being, say, McGrath, who was routinely foul-mouthed, intimidatory and spent his career looking as if he had swallowed a lemon? Or the dreadful Ponting who had a history of disciplinary problems including some on his first tour of India? Or indeed, Shane Warne? No one, so far as I know, has ever accused Ganguly of doing anything as pathetic as making dirty phone calls. Or of taking money from bookies. And yet, Ganguly was once suspended for a match for excessive appealing while Michael Slater, who actually argued with umpire Venkatraghavan after the third umpire had turned down his appeal for a catch and then advanced on the batsman, Rahul Dravid, and swore at him, got away with a caution.

The reason for this difference in perception was that spectators, umpires and the cricketing public in general had been successfully sold a certain image of the Australian team. Australian cricketers were portrayed as hardbitten competitors. The description covered a multitude of sins. Thus, obscene sledging and physical intimidation, instead of being seen for what they were—forms of illegal bullying—were transformed into signs of manly commitment to the business of winning. All aggro became machismo: in this worldview, it was fine for Colin Miller to fling the ball at the batsman's head when the batsman was neither out of his crease nor trying to take a run.

We need to remind ourselves that the great West Indian sides of the sixties, seventies and eighties didn't bother with this kind of low-life intimidation. Their great fast bowlers let the ball talk for them and their captains, Worrell, Sobers, Lloyd and Richards, neither sanctioned nor practised sledging. Steve Waugh did both: so while he remained a determined and durable cricketer and, in some phases of his career, arguably the best batsman in the world, people who held him up as an exemplary captain lost the right to criticize Ganguly.

Indians aren't good at machismo. We haven't the manner for manly truculence; clever petulance is what we do. Indian fans and cricket writers should lobby the ICC to reeducate umpires so they can recognize both as equal forms of bad behaviour. Meanwhile I, like a million other Indians, was very taken with Ganguly's stratagems for unsettling Waugh. Ganguly kept him waiting in the middle for the toss before every match, he irked him by taking minutes to set the field, he publicly rubbished the quality of Australia's opposition during its winning streak (not excepting his own team!) and, best of all, he was elaborately gracious in victory. Not all of this was cricket, but the Aussies hadn't played that game in years. The Australians came to loathe Ganguly nearly as much as they once hated Ranatunga: for that reason alone, we (and the booing crowd in Chepauk) must learn to love him.

The Indian Game

A Passage to Greatness: The Best of Indian Batting

There's a reason why there's no chapter in this book called 'The best of Indian bowling'. Unlike Pakistani cricket, which has gloried in its fast bowlers since the days of Fazal Mahmood and matting wickets, the Indian cricket fan has always looked to the side's great batsmen to pull them to victory or (much more frequently) to console them in defeat.

When *Wisden*'s hundred best centuries of all time didn't find room for any of Tendulkar's tons, the Indian cricket public wanted to know why and thus began its education in the methods of modern statistics. *Wisden*'s innings were assessed by weighted criteria and ladder ranked: judged by those yardsticks, Tendulkar's innings didn't measure up. Viswanath was there, Gavaskar was there, V.V.S Laxman was right up there—the fourth best innings of all time—Lara was severally there, but not Tendulkar.

One reason given for his exclusion was that his big innings didn't win matches for India against good opposition and the *Wisden* rankings set great store by victory. Laxman's Calcutta double hundred was fresh in our minds, a textbook example of what *Wisden*'s statisticians valued: a big innings against a great side in seemingly hopeless circumstances, which turned the match and set up an improbable victory. That it had been recognized as one of the best innings in the history of Test cricket helped soften the blow of Tendulkar's exclusion and legitimized *Wisden*'s methods.

But for the Indian fan, the weight given to victory is problematic. For us, the trouble with using victory as a touchstone for great batting is that the cricket we've watched (or followed over the radio) has been generally framed by defeat. If losing the Test match radically devalues individual performances, most of the innings that made us bite our nails and pace the floor and cover our eyes, turn out to be dross.

In countries like Australia, which have historically won more matches than they have lost, there's a better fit between individual achievement and team performance. Australian memories of a great innings by Ponsford or Bradman or Chappell or Waugh or Gilchrist are unlikely to be diminished by subsequent defeat whereas Indian fans have spent their lives salvaging individual innings from shipwrecked Tests. In the whole of our Test match history there have been two or three brief periods of success: Wadekar's team in the early seventies, Kapil's series win in England in the eighties, then the combative phase under Ganguly. These are our winning streaks. Winning sprinkles would be more accurate.

So a celebration of Indian batsmanship that concentrates on winning performances would exclude most of our cricket history, most of our batsmen and most of our memories. That can't be right. And the reason it doesn't seem right is related to the nature of cricket, not just our local predicament as supporters of a team that loses more often than it wins.

Cricket, it's worth repeating, in these star-obsessed times, is a team game. And not only is it a team game, it's a team game played out over five days and two innings. To grade a single batting performance out of a possible twenty-two (eleven batsmen, batting twice) in the light of victory and defeat, is to place on it a burden that it shouldn't have to bear. Worse, such a judgement is untrue to the moment and to the experience of contemporary spectators. Innings that subsequently seem decisive more often than not begin and end with the issue unresolved and the match in the balance. Subsequent performances by others in the team, bowlers, batsmen and fielders, build on the promise of the innings or betray it.

Since we began with Tendulkar, we can use three first-innings centuries by him to illustrate the point. In March 2001, Tendulkar scored a dour, attritional century in India's first innings against Australia in Chennai. India won by two wickets; if it hadn't been for a composed 60-odd by Laxman in the second innings, India would have lost. Six months later, on the first day of the first Test in South Africa in 2001, India batted first and Tendulkar scored 155 in 184 balls with twenty-three fours and a six. It was an innings of exhilarating aggression against the best fast bowling attack in the world with wickets falling all round him. India lost. A little over two years later, in Sydney, Tendulkar scored an unbeaten 241. It was a patient knock, notable for his refusal to off drive. India pressed Australia hard, but failed to bowl them out on the last day and the match was drawn. The best of the three in terms of the quality of the attack and sustained brilliance in stroke production was the Bloemfontein knock. The highest score of the three, made in Sydney, was an anonymous, patient knock, utterly uncharacteristic of Tendulkar in his pomp. The Chennai hundred was workmanlike and purposeful. And while the batsman making these scores was recognizably Tendulkar, the innings themselves weren't Tendulkaresque. Ken Barrington could have played them. The only one of the three innings that made full use of Tendulkar's genius was the one at

Bloemfontein where he did everything he could to set India up, yet India lost. So which of these three innings should Indians commemorate?

Wisden Asia Cricket's list of the twenty-five greatest knocks by Indian batsmen provides one answer. While Tendulkar has three innings listed in the top twenty-five, the three I've mentioned don't figure. Since the jury of cricket players, broadcasters and writers who voted for the top twenty-five chose from a longer list that they were free to add to (full disclosure: I was part of the jury), I can reveal that the Sydney innings was the only one of the three to make it to even the long list, and it came in low down at number forty-eight. I guess the size of the score helped it past the Chennai knock even though the latter helped India win. The century at Bloemfontein, one of the great attacking innings of modern times, doesn't get a mention, sunk by the all-round awfulness of the team's performance. Judging batsmanship by the match result can be a tricky, misleading business.

But overall, *Wisden Asia Cricket*'s top twenty-five is a very good list, closer to the nature and spirit of the game than *Wisden*'s top hundred because it doesn't fetishize winning. Of the top ten innings, five didn't lead to victories. Three of those five were played in Test matches that India lost. Gavaskar has three mentions in the top ten and not one of those innings helped India win: the two double centuries resulted in draws while the battling 96 he made against Pakistan in Bangalore, his last Test innings, wasn't enough to ward off defeat. And this is as it should be. After that first spasm of success under Wadekar, for the rest of his career, Gavaskar spent a lot of his time in the middle fighting heroic rearguard actions because India didn't have the batting depth to set up victories. The 221 he made at the Oval, chasing 438 to win, illustrates India's dependence on him. He fell with India within reaching distance of the target only to see the batting collapse and India fall short by 10 runs, barely achieving a draw.

It's ironical (and, in an odd way, appropriate) that Gavaskar's attacking innings and his match-winning efforts are overlooked by *Wisden Asia Cricket*'s top twenty-five in favour of the heroic losing rearguards or, as in the case of the 221 at the Oval, the 'nearly there' epic. His blitz against a West Indies pace attack led by Malcolm Marshall in his lethal prime in Delhi, where he scored 121 in 128 balls on the first morning of the match, was a truly great attacking innings, irrespective of the result of the match (which ended in a draw). But not only does the 121 not figure in the top twenty-five, it doesn't even figure in the long list of sixty-three. I can only speculate that the image Indians have of Gavaskar as the rock on which the country's cricket was built for sixteen years, is so powerful that it crowds out innings that don't seem in character.

An even more interesting omission is the century he hit to set the stage for India's greatest away win, when India scored 406 to defeat the West Indies at Port of Spain in 1976. His comrade-in-arms Viswanath, who also contributed a century (120) to the winning total, similarly doesn't make the cut with that innings, though he is represented by two other knocks against the West Indies in Tests that India won.

Examined carefully, these twenty-five innings disclose a pattern that describes the historical evolution of Indian batsmanship. Viswanath's debut in 1969 marks the beginning of Indian batsmanship's modern era. The middle-sixties were a thin time for Indian batting and Viswanath's arrival was a watershed. He scored a century on debut and went on to score many more, which laid a jinx to rest: no Indian who had made a century on debut had ever made another one.

His batting record surpassed—in terms of runs scored and centuries made—any Indian batsman before him. He first, and then Gavaskar with him, liberated Indian batsmen from the reputation of being rabbits against fast bowling. Viswanath's 97 not out is rated third in the list of twenty-five for a reason: it was made against a rampant Andy Roberts on a fast pitch in a total of 190. It helped that India won the match. With Viswanath and Gavaskar, Indian batting achieved respectabillity.

If we divide Indian innings into two epochs, before and after Viswanath, and map these twenty-five innings on either side of that division, some things become clear. Less than a third of the twenty-five innings come from the era before Viswanath. The thirty-five years of Test cricket after 1969 produced eighteen of the twenty-five innings chosen while the first thirty-six years produced just seven. That in itself isn't significant because there were far fewer Test matches played in the earlier era. What is significant is that none of those seven innings helped India win: India lost five matches and managed to draw just two. Which brings me back to my original point: for the first three and a half decades of Indian Test cricket, fine batsmen battled insuperable odds. To judge a great batsman like Vijay Hazare by the blunt measure of victory is to hold him responsible for the failings of the teams he played in. *Wisden*'s list of twenty-five best innings doesn't make that mistake; it understands Indian cricket's long romance with gallant defeat and makes room for it.

With the exception of Vijay Hazare, all of India's greatest Test batsmen belong to the later period, the era inaugurated by Viswanath. Vijay Merchant will have his supporters, but he only ever played ten Tests. Chandu Borde, Vijay Manjrekar, Dilip Sardesai, fine batsmen all, have wonderful innings to their credit, but modest career records. Polly

Umrigar had a substantial career, but there was some doubt about his ability against quick bowling.

On the evidence of this listing and their careers, the four best Indian batsmen ever are Dravid, Gavaskar, Tendulkar and Viswanath. Close behind them follow Vengsarkar and Azharuddin, with Sehwag entering a claim to future greatness. This second period itself divides neatly into two halves: the first two decades producing great all-round batsmanship with the accent on defence. Gavaskar, Viswanath, Mohinder Amarnath and Dilip Vengsarkar were capable of fine attacking play but more often than not, they played with watchful orthodoxy. With Azhar and Tendulkar, Indian batsmanship switches to a more attacking register. Sound play is sometimes sacrificed to berserker brilliance: Azharuddin's sole entry in the list of twenty-five, coming in at number twenty-two, is a wonderful example of all-out assault in a losing cause: 121 at Lords in 1990, in 111 balls. Tendulkar lit up the whole cricketing world in the 1990s with his attacking genius. Azhar and Tendulkar between them created the space for the essentially attacking batsman to flourish. If Sehwag is Tendulkar's heir, Laxman is, just as clearly, Azharuddin's.

But even as everyone from Bradman to Benaud celebrated Tendulkar's primacy in the modern game, from an Indian point of view, the new millennium saw the maturing of a cricketer who drew level with Tendulkar in the matter of consistency, and then surpassed him in the business of making big innings against powerful teams to help India win: Rahul Dravid. Dravid owns four of the twenty-five innings listed and every one of them was played in a match that India won. In some ways, Dravid is a throwback to both Gavaskar and Viswanath, all technique and concentration on the one hand and wristy flourish on the other.

It's worth noting that all the innings in the list that were played in the new millennium (there are six) were played in matches that India won. Suddenly, India's batting best is being used to win us matches, not just to salvage draws or provide silver linings to defeats. Also, it isn't a coincidence that starting with Laxman's sublime 281 in March 2001, Indian batsmen have racked up five of the six highest individual scores in Indian Test history in the last three years. Laxman and Tendulkar have built big double hundreds, Dravid has scored two more, while Sehwag has managed a triple hundred. It isn't a coincidence because India has, for the first time, four batsmen capable of greatness playing on the same team. This doesn't guarantee victory: in the home series against Australia in late 2004, all of the top-order batsmen, with the honourable exception of Sehwag, failed simultaneously. It does mean, though, that India can consistently challenge for the top spots in Test cricket in a way that it has never done before.

Embers Not Ashes: India vs Pakistan

By the time I woke up to Test cricket as a child in the early sixties, India and Pakistan had stopped playing each other. I was twenty-one when they resumed normal service in 1978. On the whole, this was a good thing. Had Tests been played nearer the two wars with Pakistan (1965 and 1971), the air would have been poisonous with chauvinism. The one-day circuses in Sharjah were a glimpse of the lunatic passions stoked by Indo-Pak contests. It was a good thing we stopped playing those matches in Sharjah: they hot housed hatred. That we lost more often than we won had nothing, of course, to do with the case.

This is a history of men taking sides. India and Pakistan have been playing cricket against each other for more than fifty years. The first Test was played in Delhi in October 1952. Half a century is a good round number, favoured by historians, but a deceptive one in this instance; for nearly half this time the two countries have pointedly not played cricket with each other. After a decade of tense but mainly tedious Test matches (twelve of which were drawn), India and Pakistan played no cricket for seventeen years between 1961 and 1978. Then, after twenty years of normal cricketing relations, India retired to its tent after the World Cup in England in 1999, refusing to do battle on the cricket pitch with a country that covertly sponsored war and bloody militancy across the border in Kashmir. Since then the two countries have played no Test matches and no one-day matches on home soil, though they have played each other at the shorter version of the game in the World Cup and there has recently been an announcement that the two countries will resume playing tests against each other in the spring of 2004.

It's hard to find a parallel for this fraught on-off relationship within the world of cricket. The Australia–England rivalry doesn't have the same nationalist edge. The Mother Country connection, the white Anglophone bond and the weird (to Asian eyes) ritual of sledging on the pitch and chugging beers in a fraternal way off it, makes the needle between the two teams seem a staged ritual rather than the real thing. You could argue that cricketing encounters between Australia and New Zealand bear a family resemblance to the India–Pakistan matches, but this is to mistake sibling rivalry for fratricidal rage. No, inter-Tasman aggro doesn't really compare.

The reason India–Pakistan matches are different is because they are fuelled by an old-fashioned dispute between sovereign nations over land. The whiff of grapeshot that attends these encounters has a nineteenth-century smell to it: blood debts, blood lust and revanchism. The rage that sustains them is found in only a few select places and quarrels: The Israeli–Palestinian stand-off and the Eire–Northern Ireland mess might qualify because of the durability of those hatreds; basically, like India, they are places that the British helped partition. Only, Palestine and Northern Ireland aren't proper countries.

Serbia playing Bosnia or Croatia at basketball might raise feelings that parallel the India–Pakistan encounter. Perhaps one way of grasping the intensity of feeling that informs cricket matches between India and Pakistan is to think of them as Balkan contests on a subcontinental scale. Partition pogroms (conservatively a million dead), three and a half wars and a vicious property dispute over Kashmir make every cricket match between the two countries a way of settling other, bloodier scores.

The way India–Pakistan matches are followed and supported is interesting. There's no one under the age of fifty in India (and India's cricket fans are mostly under fifty) who has first-hand memories of the first period of Indo-Pak cricket between 1952 and 1961. They were too young to have followed those tours and when they were old enough, there were no India–Pakistan Tests to follow. The Indians and Pakistanis who gather around their television sets now when these old enemies play, might be familiar with the great names of that time—Kardar, Fazal Mehmood, Hanif Mohammad, Hazare, Manjrekar, Mankad—but the names stir no nostalgia, no childhood images of winter mornings spent queuing outside stadiums to watch these great men play each other. The fans who follow India–Pakistan cricket, watch it in a state of frenzy, like spectators at a Roman circus, their partisanship unleavened by the affection that memory usually brings.

This is not to argue that the early Tests between these countries were festivals of generous camaraderie. The reason twelve out of the first fifteen Tests were drawn was not only that the teams were evenly matched; as important was the terror of losing a match to this intimate enemy, this severed Siamese twin. Even before the first formal war between the two countries in 1965, playing Pakistan was a fraught business for an Indian, especially if that Indian was also a Muslim. In his *History of Indian Cricket*, Mihir Bose recalls the blighted career of Abbas Ali Baig. Baig had debuted for India against the Australians when they toured in 1959–60. He scored a century in his first Test and was promptly hailed as Indian batting's bright new hope. He even made the headlines when a girl kissed him out in the middle after he completed his second fifty of the Bombay Test. In his next four innings he made 1, 13, 19 and 1. Given that he had made a century and two fifties in his debut series against the Australians, he might have survived this run of low scores in the normal course; but this wasn't the normal course, this was Pakistan and he was an Indian Muslim. According to Bose, '. . . the fantastic allegation was made that Baig had failed deliberately to help his co-religionists from Pakistan. This was monstrously untrue, but he received poison-pen letters, was dropped and only played two more Tests, six years later, against the West Indies.'

Decades later, Abbas Ali Baig's captain and friend, Mansur Ali Khan Pataudi, asked Asif Iqbal, the Pakistan captain touring India, a wicked question before the television cameras. He asked Asif if he planned to switch countries again. Asif Iqbal had played first-class cricket for Hyderabad, Pataudi's first-class team, before migrating to Pakistan. For someone like Pataudi, a Muslim, who like his father, Iftikar Ali Khan Pataudi, had captained India, Asif Iqbal's move would have seemed at the time like a defection that bore out the bigots who claimed all Muslims in India were Pakistani fifth columnists at heart. To his credit, Asif Iqbal, ambushed by a question that he must have thought gratuitous, smiled and declared himself content with his Pakistani state.

Tense and difficult though these matches were for the players, the Indians and Pakistanis who watched them were cricket fans first and nationalists later. Cricket was a popular sport, but not yet a mass market enterprise. To follow the game you had to buy relatively expensive tickets (they cost three or four times as much as a ticket to the cinema) and invest days of your time watching Test match cricket at the cricket ground. Or else you followed cricket matches on the radio which, unlike the literal immediacy of telecast cricket, required some exercise of the imagination. The chauvinism made general by the wars of 1965 and 1971, Pakistani bitterness about India's hand in the creation of Bangladesh, Indian bitterness about Pakistan's role in creating sedition and secessionism in Kashmir, the transformation of cricket into mass spectacle via television and limited-overs contests, all this still lay in the future. Cricket was popular but also oddly genteel. In his marvellous history of Indian cricket, *A Corner of a Foreign Field* , Ramachandra Guha describes the almost courtly goodwill that characterized the early tours. Five years after the horrors of Partition, Abdul Hafeez Kardar, the captain of Pakistan, a man ideologically committed to the idea of an Islamic state, could commend Indian spectators for their generosity and fairness after Pakistan's first Test match series in India, a series that his fledgling team lost two matches to one. When the Indians toured Pakistan in their turn, the president of the Indian board, the Maharajkumar of Vizianagram, reciprocated by praising the '. . . clean good sport . . .' that had characterized the series. So while a proper sense of solidarity joined Indian and Pakistani spectators to their teams, the venomous hysteria of the eighties and nineties had to wait upon events and technology.

The matches India and Pakistan played from 1978 onwards were, thanks to television, transformed into national spectacles. For the first time in the subcontinent's cricket history, millions of people with no interest in cricket, but a vested interest in seeing the old enemy humbled by their champions, were drawn into watching cricket on black and white television sets.

Indians have always been susceptible to the broadcast word: I refer earlier in the book to an Indian radio commentator who set off arson and rioting in Calcutta's Eden Gardens by suggesting on air that an Indian batsman had been unfairly given out. Now television's growing reach and immediacy created huge national audiences that followed these contests squealing, yelping, exulting and mourning, ball by ball, in massive unison.

When, in 1978, the Indian team led by Bishen Singh Bedi was comfortably beaten 2–0 by Mushtaq Mohammad's Pakistan, it could be properly described as a national humiliation, because for the first time, there was a nation watching. When Pakistan toured two years later, and Imran Khan did his hamstring early in his spell in the first Test, a pan-Indian audience exhaled in relief, not just the spectators present that day at the Feroz Shah Kotla in Delhi. Thanks partly to Imran's unavailability for the rest of the tour, the Indian team won the series handily . . . and the nation was avenged. Years later, during the Calcutta Test in 1998, when Tendulkar was run out at the bowler's end after running into the big fast bowler, Shoaib Akhtar, tens of millions of Indians sulked alongside Tendulkar, then watched helplessly as Pakistan went on to win the Test and take the series in front of an empty Eden Gardens, cleared of its rowdy, rioting crowd.

But Test cricket wasn't the chosen vehicle for the chauvinist melodrama that this new audience craved. For these neophytes Test matches were too long, too infrequent and too often drawn. One-day matches with their guaranteed results offered more opportunities for catharsis and release. The commercial potential of India–Pakistan cricket was first seriously milked by the organizers of the Sharjah circus, a bizarrely unlikely event situated in the sands of a Gulf sheikhdom. The brainchild of a cricket-loving sheikh and that canny former captain of Pakistan, Asif Iqbal, it drew expatriate Indians and Pakistanis working in the United Arab Emirates, former cricketers from the subcontinent looking for handouts, bookies, Bollywood stars, Bombay ganglords and vast television audiences in India and Pakistan.

While other cricketing nations were invited to Sharjah, they were no more than window-dressing. The stadium in Sharjah served the same purpose as the Roman arena once did: it was intended to keep Indian and Pakistani fans in a state of addicted arousal as their gladiators fought to the finish. And it worked.

The most traumatic single moment in the history of Indian cricket as registered by its fans didn't occur during some memorable Test match. It wasn't contained in the great Madras Test against Pakistan where, despite Tendulkar's heroic century, India fell 12 runs short; nor was it framed by that earlier brave defeat in Bangalore at the hands of Imran Khan's men, when Gavaskar fell in his nineties after a great innings on a vicious turner. No; appropriately enough, Indian cricket's supremely awful moment, seared into every cricket-watching Indian's eyeballs was the last-ball six hit by Javed Miandad off Chetan Sharma when Pakistan needed four off that ultimate ball to win a forgettable tournament, indistinguishable from the dozens of triangular tournaments that Sharjah hosted year after year.

It was the repeated defeats in Sharjah that paved the way for India's refusal to play Pakistan. Darkly implying that the dice at Sharjah were loaded in favour of the Pakistanis, India stopped playing there and as India–Pakistan relations declined during the nineties, cricket tours became rarer, increasingly hostage to reasons of state. Thaws in Indo-Pak diplomacy are invariably accompanied by a resumption of cricketing relations while frostier periods inevitably lead to disengagement. This latest restoration of cricketing ties again follows a competitive flurry of conciliatory gestures made by the governments of India and Pakistan in order to persuade the world that the other country is the warmongering aggressor, deaf to the needs of peace.

Over the past fifteen years, despite the stop-start course of India-Pakistan cricket, the cricket boards of India and Pakistan have snuggled up together to act in concert as a South Asian bloc in the changing world of international cricket politics. This bloc has successfully elevated Jagmohan Dalmiya to the presidency of the ICC, it has managed to strongarm the ICC into staging the World Cup not once, but twice in the subcontinent, and it has held together despite India's unilateral ban on cricket matches against Pakistan, at home or away. This ban hurts Pakistan's cricket coffers more than it does Indian ones because the Indian board has very deep pockets, but in spite of that the Pakistan board has backed Dalmiya in all his challenges to the authority of the ICC: from the Mike Denness affair where the Indian board defied ICC match referee Denness's ruling and played a suspended player, to the row about sponsorship contracts on the eve of the last World Cup.

There are two main reasons for this apparently inexplicable fraternity. One is the perceived tendency of the two founding members of the ICC, England and Australia, to carry on as if the management of world cricket ought to be theirs by right. This by itself is enough to create a kind of post-colonial solidarity. More important is the realization that the Indian television market for cricket makes it the economic powerhouse of the cricketing world. Dalmiya put the finances of the ICC on a sound footing by delivering the Indian audience and he's not about to let anyone forget that. It makes perfect economic sense for someone like General Tauqeer Zia, former head of the Pakistan Cricket Board, to back India against the ICC: why would you annoy cricket's eight hundred pound gorilla, when you live in its neighbourhood? Dalmiya, a businessman himself, understands this; his assurance to all his allies in ICC politics is simple: Stick with me; I'll make you rich. In a way that Karl Marx (a materialist himself) would have understood, economics has begun to bring together what the subcontinent's politicians would pull apart.

Our Boys

I had spent $80 for the webcast of the 2003 World Cup final in South Africa because I was living in a brownstone neighbourhood in Brooklyn which wasn't served by the satellite platform that was beaming in the match. Then Ganguly put Australia in . . . and we weren't in the match for a single over. There are moments in a fan's life (several, if you're an Indian fan) when you really hate your team. You think dark thoughts at such times. Thoughts like these.

All Indian spectators—whether they admit it or not—have noticed and regretted the inability of Indian bowlers to eyeball opposing batsmen, to intimidate them, to impose their will on the enemy. They've watched Allan Donald, Glenn McGrath, even Andrew Flintoff, bad-mouth and bully Indian batsmen. Sometimes they've cried foul because Indians find intimidatory sledging alien and distasteful, but mostly they've longed for a bowler who would pay back those players in kind.

What they've got, though, is shrill petulance or low truculence: Ganguly jumping and squealing like a thwarted child, Yashpal Sharma muttering obscenities in a language the opposition can't understand and Venkatesh Prasad pointing batsmen in the direction of the pavilion as he runs past them, like a prudent Indian motorist cursing out another after making sure that he's headed in the other direction. Indian cricketers aren't good at being bad. That alpha-male malevolence that Donald and McGrath have on tap just doesn't come naturally to us.

One explanation for this difference could be that Indians are simply better behaved, nicer, non-violent. This is hard to credit given the sectarian bloodletting chronically on show in recent Indian history. I have a more plausible theory. It goes like this: the minimum requirement for calculated aggression is the availability of an adult male. Indian cricket teams mostly don't feature adult men.

Indian Test cricketers aren't adults; this is something they share with Indian men generally. The reason for this, if you'll forgive a short detour into pop sociology, is that young Indian men know themselves mainly as brothers, sons and husbands; they see themselves as points in a grid of kin. They don't grow up confronting others to define their individual selves; they don't leave home and they don't metaphorically kill their fathers. It isn't as if they aren't competitive or self-promoting: they are, only they learn to compete covertly, behind a well-bred façade of dutifulness and deference.

To understand this you only have to compare the difference in the attitude towards captaincy between Indian and Australian contenders. No Indian hopeful will ever confess that he would actually like to be captain of India. Australian players like Warne make no secret of their ambition to lead their country. In India such frankness would be understood as the preliminary to a palace coup. Because Indian cricket teams are hierarchical and social relationships need to be lubricated by deference, ambition can only amount to disloyalty.

When Mark Taylor was replaced by Steve Waugh as the captain of the Australian one-day team and then, when Waugh was brutally canned to make room for Ponting, there was a certain amount of heartburn and bad feeling—Warne, for example, railed against the media for highlighting his off-field indiscretions, implying that notoriety had cost him the captaincy—but nobody held his ambition against him, nor did anyone expect Ponting to be insincerely surprised or self-deprecating. Contrast this with the furore that erupted when Tendulkar was reported to have said that he hadn't ruled out becoming captain again. At once the newspapers began to gossip about Tendulkar's motives and Ganguly's future.

The Indian cricket team does not consist of adult individuals acting in concert. The team is organized on the model of the Hindu joint family. More accurately, it is organized on the model of a recently orphaned joint family where a bunch of pseudo siblings are led by the captain who, on account of his leadership role, automatically becomes the honorary older brother. He becomes the karta (the executor or head) of this orphaned joint family and hereafter, as befits his seniority, always refers to his team as 'my boys'.

The same principle of seniority creates a ladder of deference within the team. Young players always call Kumble 'Anilbhai' for two reasons. First, age and seniority demand deference. Second, Indians instinctively use kinship terms to describe acquaintances and friends. Thus, the parents of friends are 'aunty' and 'uncle' and an older teammate not old enough to be 'uncle' has to be a stand-in older brother. Hence bhai.

The members of the Indian cricket team are more likely to address Jagmohan Dalmiya as 'Uncle' than as Mr Dalmiya and I'm certain none of them call him Jaggu. I bet John Wright had to train his charges to address him as 'John' since most of them would have started out calling him 'Sir'. Deference slows the transition to self-propelled adulthood so that Indian cricketers remain 'boys' right through their careers in international cricket.

You can see this in their body language: the Indian bowler's reaction when a ball is misfielded or a catch put down doesn't just indicate disappointment—it is intended to convey a sense of injury. It isn't unusual to see the bowler stamp his foot and sulk all the way back to his bowling mark. This isn't the professional sportsman's rueful acceptance of human error (a la Warne); it's the petulance of the cosseted male child and his need to fix blame, to establish to the watching world that it was someone else's fault. Ganguly is the obvious example, but Kumble and Srinath carried on in exactly this way.

The deportment and manner of Indian cricketers is shaped partly by this prolonged immaturity and partly by the middle class instincts that they bring to their job. The Indian middle class is a hold-all category that encompasses multitudes, but its values and habits of mind are those of the 'salariat' that forms its vanguard. The characteristic features of a salaried class are an obsession with stability (a permanent salaried job, marriage, 'settling down') and gentility. A white-collar class, it defers to its betters and is ruthless with the lower orders. This class has traditionally supplied the bulk of India's Test cricketers (though this is changing slowly) and its members are comfortable with the (sh)amateur organization of Indian cricket which promises the double deliverance of wealth and gentility. Cricketing success brings money and celebrity while sinecures in private and public sector companies give them the security and respectability of regular employment.

But for our middle class recruit, there's a catch: for all its complexity and sophistication, cricket is an outdoor sport and outdoor sport consists mainly of hard manual work. Azhar, Pataudi, Solkar, Jadeja and a handful of others apart, Indian cricketers aren't keen on fielding, and it shows. They concentrate on batting and bowling skills and are indifferent to those aspects of cricket where fitness and athleticism are important, like fielding or running between wickets. Again, Ganguly is the perfect example of this bhadralok disdain for the sweaty exertion required by fielding or modern training regimes. It's an open secret that Leipus and Wright were infuriated by Ganguly's refusal to follow prescribed training routines.

But Ganguly is only one example of this upper-caste unwillingness to labour. It isn't a coincidence that the best educated, most genteel, most archetypally middle class members of the Indian team, generally regarded as the sort of suitable boys match-making mamas dream of—Kumble, Dravid and Srinath—are hopeless fielders. Kumble keeling over at mid-on (diving for a ball that has long since passed), Dravid in high-stepping pursuit of leather, knees pumping but never making any ground, Srinath in the deep, turning ones into twos, are sights that the Indian spectator has grown used to.

One reason why the Indian middle class took to cricket (football and hockey in India remained more plebeian sports) is that it used to be the only game unfit people could play at the highest level. You only need to look at file photos of Vijay Manjrekar and Erapalli Prasanna to confirm the truth of this. Contrast the Indians with Australian cricketers. They've had a few beer bellies along the way: David Boon and Merv Hughes come to mind and Steve Waugh isn't exactly wasp-waisted but they are (or were) decent fielders. Australian cricketers are raised in a culture of outdoor sport. So are the South Africans. For them cricket isn't just a recreation or a career; it's a form of physical self-expression. You only have to watch Herschelle Gibbs or Jonty Rhodes or Ricky Ponting or Damien Martyn field to know that.

It isn't unusual for cricketers from these countries to have grown up playing contact sports like Australian Rules football or Rugby. They bring to cricket the hand-to-hand aggression of contact sport. This is why the South African match referee Denis Lindsay indulgently overlooked a 'bit of argy-bargy' in the ODI between England and India when Flintoff and one or two of his teammates did some sledging and shoving. Australians and South Africans bring the in-your-face aggression of the rugger scrum to the cricket pitch. Intimidation and sledging come naturally to them. Indians, in contrast, treat cricket like an outdoor version of chess, where you solve problems posed by your opponent without acknowledging his presence or making eye contact. Srinath is Viswanathan Anand with a ball in his hand.

Middle class children in India are taught to excel, and they do. You can see that commitment to excellence in the sixteen-year-olds who spend two years in coaching schools to make it to the Indian Institutes of Technology. You can see it in Dravid's meticulous attention to technique. The trouble is, the ability to excel doesn't necessarily translate into the ability to win. I think it's fair to say that Dravid, despite his batting average, doesn't intimidate bowling attacks and doesn't turn matches the way Adam Gilchrist (who has a similar average) does.

Perhaps this is the wrong comparison. Dravid, after all, is the Wall and Gilchrist is a whirlwind. Let's compare two great batsmen, both of whom have exceptional attacking abilities and fine defensive techniques: Sachin Tendulkar and Javed Miandad. They are alike in being prodigies who shouldered for years the burden of being the best batsmen in their teams and both had chequered careers as captains. In every other respect they were chalk and cheese and I think the difference in who they were showed up in how they played.

Tendulkar is the classic representative of India's middle

class cricketing tradition. He began his Test career as a child star, moved on to become world cricket's juvenile lead, and then leap-frogged Lara to become one of the greatest batsmen in the contemporary game. He personifies the Bombay school: its fine coaching, its orthodox batsmanship, its discipline, and adds to all this, his genius.

I don't know if there is a Karachi school of cricket, but Miandad didn't belong to it. No Pakistani Achrekar tended his technique: from that brutal pull to that wholly chest-on defensive shot; it was all his own. Unlike Tendulkar, who still has the manner and visage of a boy, Javed never seemed a boy, even when he was one. In that series against India in 1978, when he was still a very young man, he swaggered with the wicked maturity of a street-smart veteran. If Tendulkar came from a white-collar world, Miandad's collar (whenever he started wearing it) was blue.

When the World Cup was played in England in 1999, the English press was entranced by Tendulkar. Journalists couldn't get over how, despite his fame and wealth and standing, he was so modest and self-effacing, so impossibly well-behaved. They compared him favourably to the unbalanced Lara with his palace on a hill, with the cocaine snorting Gazza, the oafish, star-struck Beckham.

Nobody ever accused Miandad of good behaviour. The moment he swashbuckled his way to the crease and took guard, the pitch became an akhara and the match became a scrap. Miandad was so fiercely combative that he drew the whole audience into the fight. When India played Pakistan and Miandad hit a four, I took it personally. When he hit that six in Sharjah off the last ball of the match (when a four would have done), it was as if he had personally stuck two fingers up every Indian nose.

And if I'm right and if the willingness to confront an

opponent separates the men from the boys, then this comparison becomes instructive. Both Miandad and Tendulkar have had famous collisions with fearsome fast bowlers; Tendulkar ran into Shoaib Akhtar in Calcutta and Miandad into Dennis Lillee in Australia. Tendulkar, according to insider accounts, believed Akhtar had deliberately obstructed his passage to the crease to run him out. His response was to retire to the pavilion in a towering sulk, from which he only emerged reluctantly to pacify an enraged crowd.

Miandad, knocked off his feet by Lillee, knew that Lillee had deliberately moved into his path as he set off for a run and shouldered him. Unlike Tendulkar, he didn't bother sulking or getting mad: he just set about getting even. There's a magnificent photograph of that operatic scene, with Lillee on one side and Javed on the other, the latter holding his bat one-handed like a club, extravagantly preparing to knock Lillee's head off. Cricket was combat for Miandad, and he never took a backward step.

If I had to choose between the two to play for my life, I would (after making sure that he wouldn't hold my nationality against me) choose Miandad as my champion. My memories of him are crowded with epic rearguard actions and victories salvaged by will alone. Tendulkar's innings are monuments to his genius without being landmarks in the history of Indian Test cricket. Not always, but often, they're solo performances, rather like a gymnast's striving for a perfect ten on the pommel horse.

Adults compete; children perform. Miandad didn't bat to excel; he fought to win. He was no one's vision of the parfait knight, but he was a warrior. Tendulkar, on the other hand, is the best schoolboy cricketer that ever lived.

Tendulkar is only the most famous of our juvenile leads: from Ajit Agarkar to Parthiv Patel, recent Indian teams have been well supplied with child stars. Actually chronological age has little to do with the immaturity of Indian cricketers. Players get so used to thinking of themselves as 'under' fifteen, seventeen or nineteen that they forget to grow up. Indian fans, though, keep watching because despite everything, they still believe that they'll live to support an Indian team with eleven adults on board.

Anecdotage

One of the dodgiest aspects of cricket writing is the blurring of the distinction between eyewitness experience and inherited lore. Much cricket writing treats period gossip as history. This is sometimes fun to read, but it does result in a lopsided celebration of the past: the flamboyant player becomes legendary while the quiet hero becomes obscure. So the Nayudus and Mushtaq Alis prosper at the expense of someone like Vijay Hazare, who was the greatest Indian batsman of the Time Before Viswanath. Anecdotal cricket writing has also obscured the genius of the most thrilling slow bowler of my youth, Bhagwat Chandrasekhar. This chapter was written in rehabilitation.

Cricket has its historians and a handful of first-rate histories, but its followers recall its past as folklore. The certainty and unselfconsciousness with which players, spectators and writers describe players and matches and tours they haven't watched is striking—and odd. After the deaths of Keith Miller and Vijay Hazare, there were obituaries written by people who hadn't seen either play, but you wouldn't have guessed that from the vivid colour of the writing.

There's nothing wrong with writing about the past as if you had been there: historians, especially the readable ones, do this all the time. Who wants to read a history where every sentence is hedged about with warnings that the evidence for the world evoked is provisional, incomplete and second-hand? History, by definition, is written at second-hand.

But cricket writers addressing the past or invoking it, even the young ones, suffer from a peculiar affliction: anecdotage. The past is not so much reconstructed as taken on trust on the strength of inherited stories. This is a bit like medieval Muslim jurisprudence where traditions about the Prophet's life and doings were accepted as authentic, provided they were handed down through a chain of reliable human transmitters. The difference is that Muslim jurisprudence had strict rules for testing the authenticity of prophetic traditions whereas cricket writers accept the opinions of their elders and ancestors in a state of near-perfect credulity.

There's nothing wrong with this either. Being cricket-mad is a more evolved state than being beach volleyball-mad because there is a reservoir of lore that we can call our own, stories we can share with our grandfathers, myths and legends that help make us intimate with long-gone greats. So I 'know' that Grace was the founder of modern batsmanship, that Duleepsinhji's cream silk shirt billowed behind him as he walked in to bat, I can see Chapman at slip with his bucket-like hands, and I know that Woolley's batsmanship was so exquisite that had David Gower been his contemporary, he would have looked coarse in comparison. Likewise, I can keep my end up in a conversation about sticky wickets though Indian wickets have been covered in all the time I've followed cricket. Lore is good: it makes a subtle and complex game familiar.

But without a pinch of salt, the mythology of a game can mislead its followers and derange its writers. An Indian example of this is the way in which Bishen Bedi has, in the lore of Indian cricket, emerged as *the* spinner of the quartet of slow bowlers who helped India win Test matches and Test series in the late sixties and early seventies. Actually, trio of spinners would be more accurate because Venkatraghavan, though a fine off break bowler and a sharp close-fielder, wasn't quite in the same league as the others. Or should that be duo? I watched Bedi and Prasanna cut through Ian Chappell's Australians in Delhi's Feroz Shah Kotla, bowling them out for just over a 100 and winning the match for India. Prasanna, like Bedi, was an artist who dealt in flighted spin, but if you look at the record and sift through the number of wickets taken, the cost per wicket, the match winning performances, you quickly realize that there were only two Indian spinners with equivalent career records, Bedi and Chandrasekhar. But in their share of posterity's attention, there is no comparison: Bedi is regarded as the greatest modern practitioner of left-arm orthodox spin bowling, while Chandrasekhar is affectionately remembered in India as a wonderful, freakish bowler who, thanks to a polio-withered arm, bowled fast googlies and top-spinners without quite knowing how, lacked the intelligent control of Bedi, went for lots of runs, but was, on his day, unplayable. If you look at their statistics, the difference in their bowling averages is negligible (Bedi is more economical by 1 run a wicket) while Chandrasekhar's strike rate (a modern statistic not taken into account by their contemporaries) is light years better.

It isn't an exaggeration to say that in the wider cricketing world beyond India, Chandrasekhar is not much more than a footnote, better known for the number of ducks he made than the wickets he took. The thrill of watching that long-stepping, stiff-legged run-up, the venom of that windmill action, the unexpected elegance of those long floppy sleeves, neatly buttoned at the wrist, the stupid bewilderment of the batsman, bowled while shouldering arms, or just beaten by the whiplash speed of the googly, all that has faded from public memory, leaving behind a caricature, a stick figure who bears no resemblance to the real cricketer who was the most exciting 'slow' bowler of his time.

There is no conspiracy behind this unequal recognition by posterity. Bedi was a great bowler and deserves his fame. But there are reasons why cricket lore treats players differently and anyone who is interested in the game, certainly writers, should be aware of them.

Cricket is predisposed to favour the 'orthodox' over the singular. No game sets greater store by classicism, or the idea that players should embody certain templates of style. Bedi did everything that the pattern card for left-arm orthodox slow bowling demanded: he tossed the ball up, turned it enough to elude the width of the bat and catch the edge (to turn it too sharply would have been unnecessary, unorthodox and vulgar), he never stooped to bowling over the wicket like that contemporary journeyman, Ashley Giles, he didn't mind being lofted, he lured batsmen forward, then made the ball dip and left them groping, he was a classicist's wet dream.

Chandrasekhar, on the other hand, was an original which, in cricketing terms, meant he was a freak. He represented no bowling archetype, he refined no pre-existing tradition, he was a spinner who bowled fast, he was a leg break bowler who bowled googlies, he made no elaborate demonstration of guile and was allegedly more interested in Mukesh's songs than the direction of his next ball, he sent stumps cartwheeling when he should have delicately disturbed the off-bail, in short, he was fun to watch and a match winner but he wasn't a milestone: more a comet, a natural marvel that had come from nowhere and briefly illumined the game. Cricket is a game that is obsessed with pedigrees and bowlers who have no discernible forbears are mongrels who, no matter how gifted, are never to be spoken of in the same breath as thoroughbreds.

The other reason for Bedi's standing was that he was more written about in the English press because he played county cricket for Northants. For reasons of history and language, England has produced more cricket writing than any other cricket-playing nation and in the recently post-colonial world of the sixties and seventies, cricket fans in India and other places deferred to the opinions of English writers. Bedi, being the bowler he was and later, captain of India, got wonderful press (till he blew the whistle on John Lever's tricks with Vaseline) while Chandrasekhar, content to play for Karnataka and India, never received the critical attention he deserved. Apart from the lovely, enthusiastic profile written decades ago for the *Illustrated Weekly of India* by the wonderful Raju Bharatan, no cricket journalist I've read has properly celebrated Bhagwat Chandrasekhar or described his genius.

But things will change now because in Kumble, Chandrasekhar has a descendant. They are different bowlers but they confound the classical template in the same ways. By the sheer weight of wickets, Kumble has compelled writers to re-examine their assumptions about orthodoxy. There is no argument any more about Kumble being the greatest spinner India has ever produced: matches won, strike rate, cost per wicket—dice it any way you want, he comes out on top. That being so, cricket writers, driven by the instinct of their guild, will look backwards for his pedigree and find Bhagwat Chandrasekhar smiling down at them from the glory days of the early seventies, his sleeves buttoned up at the wrists.

Postscript:

Sanjay Manjrekar, fine batsman and amongst the game's most perceptive commentators, seemed to succumb to the power of county folklore in a magazine column. He wrote that the young Tendulkar '. . . ranked with the Viv Richardses, Graeme Pollocks and Barry Richardses of the world'. The first name there seems right, the second name is allowable given that Graeme Pollock had played more than twenty Tests and averaged more than 60 when South Africa was barred from Tests, but Barry Richards? Manjrekar compared Tendulkar with a man who played four Test matches! More curiously (and this is typical of cricket writing), he compared a man he hadn't seen bat with a man he had watched through his whole career as a cricketer and broadcaster.

I suspect Manjrekar thought this was reasonable because (a) the county game rated Barry Richards the greatest on account of the mountain of runs he made in that league and (b) because Bradman wrote Barry Richards into his greatest team ever. Bradman's opinion must count for something with anyone involved in cricket, but surely first-hand experience must count for more. After playing four Tests, Sunil Gavaskar, an opening batsman closer to home, averaged over 150, more than twice Barry Richards's average when his career was cut short. Manjrekar must have watched nearly every match Gavaskar played and yet the example that comes to his mind is Barry Richards who he had never laid eyes on. The point is not that Manjrekar ought to rate Tendulkar or Gavaskar above all others because they are Indians and Mumbai men: the point is that cricket writing's anecdotal influence is such that he is willing to place the unseen, mythic potential of Barry Richards above the realized careers of others and the evidence of his eyes.

At Lord's

Reading K.N. Prabhu file stories for the Times of India *from the Sydney Cricket Ground, the Queens Park Oval, Old Trafford, I used to yearn to be a cricket correspondent: a life, bought and paid for, spent watching cricket from the best seats in the house, the press-box. Then, thanks to a generous magazine editor, I was given the chance to play at being a cricket correspondent for a day at Lord's. Be careful what you wish for; you might get it.*

Exactly three weeks ago, a dream came true: I watched a cricket match from a press-box, as a bona fide cricket correspondent. It didn't hurt that the match was a one-day international against England, that it was played at Lord's, that the press-box in question was that glazed, uber-modern ovoid that stares at the Pavilion end like an eye on stalks. Best of all, we won.

It was the last day of a long holiday in Wales and England, filled with football. After cheering Brazil on for nearly four weeks, after watching England play Argentina and Denmark in pubs fizzing with hysterical feeling, it was hard to feel excited about cricket. The most rabid cricket fan would find his passion for the game dimmed in England—compared to football, it counts for so little in the public mind. Still, this was India playing, I told myself, as I caught the bus. Also, I had a pass to the press-box.

I had spent the morning on a train, riding up to London, so by the time I got on the bus the match had begun. It didn't help that Lord's was a couple of miles from the nearest bus stop, obscurely called Swiss Cottage. I got to the ground two hours into the match to find England disastrously well placed: two hundred and a few for three, with twelve overs to go. I bought myself an unwieldy can of lager from a stall, flourished my credentials at the woman guarding the lift to the press-box and rode up the stalk trying to look like a grizzled correspondent.

So I got off, frowning purposefully, trying to take everything in without gawping. The view was spectacular, right over the stumps, but we were so high up that the players were slightly foreshortened. The reporters were arranged in stepped rows behind the tinted glass façade, looking steeply downwards: the whole effect was one of sitting in a Star Trek lecture theatre built for nerveless space cadets.

I slid into a seat next to a well-set-up Sri Lankan. He was armed to the teeth: laptop, mobile phone, as well as a landline phone into which he spoke endlessly about London's night-life. All phone conversations follow a script: in this one my neighbour was the man about town and the man at the other end (who, I gathered, had never been to a nightclub) had been cast as the hick.

I watched for a while, but desultorily, because it was England batting. Besides, Nasser Hussain was on strike, so nothing was laboriously happening. That's when I noticed that several correspondents had trays of food and glasses of wine in front of them. Had these only been white correspondents I would have assumed that the refreshments were a guild privilege to which I was not entitled and done nothing, but when I saw a couple of desi journos walking in with trays I began to wonder, as Indians customarily do, whether they knew something I didn't.

I looked around me and saw that there was a buffet lunch laid out behind the viewing area and a counter from which drink was being dispensed. I slid past the Sri Lankan bon vivant and made my way to the buffet table, but not before making certain that absolutely no money was changing hands. Reassured, I picked up a plate and a napkin and had a bit of everything and many glasses of wine. This took a while. I could have carried my tray to the viewing gallery, but I decided to stay in the buffet area within easy reach of the spread, reasoning that the match I could have watched at home, but the food and drink came with the premises. And I missed nothing: there were television sets suspended over the tables. I wondered about people who insisted that there was no such thing as a free lunch; that was probably true in the normal world, but this was Lord's and the lift had likely raised us into a kind of heaven.

It was certainly peopled by godlings. There was Barry Richards perched on a table; Ravi Shastri sharply turned out in blazer and tie; Boycott in shirtsleeves and best of all, Gavaskar. I got Harsha Bhogle to introduce me to him and shook his hand.

We strangled the English batting in the last ten overs so it fell short of the 300 that had once seemed likely and then Sehwag got us off to a rocketing start. I made the mistake of clapping audibly when he whacked a ball straight for four. The Sri Lankan stopped talking on the phone to call me to order. Did I know, he asked rhetorically, that this was a press-box and clapping wasn't allowed? Why don't you mind your own business? I asked in return, not really wanting to know. I was mildly tipsy and consequently filled with indignation at being publicly chided. The Sri Lankan said something else which I didn't hear because my head was busy thinking up a crushing put-down. Why don't you stop being officious? I enquired. Feeble, I know, but it was the best I could do.

Dravid and Yuvraj played wonderfully to steer us home and I wanted to cheer, but cowed by the deadpan professionalism of the hacks all round me, I merely mimed applause. Think of watching a Test match over five days without booing or whistling or cheering! Peter Roebuck, who does the best cricket reporting I've read, was the only journalist there who looked remotely animated. The rest of them watched impassively and intermittently tapped their keyboards with two fingers, like expert zombies. If press-boxes are all like this, reporting on cricket from inside them for a living must be a kind of purgatory.

After we won I walked home because there were tens of thousands of people looking for buses and taxis. For a while I walked surrounded by desi supporters. One of them was a South Indian who kept shouting triumphantly in a kind of macho Hindustani. Every time he caught a white person's eye, he'd shout, 'Oye gorey! Kya dekh raha hai, saale, tu haar gaya!' (Oye whitey, what are you looking at, b—r?, you lost!). Then he'd neigh with laughter and look at his friends for endorsement. It was a stupid and pathetic form of solidarity, but compared to the stupor of the professionals in the press-box, it was a sign of life. So, instead of wincing each time he yelled, I smiled indulgently all the way home.

Champions at Chepauk

Cricketers, batsmen especially, talk of being in the 'zone', a sporting trance in which they do everything right. Spectators have a zone of their own: the times when their fantasies are played out down to the last detail on the ground, as they watch from the best seats in the stadium. Tendulkar scores a hundred, Laxman gets a pair of genius fifties, Harbhajan mows down the opposition and India win the match and with it a series that had once seemed lost. Like a school cricket match written up by P.G. Wodehouse but adapted to the higher altitudes of Test cricket. Reader, I've been there. I was at Chepauk when Ganguly's goers beat Waugh's world conquerors. I helped them win.

The earliest image I have of Chepauk is Budhi Kunderan beaten playing a forward defensive shot to Fred Titmus. He's at full stretch, looking back at his broken stumps, bowled 192, circa 1964. I wasn't there but *Sport & Pastime* was and it carried a black and white photograph of his dismissal. My first memory of the Australians at Chepauk has them 2 down for 19 and Mohinder Amarnath, just nineteen himself, is the unlikely opening bowler. But this was thirty-one years ago and it's a radio memory. We lost that Chepauk Test which we should have won to square the series. When I flew to Madras to watch the last Test of the 2001 series against Waugh's

Australians, I had a simple two-point plan: I wanted to watch five days of cricket at a civilized cricketing venue (basically any place other than the Feroz Shah Kotla stadium in Delhi) and, at the end of that time, I wanted us to win. I was owed a win because Chepauk had been scheduled to host the second Test of the series before it was taken away and given to Eden Gardens. Laxman's double century should have been mine to watch in situ. I'd been robbed.

The first day it took me ten minutes to get from the designated car park to my seat in the Tamil Nadu Cricket Association stand, and in that time I shook off thirty years. By the time Waugh won the toss I was fourteen again, as were most people around me. For the middle aged, Test matches are time machines: it is axiomatic that cricket fans are younger than the men in the middle because seniority in sport is a function of experience, not age. You need to bring your son to a Test match to be your age and I had left mine at home in Delhi.

The Aussies won the toss and batted, so the first day was predictably dull. As a juvenile I was under no obligation to be open-minded: I didn't want to watch the Australians piling on runs. To be fair to myself, the Australian effort was not pretty. Matthew Hayden is a massively effective batsman, but he bats in a muscle-bound style that I now associate with batsmen from settler colonies—Kallis and Cullinan play in exactly this way. Apart from Mark Waugh's second innings knock, there wasn't one moment of magic from the Australian batting line-up.

I was predisposed to dislike the Aussies because they had destroyed us on our last tour there and like a good whingeing Indian I had a whole catalogue of bad umpiring decisions that went against us lodged in my head. Through the first two Tests of the series, my prejudice had grown. The idea that the

Indian tour was a tropical ordeal by fire for the touring team, the final frontier between it and immortality, was exasperating. Here was a country that staged its national tennis open when the temperature was forty-five Celsius on court and its cricket team was going on about designer tropical wear like iced vests! Straitjackets were what they needed. Already (and they had only lost a Test, not the series), the Australian journalists covering the tour had begun to pay tribute to the gallant endurance of the Australian fast men in the face of the weather. It was a matter of time before they began writing about weight loss: this was the Kasprowicz gambit, or how India extracts pounds of Occidental flesh as a kind of touring toll.

Armed with my son's binoculars and raging prejudice, I studied the enemy carefully and saw nothing but villainy. Gillespie with his hooked nose and Mephistophelean beard looked like a bird of prey, a devilish eagle arrowing in. McGrath on the other hand looked like a mean, distempered vulture. Steve Waugh was dogged and unlovely and Warne, I noted with sour delight, was as clueless as he'd been on the last tour. For a man who once had the largest repertoire of deliveries of any spinner ever, Warne was reduced to one stock ball: round the wicket, wide of leg stump, into the rough. In Mumbai and Kolkata he had managed once or twice to turn it a mile; in Chennai even the rip was gone. He was a magician with one trick which didn't work. For variety, he bowled bouncers! Tendulkar played two reverse straight drives off those leg side deliveries past the wicketkeeper to the long stop boundary. They were miraculous shots. Then he dabbed a sad bouncer through slips for four. Laxman got stuck into Warne, then Dravid. By the end of the match, that chin-in-hand end to every delivery seemed like a charade rather than an aid to thought. It was cruel: if it hadn't been Us creaming Them, it might have been hard to watch.

Such levels of prejudice were hard to keep up in the calm surrounds of Chepauk. I watched the match from fine third man, surrounded by courtly Tamil Nadu Cricket Association members and excited children who were mildly partisan but made it a point to applaud Australian shots. It's a wonderful stadium at the pavilion end: shady, cooled by fans, its pillars strapped with television sets so you can test the evidence of your eyes against the infallibility of the camera. It isn't beautiful—they destroyed the old Madras Cricket Club clubhouse to build the concrete doughnut we were sitting in—but it works. Anyone who has watched a day's play at the squalidly anarchic Feroz Shah Kotla in Delhi will testify that a functional stadium is a wonderful thing.

The members and their families are out in force. They join in the Mexican Wave, they beat out terrible rhythms with plastic empties, they shout good-natured challenges to the knots of Australian supporters scattered amidst them, but they're quick to subside and they police themselves. The one time a rowdy throws a plastic bottle into the ground, he meets with such hissed disapproval that he shrinks and then disappears.

Chepauk feels orderly. There are no No Smoking signs up, but the word is out that you can't light up and so, with one or two exceptions, no one does. Behind the rows of seats is a wide curving corridor that houses the refreshments stalls. Pizzas, tayirsaadam, tamarind rice, colas are queued up for and dispensed. The crowd of people eating is dotted with cricketers you have seen or heard of: I stand respectfully at the fringes of expert discussions, listening to W.V. Raman who opened for India, Ram Narayan, who spun off breaks for Tamil Nadu, and Saad bin Jung who was a Test prospect when I was at university. There's some discussion about the legality of Harbhajan's present bowling action. The consensus is that he probably doesn't chuck any more. I don't mind if he does, on the time-tested principle that if he is a chucker, he's one of ours and at his speed he can't hurt anyone. The relaxed matter-of-factness of these cricketers is disarming; their counterparts in Delhi would be speechless with self-esteem, dunghill panjandrums who commune only with their cellphones.

Watching a Test match in a stadium over five days is nicely exhausting. Your face changes colour, your eyes get set in permanent crinkles, you move quickly from depression to exhilaration, from lethargy to a strung-out alertness. Unconfined by camera angles and commercials, your enjoyment of the game is more leisured and expansive. You can feel the game changing its rhythm—time stretched out by dour defence, then time telescoped by a flurry of shots—in a way that you can't on television because the commercial breaks divide the match into equal bite-sized pieces.

Two fifties by Laxman . . . he's taken the cramps out of Indian cricket by seeming boneless. Can he repeat this easy domination on foreign pitches? Perhaps he can; what an awesome thought! Tendulkar's century is wholly different from Laxman's shorter essays. Tendulkar is much the greater batsman, but sometimes he labours because once he has set himself a task he won't let himself into the 'zone' lest he get carried away. This time he has ordered himself a century and genius being risky, he has put his on hold. Watching him play percentage cricket is fascinating because it is against his nature. Runs come in isolated bursts because he isn't Gavaskar and every now and then he has to have a go. It is a measure of his greatness that he can suppress inspiration and still get a hundred.

The last half hour of the match after Laxman's dismissal is impossible to watch because I'm convinced they'll lose just to spite me. I watch till the bowler gets into his delivery stride, then shut my eyes and ask my friends what happened. It works most of the time because we don't lose all our wickets and in this way I help India win. There's a lull between Harbhajan's winning shot and the prize distribution. Politicians, officials and trophies are arranged in rows on a rostrum like ugly ornaments on a mantelpiece. Ravi Shastri, the master of ceremonies, dabs at his face and primps. Waugh strides out with his team to warm Chepauk applause. I clap too. Then Ganguly emerges to universal booing. I boo. It doesn't really matter . . . we've won.

Hope and the Indian Spectator

Indian fans aren't just optimists, they're connoisseurs of hope. They stalk hope, they note the best times for savouring it. They've learnt there are grades of hope: the thin, ultra-refined sort, the hope against hope when all is lost unless Bedi hits a hundred and Chandrasekhar bats out two sessions against Andy Roberts. There's the middling, cold-pressed kind when, in the middle of a first innings batting collapse, you dream of redemption in the second. But the rarest sort, extra virgin hope, is only found in beginnings. The two pieces below (written five years apart) were composed as the action unfolded so they don't mention the results of the Tests in question. But you can probably guess.

Bloemfontein, South Africa, 3 November 2001, first day, first Test:

India will bat. It's two in the afternoon and that time of the year again, that perfect blank slate moment when India begins a series, batting first. Harbhajan's not playing and that's a blow, but Pollock has put India in, so the business of bowling is in the future; right now there are two Indians in the middle with bats in their hands. It's the first innings of the tour of South Africa, 2001, no wickets down, no matches lost, that fragile bubble of time in which even middle aged men can allow themselves to believe that anything's possible. A hundred before lunch, 414 for no wickets at lunch on the second day, with Laxman and Tendulkar to come.

Actually Laxman's in already because Dravid's gone, so this time round the window for perfect optimism stayed open for about ten minutes, which has been par for the course for twenty years, ever since Sunil Gavaskar and Chetan Chauhan stopped opening the batting together. The closest India ever got to experiencing the joys of bourgeois order and development was in the middle passages of the long partnerships staged by Gavaskar and Chauhan. I look at young people who have never watched Gavaskar play and I feel for them; they'll have to emigrate to experience the sense of calm well-being that he induced in us, that first-world certainty that progress is inevitable.

Tendulkar's in now because Das has shown us once again what Gavaskar might have been without the genius: a short, well-organized batsman, shaky against the short ball. Gavaskar played the short ball like the immortal he was, swaying minimally to get out of the way or up on his toes, riding the bounce, nailing the ball into the ground. Tendulkar, even with the genius, isn't money in the bank like Gavaskar was. More like the stock market, up and down. He has just played an over by Ntini that perfectly illustrates my point: he has taken 16 runs off it with three boundaries, the last of which was a zero percentage shot that he tipped over second slip for four.

They've gone in for lunch now. I can't believe the score: 127 for 4 in two hours. Anyone who thinks the one-day game hasn't transformed Test cricket should take a look at that statistic: four wickets down and yet faster than a run a minute throughout that opening session. Tendulkar has scored 43 off forty-five balls and I regret the interruption for lunch. Lunch might remind him that Test cricket is a five-day game and in any case, he will want to play himself in after the interval. He should go for it: it has been years since Tendulkar produced a truly masterful century on tour against worthy opponents.

If it's possible to find polar opposites in the art of batsmanship, Laxman has to be the perfect foil to the Bombay school. He is tall and slender where Tendulkar and Gavaskar are short and thickset. When Laxman plays through the off side (and his cover driven boundaries off the back foot in his cameo before lunch were the purest silk), he never gets behind the ball. He just leans into the ball, firm-footed, and it speeds away. The shots played by Laxman in his 32 runs were—and there's no cleverer word for it—sublime. He made every shot played by the rest, even Tendulkar's best, look mortal, functional. Of late, the trouble with Laxman has been that his innings have been wholly unmixed with the base metal of defence or doggedness. He deals in the purest gold and there's only enough of that around to fashion perfect cameos. But it's hard to see how we can blame him for the way he plays because that's how he played throughout his majestic 281 against the Australians; the greatest innings ever played by an Indian batsman and one of the greatest in the history of Test cricket.

The amazing thing about that innings was that never once did Laxman indicate by his demeanour at the wicket or his stroke play that he was playing to save the match for India. At the other end, Dravid produced an object lesson in disciplined tenacity. Laxman was, well, unearthly; producing a stream of unhurried, lovely shots, all played it seemed, in the cause of beauty rather than the competitive object of saving or winning a Test match.

Well, Laxman's gone, but Tendulkar's just on-driven Pollock for a four to get to one of these curious Bill Frindall landmarks: 7000 runs. He's on 83 and Sehwag's playing steadily. Their partnership is worth more than a hundred. 176 for four. I can see the score tomorrow at lunch: 450 without further loss, Tendulkar within shouting distance of his first triple century. I begin to get that first-day feeling again: anything's possible.

Five years on

Durban, South Africa, 27 December 2006, second day, second Test:

This time hope lasted less than an over.

You know how it is: each time India's openers go in, just before the first ball's bowled, I warm myself with the thought of those ten wickets stacked in the bank, I finger the averages of India's best six (three over 50), I total the centuries they've made (Sachin thirty-four plus Dravid twenty-three plus Sehwag twelve plus Ganguly twelve plus Laxman ten and Jaffer two—but one of them was a double), I remind myself that the Test record for the first wicket (413 by Pankaj Roy and Vinoo Mankad) still belongs to India and then allow myself to silently mouth that sustaining motto: anything's possible.

Possible in a good way, naturally. I'm not thinking that India could be 0 for 4 wickets (Pankaj Roy had something to do with that score too); more along the lines of 513 for none, Sehwag 420, Jaffer unbeaten on a sticky 93. Most of the time this is more fantasy than hope, especially when India is touring. The standard touring story is that India loses the first Test by a lot, then loses the second Test by more. In this scenario, the anything-can-happen mantra is less optimism than forlorn swagger, desperate fans whistling in the wind. But once every decade, the team does so well that the automatic hope of the Indian fan becomes reasonable. Because this happens so rarely, these moments of rational, founded fantasy are precious and you want them to last, to grow. I never actually believe that we're going to get to 513; I'll settle for 120 for one, but I want that moist glimmer of hope to last long enough to become a puddle of expectation.

This South African Test series has been one of those high points of fandom. I can't remember the last time we took on a proper Test side on a fast pitch in a foreign country and won. Not just won: won big and via our seamers. Generally it's our batsmen who win matches for us or our spinners. This time the South Africans had picked five fast bowlers for a lively pitch and we destroyed them at their own game. Sweet.

So in the gap between the first Test at Johannesburg and this one in Durban, I counted the days. Christmas took forever coming and the morning of Boxing Day wouldn't end. Southern hemisphere Test matches are best conducted in Australia. They begin at a reasonable hour in the morning (5.30 or thereabouts) so I get to watch most of two sessions by the time I have to leave for my first lecture. South African Test matches begin, unnaturally enough, at lunch.

By the time we had reduced South Africa to 29 for 3, I was in a fever of expectation. We hadn't just won the first Test of a three-Test series, we were about to win the first day of the next match too. If a winning start in a foreign series happens rarely, a winning start in the following Test NEVER happens. (I know some tactless fool is going to say that Sehwag did get us off to a winning start with 195 against Australia at Melbourne in December 2003 but only insensitive nitpickers use tragedy to score points. Experienced Indian spectators know that some matches need to be airbrushed from our collective memory.)

Okay, so 29 for 3 was too good to last, but middle aged

fans have a lifetime's experience in keeping flickering hope alive. Like veteran smokers, we cup our hands around the flame and eke it out till it burns our fingers and, to be honest, if someone had offered us South Africa, 258 for 8, at the end of the first day's play before it began, we'd have taken it.

The second day's morning session was depressing but not desolating. It was a set-piece that Indian spectators know by heart, tail-end partnerships that allow the opposition to bulk out meagre scores into respectable totals. In this way did 250-odd for 8 become 328 all out. Still, they were all out and the moment I had been waiting for since we won the first Test was at hand: the start of our innings.

Fantasy said we'd make 550, but the reasonable optimist, calculating that Sehwag was due an eighty-ball hundred after his poor run while Tendulkar, not having crossed fifty in the thirteen innings he had played since his last century, was owed a big one, settled for 450 which would mean a lead of 122. Given that the pitch was bound to deteriorate by the fourth day, that lead would be enough. Kumble would kill them on a Durban crumbler.

The sun was out between innings, the pitch, according to the local experts, Pat Symcox and Allan Donald, had been baked into a belter for batsmen (which explained why their tail-enders had put on 70 for the last 2 wickets) and we were one up in a three-Test series in a foreign country. The stage was set and for once, no one could accuse the Indian fan of delirious hope. We were playing, after many months, our best batting line-up. Ravi Shastri's insane suggestion that Jaffer be dropped for Irfan Pathan had, fortunately, not been accepted by the team management and barring some freak decision by Chappell to send V.R.V. Singh to open the innings in the interest of flexibility, Virender Sehwag and Wasim Jaffer were about to commence their century partnership.

Actually even fifty would do so long as Jaffer went first: Sehwag, Dravid, Tendulkar, Laxman and Ganguly would, between them, manage the other 400.

That little bubble of perfect hope that we had reason to believe would balloon till it was big enough to roof the Kingsmead stadium, the virgin hope of true believers, dear reader, lived for less than an over. Five balls, to be precise. On the fifth, Virender Sehwag, who has twelve centuries and twelve fifties and a batting average of over 50 and a strike rate in the seventies, waved his bat at a ball outside off stump bowled by the wild-eyed and certifiable Andre Nel and someone called de Villiers caught him at slip.

Hope died, I was about to say, but that would be a lie. Indian fans never stop hoping. I shifted gears and pinned my faith in Dravid, this Titan with a batting average that topped 58. An unbeaten double hundred, I reasoned, and not only would we win the match but Dravid would push his average over 60 and lay claim to being the greatest batsman of modern times. So hope there was, but it was a tarnished hope, smudged by that early wicket and limned with foreboding of worse to come. Which came. An idiot umpire judged Dravid leg before to Nel after spending the whole of the South African innings pretending that lbw wasn't a legal way of dismissing a batsman. Then Jaffer left us.

As I write this, Laxman and Tendulkar occupy the crease. I worship both of them, but I can't watch the telecast continuously any more. I keep my eyes open till the bowler's delivery stride, then keep them closed till I'm sure no one is out. We're 93 for 3, Tendulkar's in the late thirties, Laxman that colossus of Calcutta, is on 7. Graeme Smith, he of the enormous body and tiny face, has just dropped a sitter at slip. Tendulkar's been given a life. Surely, this is a sign.

Home Advantage

When Kumble took all 10 wickets in an innings against Pakistan in Delhi, my joy was qualified by an automatic thought: he had done it at home in a game supervised by Indian umpires (neutral umpires not being in vogue then). On the way home from Feroz Shah Kotla, I thought about the only other time a bowler had managed all 10: Jim Laker at Old Trafford against the Australians. In all the many descriptions I had read of his amazing achievement (19 wickets in a match), I couldn't recall any that suggested his performance was diminished by home advantage. Encouraged by that, I settled down some years later to exorcize this ghost.

Towards the end of the Delhi Test between Sri Lanka and India in December 2005, a television commentator was told by his statistician that Anil Kumble had become the second man in history to take 300 wickets in 'home' Tests, that is Test matches played in the bowler's own country. Sitting in front of the television, I instinctively wished it had been the other way round—I wanted the 300 wickets in the 'away' column. In this I was typical.

South Asian cricket teams and their supporters are sensitive to the issue of home advantage. The charge that subcontinental teams are poor tourists is acutely felt. After Chetan Sharma's spirited and surprisingly brisk bowling won us a rubber in

England, no Indian team has won a Test series there. Every Indian fan, commentator and pundit knows that the Indian team hasn't won a Test series outside India for twenty years or thereabouts. What about the win in Pakistan in 2004, someone asked? Same subcontinent: doesn't count as abroad. And Zimbabwe the following year? A two-Test series against the worst team in the world, purged of its best players? Be serious. Despite Tendulkar and Dravid and Azhar and the rest, Indian pundits conclude that Indian cricket has been fundamentally unsound for twenty years.

Indians console themselves by thinking that the Sri Lankan record is even more lopsided. They win everything at home and nothing abroad. Mahela Jayawardene's Sri Lankan record is Bradmanesque; outside his country he shrinks into a goodish batsman. The same is true of Atapattu. And Murali? Well, says the hard-nosed, undeluded, subcontinental cricket writer, there's a reason why the bowler who beat Kumble to 300 wickets at home was Murali. Those Sri Lankan glue-pots are made for the man.

We need to cease and desist. Indians, Pakistanis and Sri Lankans should stop apologizing for doing well at home. If this self-flagellation is meant to prove to the world that we're grown up and unillusioned and mature, I have news for you: there's no one listening. Our obsessive need to talk down our performances at home isn't self-awareness, it is a form of self-hatred that we should have outgrown.

Our tendency to discount home performances when calculating actual cricketing ability is based on the idea that the rest of the cricketing world judges its teams and players by their all-weather abilities on sporting pitches. That, the story goes, is how they tell the men from the boys in the West Indies, in Australia, in England and in South Africa.

Actually, that isn't really how they do things Over There. You shouldn't believe everything you read.

Your average English or Australian player, journalist and fan does not see failure in the subcontinent as damning. He doesn't believe that defeat in India or Pakistan defines his team's ability or the standing of its individual members. Steve Waugh nominated India as the final frontier because he was bidding for cricketing immortality, for the right to claim that the team he captained was the greatest team in the history of the game. When he lost that extraordinary series, when Ponting barely made double figures in three Test matches, when Warne was caned into comic relief, the Australians didn't become self-abnegating wrecks. They didn't apply to have Warne's name removed from *Wisden*'s five greatest cricketers ever. Nor did they decide that Ponting wasn't as good as his career average suggested because he had averaged two or thereabouts in India.

So why are we in South Asia so keen to make success outside the subcontinent the measure of a man or a team? The obvious answer is that it is natural to want a good side to prove itself in every circumstance, the all-weather test. And, as I said, we believe that is how more successful teams assess themselves. Only they don't.

The English, for example, have developed over decades of failure in the subcontinent, an epic of extenuating circumstances, *The Alibiad*. It goes like this. We (the English) couldn't compete because the food was inedible, the hotels roach-ridden, our stomachs upset, and the nightlife non-existent, the heat too hot and the dust too obscuring. These were the off-field handicaps.

As far as playing conditions went, the pitches were dust-bowls or rolled mud, they kept low, they turned square, the ball didn't come on, its seam wasn't right, the crowds were too noisy, the toss too important, the umpires were bent and the home team cheated.

Central to our anxiety about home conditions is our acceptance of the Anglo-Australian definition of a 'sporting' wicket. The good pitch has a light covering of grass, it has bounce and movement for the fast men, it doesn't turn till the fourth day, the ball comes on and *it has something for everyone*. Anything else is either a feather bed or a vicious turner, not a fair Test wicket.

Why a pitch that turns from the first day is a bad thing is not clear. Why this is worse or more unfair than a pitch where the ball bounces throat high or swings like a banana from start of play is even more obscure. Why is a hot day in Delhi harder to deal with for a touring side than the finger-numbing cold of Trent Bridge in the first half of the English season? Do you see the English discounting their 2005 Ashes win as a bad case of home advantage? I don't think so.

So long as both teams have to cope with the same sort of turn and bounce and weather, mastery of home conditions is something to be admired, not disparaged. The cricket publics of South Asia need to remember that the greatest skills in contemporary cricket have been developed by Sri Lankan, Pakistani and Indian players in creative response to subcontinental conditions.

Saqlain Mushtaq invented and Murali perfected the doosra to counter hard-charging, bludgeon-bearing modern batsmen who were threatening to make finger-spin obsolete. Sarfaraz, Imran, Wasim and Waqar invented reverse swing to move the ball in conditions that English seamers had only whinged about. To watch Tendulkar and Sidhu and Laxman destroy Warne on turning tracks by reading him from the hand, skipping down the wicket and hitting him inside-out from the leg stump rough through cover, was to be given a masterclass in batsmanship. And conversely, to watch Murali bowl doosras around the wicket in Delhi and utterly bewilder those same Indian batsmen, the best players of spin bowling in the world, was to be present at one of those pivotal moments when the game makes an evolutionary leap.

So the next time one of our gladiators reaches a landmark at home, we should celebrate without being modest on his behalf. Hail Kumble! Ave Tendulkar! All hail.

Acknowledgements

Nearly all the pieces in this book were first published in newspapers and magazines. Most of them were written for two publications: *Wisden Asia Cricket* (and its successor, *Cricinfo Magazine*), and the *Telegraph*, Kolkata. The rest appeared in *The Hindu*, *Mansworld*, *Wisden Cricket Monthly* and the *Hindustan Times*. One of these essays, 'On Walking', was, much to my delight, reprinted in *How's That?*, the official journal of the Association of Cricket Umpires and Scorers! I'm grateful to all these publications for their permission to use these pieces in this book.

Editorially, my greatest debt is to Sambit Bal, the editor of *Wisden Asia Cricket*, *Cricinfo Magazine* and Cricinfo.com. If he hadn't magicked out of nowhere a wonderfully literate cricket magazine, there would have been no reason to write the reports and arguments and commemorations that make up *Men in White*. His colleague at *Wisden Asia Cricket*, Leslie Mathews spotted ludicrous mistakes I had made before they saw print, for which many thanks. Rudrangshu Mukherjee and Bhaswati Chakravorty and their colleagues who run the editorial pages of the *Telegraph*, were, as always, generous and vigilant editors.

Special thanks to V.K. Karthika, my editor at Penguin, for turning a bitty manuscript into a respectable book and to Anurag Basnet for completing the job.

Anyone who writes about cricket in India is in Ram Guha's debt; my debt is made larger by thirty years of talk about cricket and other things. Mukund Padmanabhan, contrarian, friend and fellow enthusiast, is due undying thanks for finding a way of getting me into Chepauk to watch us beat the Australians in the deciding Test of that epic series of 2001.

My greatest debt as a cricket watcher is to Hari Sen in whose slipstream I've sidled into Feroz Shah Kotla's pavilion seats more times than I can count. My initiation into cricket was the handiwork of my father, who raised me on visions of Larwood and Duleepsinhji; he would have approved of *Men in White*, I think.

To Arun, Raghu and Tara who have followed *Men in White*'s gestation with amused indulgence; look, the thing's done!

Index